JOHN COLTRANE

by

Bill Cole

SCHIRMER BOOKS
A Division of Macmillan Publishing Co., Inc.
NEW YORK

Collier Macmillan Publishers
LONDON

Schirmer Books
A Division of Macmillan Publishing Co., Inc.
866 Third Avenue, New York, N.Y. 10022

Collier Macmillan Canada, Ltd.

Library of Congress Catalog Card Number: 76—14289

Printed in the United States of America

printing number

2   3   4   5   6   7   8   9   10

Library of Congress Cataloging in Publication Data

Cole, Bill
    John Coltrane.

    Bibliography: p.
    Includes indexes.
    1. Coltrane, John, 1926-1967. 2. Jazz musicians--
United States--Biography.
ML419.C645C6   788'.66'0924 [B]   76-14289
ISBN 0-02-870660-9

78149

CONTENTS

PREFACE

There are two things in particular that I would like to get at in this book: John Coltrane as a musician, and John Coltrane as a religious person. And both these aspects of Coltrane are intimately bound up with his being an African-American. I had an inkling early in life of Trane's greatness as a musician, but his merits were more clearly pointed out to me by my teachers: Nathan Davis, Clifford Thornton, Sam Rivers, Warren Smith, and Jayne Cortez.

In regard to Coltrane in a religious context, I was perplexed about this aspect of his genius for quite a long period of time until I had the privilege of meeting, talking with, and corresponding with Professor Fela Sowande, the great Nigerian composer and folklorist.

Professor Sowande is over seventy years old, and the work he has done among the tribes of his own people—the Yorubas of Nigeria—as well as other tribes, collecting not only the music but the folklore, mythology, and religious patterns and concepts of West African people, is invaluable in its own right, as well as highly relevant to the understanding of the works of John Coltrane. I have included excerpts from Professor Sowande's writings throught this book, and I hope they prove as stimulating to the reader as they were to me.

I have also included in this book many examples of what John Coltrane actually played, as transcribed by Andrew White of Washington, D.C. I believe that any tenor saxophonist who is interested in Coltrane's transcribed solos would find Mr. White's work a tremendous resource.

At the back of this book is a chronological discography of John Coltrane's recorded output, "Recording Dates and Personnel." This is followed by an extensive two-part bibliography, "Works Cited" and "For Further Reference." All of these should prove interesting and helpful to the ardent Coltrane fan or researcher.

There are numerous people to thank and to acknowledge. However, it was David Baker of Indiana University whose enthusiasm for my original dissertation helped me to continue in this quest for John Coltrane and gave me the confidence to write this book. I also want to thank Mary Ann Reifenstein, whose technical assistance was crucial to the expression of my ideas, and to Ken Stuart for believing in those ideas.

—W.S.C.

ACKNOWLEDGMENTS

Acknowledgment is gratefully given to Joe Alper for the use of his photos (courtesy of Jackie Gibson Alper), Fela Sowande for the excerpts from his writings, and Andrew White for the use of his transcriptions of Coltrane's music.

INTRODUCTION

Jimmy Garrison, John Coltrane and McCoy Tyner — March, 1963, recording session.

can recall, almost as if it were yesterday, the first time I saw John Coltrane play. It was in Pittsburgh—the year was 1955—and he had just been hired by Miles Davis to become a member of what was really Miles Davis's first band. They played as part of a "package deal" in a touring show. I can't recall now the other bands in the tour but I remember my great enthusiasm to see Miles Davis.

Miles was the idol of all the people that I ran around with at that time—not only from a musical standpoint but also from the way he was as a personality: the whole mystique that he carried with him even in these days. I was eighteen at the time and had been listening to Miles Davis intently for about four years. But this was the first time I was seeing him in person.

The tour played in a hall called the Syria Mosque. It was a rather large hall, too big for a quintet to play in, but it was certainly better than listening to a band play in a bar. It had two balconies. The *second* balcony had good sightlines with no obstructions. However, I was only able to get my seat on the day of the concert and found myself behind a pole in the *first* balcony. That was OK, though, because I was always more into listening than actually seeing the band.

This was in the fall of 1955, at which time the quintet was made up of Miles playing trumpet, Philly Joe Jones on drums, Paul Chambers on bass, Red Garland on piano, and Trane on tenor saxophone. I can't remember now which order they appeared in on the bill, but the band was very businesslike when they came on stage. Philly Joe quickly set up his drums, and as soon as he had them arranged the rest of the band came out and began to play. I remember at first being startled at the increased tempo of the pieces they played, compared to the recorded versions I was used to. Some pieces were even taken twice as fast as when Miles had recorded them. Even though they hadn't really been together that long, the unit was crisp and precise in its execution of the music. Miles would take the first improvisation, then Trane followed by Garland; and on one piece Chambers played a solo, and on another Jones played a solo. Outside of the Clifford Brown/Max Roach Quintet, this was truly the best band around. Each player was not only "on time" in ensemble playing but they were all excellent improvisers.

It was Trane, though, who caught my attention. He was the person who made me bend my neck around the pillar to see who it was that *sounded* so different. This was the time when reed players were trying to develop a stylized sound, a sound that was reaching toward a classical tone—something pure, defying any kind of individuality.

1

Trane's sound was the antithesis of all that. He really sounded like no one I had ever heard before. His sound was clearly an extension of his own voice—an expression of Trane himself coming through the horn. I wasn't really aware of what was happening to me at the time, aware that this individual was pulling me towards him—but now I know that his voice was rooted firmly in the context of the traditional African that Fela Sowande describes in *The Role of Music in African Society*: "The magical powers inherent in Sound is one of the basic fundamental beliefs of the traditional African."[1] The image I have of that occasion now is only a vague one; but the impact that John Coltrane had on me from that very moment has stayed in my mind now for twenty years. He had, and I knew from that moment that he had, a magnetic quality. And, as is so often the case with young people, I felt my allegiance transferring from Miles to Trane. This was the first time I had heared him play. Even though he had been a figure talked about in the community, I had not heard him at all before this moment. The emergence of any great musician is always first propagated in the community, and if a person grows up in an isolated city like Pittsburgh sometimes it is possible to hear about a player for months before you actually see him in person or hear him on record. This was my particular case with Trane.

The next year, 1956, was the first year I went to New York. My brother and I had saved our money and we thought we would try New York. I was wildly enthusiastic when I saw that Miles was playing at a club in Greenwich Village called the Cafe Bohemian. The club itself was right off Sheridan Square—one of numerous jazz spots that had emerged in the Village. My brother and I couldn't wait to see the band. Our disappointment was tremendous when we finally got there and saw that Trane was no longer in the band. In fact, Miles's relaxed context only served as a further "down" in the situation. Sonny Rollins was on tenor saxophone and Tadd Dameron had replaced Garland on piano. Miles did very little playing that evening, and, unfortunately, this seemed to be one of the band's off nights.

It would be almost two and a half years before I would see Trane again. This was after Miles had rehired him at the beginning of 1958. The personnel now included not only Miles and Trane on trumpet and tenor saxophone respectively, but also Julian Cannonball Adderley on alto saxophone. Bill Evans now played piano and Jimmy Cobbs was on drums. The only holdover from the first band was Paul Chambers. They were playing in a dark, dingy bar called the Midway Lounge in the downtown section of Pittsburgh.

2

During the late 1950s the Midway Lounge was the only place in Pittsburgh where jazz could be heard on a regular basis. It was a singles "low life" bar inhabited mostly by young people who were by and large under the legal age for drinking. It was a long, thin room with the bar itself extended along one whole side of the lounge. The musicians played on an elevated stage behind the bar. The stage only held four people comfortably, but most of the time it was crowded with more than that number. I had seen many different bands there: the Clifford Brown/Max Roach band; Art Blakey's Jazz Messengers (at the time when that band included Horace Silver on piano, Kenny Dorham on trumpet, Hank Mobley on tenor saxophone, and Doug Watkins on bass); Dizzy Gillespie, who played there several times; and many others who came through Pittsburgh. In fact, the only time I had ever seen pianist Bud Powell was when he played there. Ironically, his drummer at that time was Elvin Jones who, of course, would become Trane's primary drummer during the sixties.

The Midway Lounge really held many beautiful musical moments for me. It was there that I had a chance to speak to Clifford Brown, just months before he was killed in an automobile accident. He was one of the most beautiful persons I had ever met, and he spent all the breaks he had between sets sitting with me. We talked about music, mathematics, and his life in general. It was his insistence that allowed me to stay that evening, because the woman who managed the bar recognized that I was underage and was trying to get me to leave.

It is important that people understand the kind of situations that Trane played in. Even though the Midway Lounge was the only place to hear good music from outside the city, it was a place where minors were almost openly served alcohol, where drugs were passed between peddler and user without anyone so much as blinking an eye, and where "ladies" were always around—and more than willing to be picked up. Most of the women who visited this bar were underage and were interested in the musicians that were playing. So there was a lot going on besides the music itself.

This was—in 1958—the second time I had seen Trane play; and he was by this time the most dominant figure in the band. Where earlier he had seemed to be still groping, now he was completely fluent on the tenor saxophone and was certainly taking the longer solos. He was beginning to play rhythmic patterns over and over again. I remember him playing one phrase in particular twenty-nine times, and then seeing Miles pull the cuff on Trane's pants so he would move into something different—at which point Trane sprang into a completely new line, like being launched out of Cape Kennedy. This was the last time I saw Trane in the Miles Davis context. Trane had by this time become the most dominant musical figure in the minds of all the people that I hung out with. Every new album that he made either under his own name or with Miles Davis was a "must" for me and my companions.

It wasn't until 1960 that I saw him play again, and, except for two occasions, I always heard him play in a place called the Crawford Grill #2. The Grill, as it was known, was located deep in the heart of the largest black community in Pittsburgh—the Hill District. The Grill #1 was also located in the Hill District, but in the poorest section, and it was eventually cleared away by urban renewal. Grill #2 was supposed to be a "high-class" bar as opposed to #1 which was situated in the most notorious part of the Hill District.

The Grill #2 was actually a restaurant-bar. It was owned by a gambler named Joe Robinson, and his son Buzzy was the manager or producer of the music. Buzzy was a cousin of a good friend of mine, so even though there was always a cover charge to get in when bands were playing I was accustomed to getting in free. Trane played this bar for the next six years, three or four times a year, and I tried my best to see him every night of the week he would play. There were only two members of his band who played every time I saw him. They were McCoy Tyner and Elvin Jones. The first time I saw Trane play at the end of 1960 Steve Davis was the bassist, and I felt that, with the exception of Art Davis, Steve was Trane's strongest bassist. He was very much out of the Paul Chambers mold—light touch and very consistent all over the bass. He seemed to have great intuitive skills, knowing at all times in what direction Trane would be moving.

On the first occasion that I saw Trane at the Grill I had gone down with my friend Kenny who was a tenor saxophone player. The bands always started playing on Monday and played from Monday through Saturday, Sunday being an off day because of the blue laws in Pennsylvania. It was only on very rare occasions that any one band would be held over for more than a week. Kenny and I had gone down to see the band play on the Monday that they arrived, and between sets Kenny had asked Trane if he could practice with him sometime during the week. This was always the situation. The younger musicians of any particular town would always ask the performer whether it was possible for them to sit in and play sometime when that particular performer was practicing. Trane took down Kenny's telephone number and told him he would call him during the week. We

4

had gone down every night during that week and my friend was still waiting for Trane to give him a phone call. Finally, on Saturday morning, Trane called Kenny and asked him if he would be ready in an hour to start practicing. Kenny called me up and together we went to Trane's hotel room and they started practicing.

Much has been written about Trane's practicing habits. But I can tell you firsthand that they started at 9:00 in the morning and, with an hour or so for lunch, they played until 4:30 in the afternoon. There was very little conversation. Trane would play a scale through the different registers of his instrument and then he and Kenny would play those scales in unison, each time playing faster and faster. Then they would go to another scale. Trane often would move through not just the diatonic scales, but many other different-numbered scales: heptatonic, pentatonic, et cetera. The whole atmosphere was not as if my friend was practicing with a master musician, but as if these two individuals were practicing together as equals. Trane would occasionally stop and show Kenny how to get around certain scales easier; he would show him ways of modulating through different scales using all kinds of formulas—not only established formulas, but those he had thought of himself. This is something that all master musicians do. They are constantly working out ways in which they can articulate themselves more fluently. When we walked out of Trane's hotel room we both felt as if we were ten feet tall. I know I felt just as good watching and listening to them play as my friend felt playing. Trane, however, was not unique in his openness to young musicians. Almost without exception the people I have seen and heard play—and especially when those persons played in community bar situations—always seemed to display an openness to younger musicians.

The Grill, like almost all bars where music is played, was more interested in making money than it was in having musicians play. There was constant harassment from bartenders to buy drinks, and there was a lot of ongoing chatter. So, except for a very few minutes, the music was very hard to hear. When Trane first started playing there in 1960 he was playing the rather conventional set of about forty-five minutes to an hour and taking a break of about twenty minutes. However, by the time I saw him in 1963 and 1964 his sets had become longer and longer. Often he would play only one piece a set, but that piece could go on for as long as two hours. I can remember actually clocking him when he and Elvin Jones played a duet that lasted for an hour and forty-five minutes. His strength was really incredible.

Trane and the quartet had a very loose format—and this is especially when the band included McCoy Tyner and Jimmy Garrison on bass. Sometimes McCoy would start off a set playing solo, and then Jones and Garrison would start to play and then Trane. Often Garrison would begin a set with Tyner and Jones, and then Trane. But always Trane and Jones would end every piece. In fact, a quarter of a way through Trane's solo, Tyner and Garrison would "lay out" and Trane and Jones would go on and on and on. There are really no words to describe the energy that these two men would exude. After each set they would literally be drenched with perspiration, and I often wondered how they could possibly do this over and over again without catching bad colds or even pneumonia. Just before Pharaoh Sanders entered the band, I remember beginning to watch Trane and wondering how much longer he was going to be able to put out that much energy—not only night after night, but set after set. As hokey as it sounds, I felt that if he continued this outpouring of himself to the people something would soon happen to him. When he played, his intensity was almost unbearable to watch. He seemed to almost want to envelop the instrument, whether that instrument was soprano or tenor saxophone. His face always seemed to be straining to its utmost capacity, and the veins in his face seemed as if they would pop straight out of his body. He was truly an awesome figure to watch. And as intense as Trane could be, Elvin Jones was certainly his equal. Jones was demonic, constantly whipping and interchanging with Trane during the solos. It wasn't just John Coltrane and Elvin Jones: they were a pair—and they both put out an equal amount of energy to the people.

Another musical companion of Trane's was Eric Dolphy. I only saw Dolphy play with Trane once. He played all three instruments at that time—the bass clarinet, flute, and alto saxophone—and he was fluent on all of them. His bouncing, jumping style of moving through the registers of his instruments contrasted with Trane's fluid style. They complemented each other beautifully. Yet they were two strong, individualistic players. On the other hand, the time I saw Sanders play in the band I felt that Sanders more often would take an accompanist role to Trane. Trane at the time also didn't seem to be as strong physically, and Sanders certainly more than carried out his responsibility in the band. His role was more of the student than Dolphy's was. However, one has to remember that Dolphy had known Trane from the middle fifties and that they were closer in age than Trane and Sanders were.

I only saw Trane two times outside of the Crawford Grill situation. Once was in 1963 when he was playing a club in San Francisco called

6

the Both/And. Opportunely, Roland Kirk had come in to sit in on a set on the night I went to see them play. On the last piece they played together, Trane broke into a long improvisation in which Kirk held one note without taking a breath. After Trane had finished his improvisation and stopped playing, Kirk immediately sprang into a long improvisation himself—still without taking a single breath. He had by this time really developed his cycle breathing. After Kirk had finished his improvisation and both men had come down from the stand, I can remember Trane asking Kirk how he did that and Kirk simply saying to him that because he was blind he had this sixth sense; and both of them began to laugh.

The only other time besides this that I saw Trane again, outside of the Crawford Grill situations, was in 1966 in a concert in New York at which he and a whole host of other musicians played a long free improvisational number. I must in all honesty admit that this was at my most reactionary point in terms of understanding Trane's music, and the complexities of what they were playing were very difficult for me to get into.

There were, especially during the early part of the 1960s, two camps of jazz lovers developing simultaneously. One camp was submerged in the hard bop of the 1950s. The other had just as much love for that tradition but was also vanguarding the music represented by Ornette Coleman and his followers. Trane, for a long time, was on the fence—or at least he was thought of as being between these two camps. However, I think that this observation was inaccurate because the music that he was putting on records (at least those records that were being released by the record companies) was far different from the music that he was playing in clubs. I think this was the biggest problem that Trane was having with his constituency. On the one hand, a person could go home and put "These Are a Few of My Favorite Things" on the record player and feel very comfortable with what Trane was playing, but when Trane actually played this piece in person it became just another vehicle to spring him on to one of his long improvisations. Before he would get a quarter of the way through his improvisation—and especially when Garrison and Tyner would lay out—one would completely forget the piece that he was playing. Trane used lines to develop other lines. He certainly had centers which lines would spring from, but those centers would constantly be changing. It's apparent to me now that a musician of his quality would always be moving forward and would never be content to keep playing the same thing the same way. And this was the perplexing problem that his audiences had to try to deal with. So, even though it may have seemed that for a while he represented just the hard bop tradition, those of us who were fortunate enough to hear him in person knew that his music was continually moving and developing and expanding in a multiplicity of directions.

I have to admit that the music that he played during the very end of his career, and especially the pieces he played in conjunction with Pharaoh Sanders, often baffled me; and it wasn't until I began to write my master's thesis in the spring of 1968 that I truly recognized what an incredible wealth of music he had left for all of us to listen to.

Although the subject of both my master's thesis and the subsequent book that emerged out of that was Miles Davis, it became clear to me over a period of time that John Coltrane was the individual I was mostly listening to. My interest was only further stimulated and increased by these two documents. In the fall of 1970 I entered Wesleyan University as a Ph.D. candidate. What had been started and finished as a master's thesis on Miles Davis had become a full-blown idea on how to deal with the music of John Coltrane. Nathan Davis at the University of Pittsburgh had given me some clear ideas on how to begin that search. But Clifford Thornton at Wesleyan University provided me with an ongoing commentary on how to successfully deal with a figure of Coltrane's stature. I had kept up an interest even before 1968 because I recall being very aware of Trane's death and what I was doing at that very moment. But this was the first time I had made a solid, concentrated effort to get at this man at his root sources.

During the year and a half that I pursued my academic work at Wesleyan I thought at great length about how I should try to put down my ideas on Coltrane as a doctoral dissertation. Finally, in the spring of 1972 I first heard Fela Sowande, and I knew from the very first moment I saw him that he would have concrete directions for my questions.

In the fall of 1972 I created the John Coltrane Memorial World Music Lecture/Demonstration Series at Amherst College. The series was designed to support the world music courses that I teach. It also gave me an excellent opportunity to bring Professor Sowande to the series and to expose his ideas to the student body. He has lectured in the series during each of the subsequent three years that it has existed. On one of his visits, in the spring of 1974, he began to share his writings with me. And those writings helped me to complete my dissertation.

This book is a logical outcome of my dissertation on John Coltrane. It had become obvious long before starting the dissertation that John Coltrane could not be treated fully, even in a book of more than normal length—much less in a dissertation. Moreover, because of the time and space limitations imposed by an academic paper, much that was highly relevant had to be left out of the dissertation. But I was determined to pick up the threads again once the hurdle of the dissertation had been cleared and I was free of all limitations except those dictated by relevance, evidence, good taste, and propriety. Such is the genesis of this book.

In the interval, *Chasin' the Trane: The Music and Mystique of John Coltrane,* by J. C. Thomas, and *Coltrane: A Musical Biography,* by C. O. Simpkins, were published. Both books are extremely capable, with Thomas having a complete discography at the end of his book and Simpkins including an excellent appendix in his. However, the publication of these two books only served to intensify rather than diminish my urge to write, for reasons that will be apparent in the pages that follow. In any case, Trane is far too vital, and far too much of a key figure in the historical development of African-American music, to be evaluated completely within the pages of any one book—no matter how competent the author or painstakingly thorough and minutely detailed his researches and original information resources.

This book then will deal with John Coltrane the musician, the African-American, who not only recognized but was more than ready to accept—and quicker still to claim—his African origins and heritage, and who went that final step beyond even this, in that he saw clearly, acknowledged fully, and paid tribute to that universal essence in all folk music, through which the music of India and of Africa complement and fulfill each other, each providing him with so much more insight into and appreciation for the other, to the advantage of his own African-American music, and even more, to the enrichment of his own personal life. If that life was sometimes one of sorrow and frustration and loneliness, that is the price demanded of the artist by the creative energies that use him for expression. These energies make two demands on him: the first is that his mastery of the techniques of his particular art form must be as perfect as humanly possible; the second is that that perfected technique be placed entirely and completely at the service of the creative forces which the artist serves.

It is futile, therefore, to look for the explanation of Trane's music in his technique, although without that technique he could never have become the master musician that he was. The "technique" is the *container* of something else, and it is not to be confused with what it in fact contains. To put it another way, the structural *form* through which artistic ideas and poetic content manifest themselves is like a vehicle in which a human being is traveling. Each serves a specific end, and each is important at its own level, but the most minutely detailed and thorough examination and analysis of the vehicle provides absolutely no clue as to the core of being or spiritual essence of the individual whom it serves as a means of transport.

But, of course, the use of analogy in a context of this kind is self-defeating. Nevertheless, it has seemed necessary to draw some analogies, because of the by no means rare tendency to let our proper admiration and respect for Trane's technical mastery and effective command of his instruments remove Trane-the-artist from the focal center of our field of vision.

It thus becomes essential to underscore the fact that sustained and concentrated attention on the steps through which a young artist evolves into a recognized master can be of incalculable benefit to a mind that is eager to learn and willing to be taught.

But that mind—that young artist—has to be prepared; he has to have evolved to a level at which the discoveries that he may unearth will be within the grasp of his understanding and intellectual comprehension. He must furthermore be prepared in the sense that he is fully determined to find in himself and give *whatever* it may take to attain to the state of a master.

That mind—that artist—must also be sensitive, so that his priorities are in the right and most profitable sequence, in ensuring his own mental, moral, and spiritual development as an unavoidable by-product of the same process; moreover, he must above all be sufficiently sensitized, so that he can hear and register—clearly and accurately—the silent communications of the "spirit of the master" enshrined, alive, and actively functioning in the works he left behind. And to understand Trane—a master musician—it is necessary to recognize and take into the fullest consideration that behind his art was his philosophy, and that this philosophy determined *everything* he did and how he did it. Trane was by no means a merely cerebral artist; that is, though he certainly was a thinking man, and there was definitely in all his music a solid underpinning of intellectual searching and working out, at the same time there was his philosophy—a philosophy that included a deep, an almost mystical feeling of love for and community with his fellow men and women.

Wherein, then, lies the magic of this man's music? The answer, from my point of view, is that it dealt with human problems in human terms for human beings in a human world. If there is "turmoil" in his music, it includes the turmoil in the hearts and minds of ordinary men and women. It includes the turmoil and violence of the times through which Trane lived. But the magic in Trane's music also must derive from the "peace which passeth all understanding" that was in this man's heart.

As Trane himself said in an interview in 1962, five years before his tragically early death:

> There are so many things to be considered in making music. The whole question of life itself: *my* life in which there are many things on which I don't think I've reached a final conclusion; there are matters I don't think I've covered completely, and all these things have to be covered before you make your music sound any way. You have to grow to know.
>
> When I was younger I didn't think this would happen, but now I know that I've got a long way to go. Maybe when I'm sixty I'll be satisfied with what I'm doing, but I don't know . . . I'm sure that later on my ideas will carry more conviction.
>
> I know that I want to produce beautiful music, music that does things to people that they need. Music that will uplift and make them happy: those are the qualities I'd like to produce.
>
> Some people say "your music sounds angry," or "tortured," or "spiritual," or "overpowering" or something; you get all kinds of things, you know. Some say they feel elated, and so you never know where it's going to go. All a musician can do is to get closer to the sources of nature, and so feel that he is in communion with the natural laws. Then he can feel that he is interpreting them to the best of his ability, and can try to convey that to others.

Responsible, mature musical commentators have often expressed the view that the role of an artist is to keep in the front of man's mind the clear vision of the ideal world, of the world as it should and could be. But when mankind is as dangerously close to passing the point of no return as he has been for at least the last several decades, then the duty of the responsible artist is to hold a mirror up to humanity in which the naked truth is so sharply reflected that there is no mistaking the dire consequences that are certain to follow if he does not change his ways. When the realities of life are harsh and forbidding, sweetly sonorous and placid art (for example, the jazz style associated with the years preceding the outbreak of the Second World War) is an anachronism. It lacks meaning and relevance for the times.

Even the most vitriolic traducer of John Coltrane cannot convincingly state that he was a madman; and certainly Trane was no fool.

Neither can there be any doubt whatsoever, except to the uninformed, that his self-discipline and application to hard, grinding work was as awesome as it was musically productive, both in terms of the areas he covered and the depth to which he plumbed each area.

If, then, Trane adopts a tone which offends the ears of some music critics and listeners, obviously there must be a reason for it, and it is doubtful whether even Trane himself could have accounted for it in a satisfactory manner. But consider that every individual human being has an irrational as well as a rational side to his nature. What is more, the more highly developed the rational side is, the more aggressively functional the irrational side becomes. Where the individual attempts to put a lid on that irrational side—and succeeds in doing so—he is in deep, deep trouble. It is from this irrational side of the artist that his instinctual guidance derives. It is the channel through which his muse (or genius, or whatever you want to call it) communicates with him. Thus, even the artist himself has no other course but to hunt for rational reasons to explain his irrational (or extrarational) actions and attitudes. So that even Trane might not be able to explain why his tone is what it is, except in terms of the plain fact that it turned out to be precisely what it was.

J. C. Thomas, in his book on Trane, quotes Whitney Balliett of the *New Yorker* as saying, "That ugliness, like life, can be beautiful is the surprising discovery one makes after attempting to meet the challenge offered by Coltrane. Coltrane's tone is harsh, . . . unexpected."[2] Balliett misses the whole point: ugliness is not beautiful, and Trane was not out to prove that it was. Trane's "ugly" tone is more likely to be an expression of the pain that for far too long far too many blacks have had to contain, and from which some relief may be felt by the simple fact of its finally being brought out into the open—precisely through the "ugliness" of Trane's tone.

But the typical music critic is completely out of his depth when faced with the kind of situation Trane presents him with. It has been said with justification—and this is particularly applicable to music deriving from or related to traditional African music—that there are two aspects to musical intervals: the mathematical (from which acoustics derives) and the symbolic and psychological (from which derive music's expressive qualities). Furthermore, these two aspects originate from the same principles and come together in a unity that is beyond the understanding of many people trained in the Western "scientific method." This is the unfortunate intellectual bias which forces on them the illogical situation of always leaving aside one aspect of experience whenever they study the other, "as if the laws of acoustics and those of musical expression did not refer to the same sounds."[3]

Thus we find reviewers who fault Trane for "repeating figurations time and again" to no purpose. Apart from the fact that these figurations are legitimately derived from certain types of traditional African music and properly incorporated by Trane into his playing, where would any of us be without the "repeated figurations" of our individual hearts, or the "repeated figurations" of our in-and-out breaths?

The harm done to artists through the "informed ignorance" of so many people who write "authoritatively" on matters beyond their comprehension is beyond reckoning. That it is unconscious and not the end result of deliberate ill will makes no difference whatsoever in its effects. It is an unfortunate situation. Trane survived it, but many budding Tranes do not.

But now let us focus on Trane's philosophy of life. Here is where the symbolic and psychological aspects of his music unfold clearly. These aspects provoked a question that hounded me for a long time—how to get at that vital issue—because this is where Trane's music becomes a living vehicle. It is clear to me now that without a reference to his source one will never be able to experience the real essence of the music that John Coltrane played.

My feeling is that one can only understand this in the context of the way of life of the traditional African, that is, the traditional man. The traditional man is everywhere; and everywhere that he resides his concepts of reality are consistent. For the traditional man "reality is a function of a celestial archetype: reality is conferred through participation in the 'symbolism of the center': cities, temples, houses become real by the fact of being assimilated to the center of the world; and rituals and significant profane gestures acquire the meaning attributed to them and materialize that meaning only because they deliberately repeat such and such acts posited originally by gods, heroes, and ancestors."[4] So reality for the traditional man is existence through the repeated actions of the gods. In this reality there are no profane acts and this concept most clearly defines the philosophy embodied in the lifestyle of John Coltrane.

However, all of this would be suspect if there were any evidence that there has been no awareness on the part of the African-American of the African. It seems to me that there has been an ongoing evaluation of evidence ever since the beginning of this century concerning the real lifestyle of Africans. The author Alex Haley has successfully worked his way back through several generations to find relatives in

West Africa. But a general concern for African roots was first demonstrated through the work of Marcus Garvey in his Universal Negro Improvement Association. Mr. Garvey advocated a mass emigration to Africa and through his efforts many African-American people became more aware and more sensitive to their heritage. This was in the early twenties, right after the First World War. At the same time, the Harlem Renaissance, a collective of black artists, was beginning to develop in New York City.

The next consciousness-raising event was the organizing of the nation of Islam by Elijah Mohammed in the late thirties. This event had direct implications on John Coltrane because he was exposed to the religion from the time he moved to Philadelphia in the middle forties. Yet, in spite of all the criticism it has received, the nation of Islam has long been a symbol for black self-determination; and its record for rehabilitating human beings is extraordinary. Both Thomas and Simpkins make it very clear in their books that the nation of Islam had a positive impact on John Coltrane.

More than anything, the nation of Islam opened Trane up to Africa and his awareness of Africa, not merely as some far-distant continent where his descent could be traced from, but as a real and living source for him, irrespective of where he might be. His acknowledgment of that was spelled out in several ways: in the many pieces that he composed and gave African names to; in the fact that he was in his time one of the foremost rhythmic players in jazz; and, perhaps more than anything else, his world view concepts. He realized the vastness of the universe and in that vastness he was a minute organism. His awareness of that is evident especially through the names of his later compositions. (The actual dates, times, and names of compositions are listed in the discography.)

In 1957 Trane went through an experience of spiritual rebirth where, in his own words, he communed with God. Clearly, when he emerged for the second time he had developed a sense of direction, with his music right at the heart of that direction. But his life was more than just *making* music: it was the offering up of this music from a now spiritually mature musician to God, and to the uplifting of people everywhere. His religion became the innermost awareness of the relationship in the unity of God, nature, and man. He developed a reverence for life, and he articulated this reverence not only through his music but in his whole being.

If one wanted to objectify this and understand it more clearly, I think one would have to refer to the graphic representation of the four

14

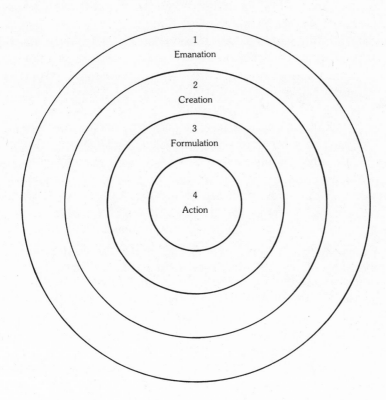

worlds of the traditional man as seen in Diagram A. There are four concentric circles. At the center is what the traditional man calls the world of action: this is essentially the material world, the fourth world seen through the eyes of the flesh rather than through eyes of the spirit, the world of oppositeness. In this world divisiveness and the logical masculine mind reside abundantly. It is a world more often experiencing chaos rather than order.

The third world is the world of formulation: this is the world that the traditional man believes can only be reached through meditation. It is the world of polarity, of positive and negative, each of which complement one another. It is a world where the masculine and the feminine minds meet in order to bring forth "new beginnings."

The second world is the world of creation: it is here where the archetypes live. That is where the "first" reside, a concept so important and central in understanding the way of life of traditional people.

The first world—the outermost of the concentric circles—is the world of emanation, the world of God, perhaps interpreted best by the Hindu who says, "Thou canst not know the Knower of knowledge, thou canst not see the Seer of seeing, thou canst not hear the Hearer of hearing, thou canst not comprehend the Comprehender of comprehension." It is my belief that Coltrane was able to penetrate the second world and that he demonstrated this penetration through the love of (and in) his music.

What this all means if interpreted through the music of John Coltrane is that he was able to connect successfully what Sowande calls the western lobe or the intellectual side of his brain with the eastern lobe or the intuitive side. The western side, the intellectual half, can be documented and seen through transcriptions. The eastern or intuitive side can only be understood through the symbols that are left and perpetuated through the art itself. If we consider only the intellectual half then we can easily move to Thomas's *Chasin' the Trane*[5] and speculate as to what Trane's concerns were about Einstein's theory of relativity in terms of music—and how he used a mathematical system to figure out musical problems that he had. Since Trane was a very evolutionary, developing artist one could see the different structures of his compositions and realize how he moved from playing through chord changes to playing free. But nothing would be known about the content that he expressed through this evolution.

The diagram by Fela Sowande (Diagram B) gives a clearer formula for trying to interpret this great musician. His art of course always appears at the top, and there is a direct line connecting the art with the imagination. Then there is a direct line from the imagination to technical proficiency. So we have, so far, music and the most fertile imagination of John Coltrane, together with his ability to play the instruments he chose to play. On the intellectual side or the western lobe, *will* (the desire to do a thing) and *form* (the essence of the material existence of that thing) can be seen and articulated. The will to do something and the form and shape that that something takes are all collectively visualized through signs. In the eastern lobe in the diagram, *idea* (the germ of the substance) and *content* (the essence of the substance) collectively meet and are expressed through symbols. Both this diagram and the diagram of the concentric circles are material vehicles by which I hope a better understanding of John Coltrane can be arrived at.

Before going into closer scrutiny of Coltrane's music it seems more than appropriate to deal with the form that he played in. This form known as "jazz" derives idiomatically out of the whole spectrum

16

Diagram B

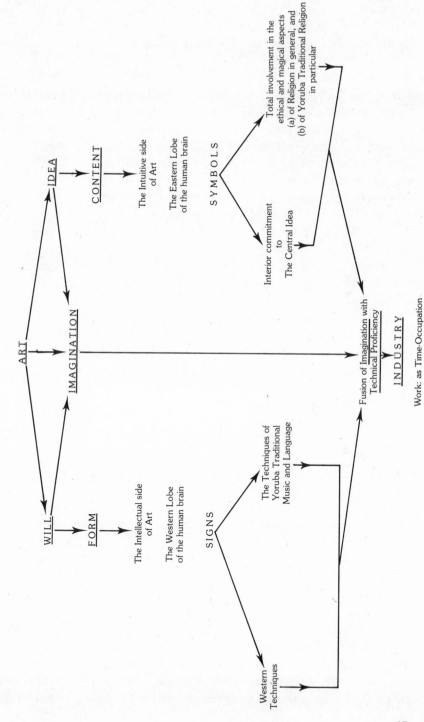

ART

IDEA

CONTENT

The Intuitive side
of Art

The Eastern Lobe
of the human brain

SYMBOLS

Total involvement in the
ethical and magical aspects
(a) of Religion in general, and
(b) of Yoruba Traditional Religion
in particular

Interior commitment
to
The Central Idea

IMAGINATION

WILL

FORM

The Intellectual side
of Art

The Western Lobe
of the human brain

SIGNS

The Techniques of
Yoruba Traditional
Music and Language

Western
Techniques

Fusion of Imagination with
Technical Proficiency

INDUSTRY

Work: as Time-Occupation

of African-American music. In the first book I wrote (about Miles Davis), I purposely left the word jazz out because there seems to have been some misuse of the word throughout its history. However, believing now that everything has its complementary side, and through further scrutiny into the meanings of symbols, I have found that the word jazz in describing the form that John Coltrane played in is suitable. It is a fact—as well as something of which I am personally convinced—that symbols play a real part in the lives of almost all peoples, but perhaps especially African-American people. Through my readings I came across a book called *The Sufis* by Idries Shah in which there is a chapter called "The Secret Language." In that chapter the word jazz—spelled "jass"—is decoded to mean "to inquire after a thing: to scrutinize (hidden things); to ascertain (news)." If this meaning were to describe Trane's relationship to his form then jazz would certainly be the word. Trane's energies were certainly directed into inquiring into the nature of his art, into scrutinizing the hidden things in music, and into "making new"—that is, arriving at new ways to say things in music, and saying them with such authority that he is entirely convincing—a true originator.

Historically, jazz has been spoken of as developing through certain style periods: from ragtime (piano music period), through Dixieland, the so-called "jazz age," swing, bebop, hard bop, free but played in tempo, and finally free with rhythmic tempo and melodically independent movement. But these style periods only took up about eighty-five years. If one looks at this in the context of "real" time (that is, the historical time of traditional people) this would represent no more than a few minutes. I would rather say that these were collective periods in which the music was and is in fact developing. Not too long ago I read a book on Indonesian music by Donald Lentz in which he talks about the music of Java having taken three centuries to develop: even in this context eighty-five years is a relatively short span of time.

It seems that in each of these periods different instruments developed. When I say "developed" I mean that fluency was becoming more and more evident as the knowledge of the original use of the instruments became apparent. Because the instruments (piano, trumpet, saxophones) were tempered instruments, the system that they were developed to be used in—the Western harmonic system—had to go through an examination period which culminated in the years 1955—1960.

Jazz took instruments and—through a series of developments which over a long period of time were harmonic developments—jazz

18

musicians learned to play those instruments with such great fluency in tempo and rhythm that finally an instrument in the hands of an individual like John Coltrane could practically communicate thought forms to an audience. And this music was, in its way, a chronicle of the African-American people. And you cannot look at John Coltrane in the context of this chronicle without recognizing where he came from—who those persons were that he identified with as a player, that he was an extension of them, and that the players who came after him were naturally an extension of him. Because we have empirical facts we know that Trane was weaned on bebop, grew to maturity with hard-bop, and then, through a spiritual rebirth, emerged as the strongest player of his time, completely revolutionizing the instrument that he played.

There would be no clear understanding of the sound and the validity of Coltrane's music without realizing one last fact: that the descent of his music emerged through his use of the natural scale. This alone immediately clashes with the idea that John Coltrane played a tempered instrument—that is, an instrument that was designed to modulate through keys. Because the harmonics of a natural sound clash with the modulation through keys that is intrinsic to the European harmonic system, instruments were developed which are essentially out of tune with the natural scale. But Coltrane found the means to go beyond this essential aspect of Western music—into a "free jazz" that was, in a sense, more African than European—by learning to play the entire scope of any specific tone. He developed this through, first of all, enormous practice and, second, a will to play finally what he wanted to play. It was through this expansion of the parameters of a tone that he was able to communicate in as brilliant and revolutionary a manner as he did.

Jazz has always been a people's art form. It has always been accessible to those who want to play it. It is a music of choices, and through a complex code communicates the spirit of the times: in the hands of a player like John Coltrane it prophesies the future. The great players who have emerged out of this music have emerged through a natural hierarchical system. It has endured in spite of attempts to prostitute it or to redefine it out of existence. It has endured in spite of the fact that its leading exponents have far too often had short lives. It has been a music that has emerged out of the profanity of the brothels into the spiritually profound reality of the art of John Coltrane.

1

Religion is the inner awareness of a factual dynamic relationship between the individual on one hand, and the Cosmos and the World of Nature on the other.

Philosophy is the articulation of that relationship in a meaningful intelligible way, as a guide to practical living.

Drama is the enactment of that relationship, in movement and speech.

Art is the meaningful expression of that relationship in any medium whatever.

History is the factual record of that relationship in its process of becoming; not as mere statistical facts, but as the detailed diary of the contacts between Man, Cosmos and Nature, from which were eventually distilled that clear awareness of the interdependence and the unbroken continuity between the three worlds.

The science of social organization is an accurate reproduction of that same relationship, in terms of human society.

The science of government is the codification of that relationship and its application in that society, its purpose being to subserve the science of social organization.

Economics, Family structure, and the Individual within the Family, are determined by, and subserve, the science of government and the science of social organization. [1]

—Fela Sowande

John Coltrane — 1965, Newport Jazz Festival

John William Coltrane was born in Hamlet, North Carolina, on September 23, 1926. He died July 17, 1967 in Huntington, Long Island, two months and six days before his forty-first birthday. Because he was an African-American, the primary source of his music was in another part of the world, in a land which he was unable to visit during his own lifetime but whose life forces transcended bodies of water and land, compelling him to respond to the patterns of traditional African societies.

His birth was on the day of the autumn equinox, on the cusp on Virgo and Libra, one of the two days during the year in which night and day are in perfect balance. Not to take this into account would be to ignore something that in fact Trane knew. He was perfectly aware of the meaning of astrology, and when he started publishing his own music the names that he gave specific pieces acknowledged this fact: Fifth House (1959), Equinox (1960), Crescent (1964), Sun Ship (1965), Cosmos (1965), Leo (1966), Mars (1967), Venus (1967), Saturn (1967), and Jupiter (1967).

When he experienced his spiritual rebirth in 1957 it was a rebirth from a materialistic high person to a spiritually high one. Coming out of Virgo into Libra—moving from the first half to the second half of the total zodiac sign—can be construed as a symbol of moving from the human to the spiritual aspect of man's development. On the more practical side, perhaps seeing the way he was able to keep three men together in his band over a period of four years showed his sensitivity to feeling the different spiritual weights of other individuals. He was constantly taking the band into the studio, often to make sure that Tyner, Jones, and Garrison were working steadily.

In traditional societies, rebirth or regeneration is an essential belief. And the spiritual maturity that Trane arrived at usually comes only to "older" souls—those who have come back many times in the cycle of rebirth. Sometimes a person is said to experience reincarnation five times, and sometimes seven, depending upon which traditional culture we are considering. But the concept is undeniable. It is the basic belief of traditional Africans throughout the continent; and it was a basic belief that they brought with them to America.

When John Coltrane was just a few months old he moved with his family from Hamlet to High Point, North Carolina—a town in the north central part of the state. The town was originally founded by Quakers, who had a direct interest in the black population of that small community. In 1891 the Society of Friends founded a "school to provide education for Negroes." Ironically, the school that Trane attended—William Penn High School—was located on a site that had at one time been used as a slave market, and which during the Civil War had been a mobilization camp for Confederate soldiers. I think Trane may well have felt the vibrations of the souls who had either experienced or viewed the many atrocities that took place on that spot.

When a Yoruba man of Nigeria goes to select a tree suitable for the framing of a drum, he first picks one near the village so that the tree will have heard the people's voices. It is having heard the people's voices that enables the drum to "speak" well. Coltrane lived close to the people, and their voices emerged—almost gushed—from his instruments. When Trane was a small child he was exposed to the religious music of the southern African-American church. Both of his grandfathers were ministers of the African Methodist Episcopal Zion Church.

> The peculiar development of African culture in North America began with the loss of the drums. The Protestant, and often Puritan, slave owners interfered much more radically with the personal life of their slaves than did their Catholic colleagues in the West Indies or in South America. The slaves were allowed no human dignity and their cultural past was ignored; or else it was considered a humane task to educate them into being "better" human beings, and this process was initiated by teaching them to be ashamed of their African heritage. And to forbid the drums was to show a keen scent for the essential: for without the drums it was impossible to call the orishas, the ancestors were silent, and the proselytizers seemed to have a free hand. The Baptists and Methodists, whose practical maxims and revivals were sympathetic to African religiosity quickly found masses of adherents.[2]

The Baptists and the Methodists were the first to accept wholesale numbers of blacks into the church and because of the participatory aspect of these two denominations it was very much in keeping with the context which the African called his Orishas. Trane saw this every Sunday—the movement between the minister and his congregation—and from this he saw the cycle of the breath of life. I recall that Aretha Franklin once described her father as the individual who had showed her how to involve a whole congregation in the overall participation in church—actively—through using the voice, through the in and out mechanism of breathing.

Trane also saw and heard the spirituals in this church, the pieces with their coded double meanings which had historically expressed the whole emotional psyche of the people. Besides this, his maternal grandfather, Rev. William Blair, was known throughout North Carolina both for his ability to evoke responses from his congregation and as a champion for the rights of African-American people. He grew up in this great man's house, and there was always plenty of family around for him to interact with. His grandfather naturally had great responsibility in the community, so to the eyes of this young sensitive individual was presented right from the beginning a strong elderly male, a man who first presented him with the concept of God.

Those people who believe in the concept of rebirth say that children up until the time that they lose their first teeth are going through a strong imitating experience. After the age of seven—up until the time that puberty starts around twelve or thirteen, when the individuals are gaining their permanent teeth—they are very much struck by authoritative figures, and the impressions made on them at this time are usually very strong. Trane was not only under the influence of a strong grandfather, Reverend Blair, but he was also fortunate in having extremely sensitive and musical parents. His father played the ukulele, violin, and sang; his mother—who had unfortunately been unable to pursue a career as an opera singer—played piano in church and also sang with the choir. All around Trane as a child were positive vibrations which helped to stimulate questions concerning the meaning of life.

Trane got his first instrument at the age of twelve. It was a school instrument, a clarinet. So from the first time he started to play he played reeds. He listened and practiced furiously, sometimes annoying the people around him; however, they never acknowledged this fact, since it was obvious even then that Trane was serious about music.

In 1939, when John was only thirteen, first his grandfather and soon afterward his father died. His mother moved to Philadelphia a few years later in order to get employment; but Trane stayed in High Point in order to finish high school. He had been an excellent student in elementary school, but almost as soon as he got his first instrument he began to lose interest in some of his school work. So what had been strong academic talent seemed to be diminishing at this time. Simpkins points out very clearly the two reasons for this. Certainly, the death of the two strong men in his family had some impact on him; but more than anything else this was the beginning of Trane's ongoing dedication to musical study.

On the advice of his high school band instructor his mother had bought him an alto saxophone a year after he had started to play the clarinet; and when he first arrived in Philadelphia in 1944 that was the instrument he was playing.

Philadelphia became Trane's real musical center. It was in

Philadelphia that he first began to know other musicians, other people who were actually involved in the vocation that he was beginning to embark upon. It was in Philadelphia that he began a simultaneous formal and social education of music. He spent a short period of time at the Ornstein School of Music but then moved to Granoff Studios. At Granoff he won scholarships both for performance and composition and was later remembered as one of their best students. He apprenticed from 1945 until 1959, playing for the most part in other men's bands. The traditional Yoruba priest learns his trade for twenty-five years or more "so that with the access of Power there shall already have been enough wisdom to enable the individual to withstand every and any temptation to misuse such Power."[3]

Looking at this period one can clearly see Trane's natural evolutionary stages of development. First he played in cocktail bars. Then he was drafted into the Navy where he spent a little under two years playing in the Navy Band in the Pacific. Any special service in any of the armed forces is hard to get into. Being accepted into one of the Navy dance bands, as Trane was, showed his proficiency even at this early time of his career. When he came out of the service he came back in Philadelphia and started developing a collection of musical friends and colleagues that he would tap for the rest of his life.

He first entered the Joe Webb Blues Band with Cal Massey. At this time Joe Webb had Big Maybelle in the band, and it was a top notch blues band. Listening to this young woman sing night after night filled Trane's head with what a sound is and how a sound can be developed through the voice, and how this in fact could be translated into instrumental playing. From Joe Webb he moved to King Kolax, and then around 1947 he had the opportunity to play with Eddie Cleanhead Vinson where he was persuaded to change from alto to tenor saxophone. It was also in 1947 that he first met Miles Davis and played with Miles and another contemporary, Sonny Rollins, in New York. These, however, were only very short engagements, and soon Trane was back in Philadelphia playing in a band directed by altoist Jimmy Heath. His early apprenticeship then, up until the time that he and Heath entered the Dizzy Gillespie Band, had been in blues-based bands and playing with his local contemporaries in Philadelphia. He worked with all of the Philadelphia reed men, including Heath, Bill Barron, Jimmy Oliver, John Glenn, and the exceptionally talented writer Benny Golson. When he joined the Dizzy Gillespie Band, though, he was moving for the first time into a situation with one of the foremost band leaders in jazz.

26

Dizzy Gillespie, along with Charlie Parker, had been one of the architects of bebop. In the late forties he began to bring Cuban percussionists into his band, and this gave Trane the opportunity to play in a situation where there were multiple rhythmic influences.

However, this also was the period when Trane began using drugs; and slowly but surely his addiction to heroin preoccupied his mind. In the early fifties Gillespie broke his large band down into a smaller unit and Trane played in that band for a short time; but Gillespie finally had to get rid of both Trane and Heath because of their drug problem. Trane constantly found himself stranded out of town and had to seek out other musicians so that he could borrow enough money to get back to Philadelphia. In 1952 he found himself stranded in Los Angeles while playing in the Earl Bostic Band and it was at this time that he first met Eric Dolphy, who gave him the money to return to Philadelphia. Earl Bostic was a tremendous player—an outstanding technician on his instrument—and sitting in the band with Earl as the lead player gave Trane the opportunity to hear a lot of things that he knew he couldn't play on the instrument yet. After the Earl Bostic job, he joined the tenor saxophonist and vocalist Gay Crosse and at this time met the young Pittsburgh trumpeter Tommy Turrentine. He was, however, still heavy into drugs and also beginning to drink a great deal.

In 1954 he began playing in Johnny Hodges's band. Hodges, of course, had been for a long time a mainstay in the Duke Ellington Band. He was an astoundingly lyrical player, not only on alto saxophone but also on soprano sax. The Ellington band was one of the first orchestras that John Coltrane had listened to when he was a kid; so that Johnny Hodges, along with Lester Young, were two of his earlier influences. Hodges's influence, in fact, was a dominant factor in the tremendous lyricism that came out in Trane's music in the late fifties, especially in the numerous ballads that he played during that period.

2

It is the LIVINGNESS in Art that makes it art. Form, style, structure, craftsmanship, are of the highest degree of importance to the creative mind in man, for meaningful ideas have nothing to say to the man who has not mastered the tools of his trade. Nevertheless it is only when even superb craftsmanship has been successfully wedded to—and has become a channel for—a "Poetic Content" that adds new dimensions and insight, greater depth and clarity, to man's awareness and understanding of himself in relation to a dynamic Universe of which he is an integral and indispensable unit, that we have Art in which there is that Livingness that makes it art. Only in terms of that "Poetic Content" can that Art be profitably approached, examined, and appraised. Only by being in the final analysis primarily concerned, not with the formal and structural elements, but with the LIFE-QUALITY in that Art can one be certain that he is handling the Art itself and not its mere container.[1]

—Fela Sowande

John Coltrane — December, 1961, Jazz Gallery, New York City.
Meditation to the level of formulation.

Thus, when Trane emerged in the Miles Davis Band, he was a unique player. He *sounded* different. He was authoritative with the tenor saxophone. He didn't just work the combinations of key stops—he played them. When influences appeared in his playing, he always acknowledged them: Lester Young, Coleman Hawkins, Ben Webster, Dexter Gordon, Bill Barron, Jimmy Oliver, Jimmy Heath, Gene Ammons, Johnny Hodges, Eddie Cleanhead Vinson, Wardell Gray, and Charlie Parker—who indirectly moved him from the alto to the tenor. It was in the playing of Coleman Hawkins that Trane first noticed the work of the arpeggio or the third moving line. Throughout his own playing the 1-3-5 combinations are everywhere.

To be hired by Miles Davis was a terrific opportunity for Trane. Interestingly enough, joining Miles Davis's band and getting married for the first time happened almost simultaneously. Trane had met his first wife, Naima, in 1954; they were married on October 3, 1955, right after Trane entered the Miles Davis Band. Just looking at the number of record dates that Trane had before he joined Miles and right after shows the great influence that Miles not only had on Trane's playing but on Trane as a personality as well. Miles Davis, in 1955, was one of the best-known and most admired musicians among his peers. To be in any way associated with him was very prestigious indeed.

What Coltrane did in Miles's band from the very beginning was to absorb his influences, dispersing them into his own maze of lines. In the solo of "Ah-Leu-Cha," recorded on October 27, 1955 for Columbia Records, most of his lower register playing sounds like a polished Gene Ammons, especially between bar nineteen and bar twenty-three in the first chorus of his improvisation, where a line, played off a preceding sequence, has intermittent rests (Example 1). Further on in the solo, between the second half of the eighth measure and the tenth measure of the second chorus, a short phrase which Coltrane used to end off the preceding line is profoundly reminiscent of Ammons (Example 2). It is a whole, round tone with, if one listens closely, a

First Chorus

Example 1

slight vibrato. However, these short phrases are difficult to pick out, even though they are a definite departure from Trane's crystallized articulations. Coltrane knew Ammons's sound. He could hear it and play it as fast as Ammons. One can imagine what he was hearing in 1955: look at what he was doing in 1967.

Second Chorus

Example 2

At this point perhaps we should try to examine what an "influence" is. I don't think that a man of Trane's potential would listen to what another person is playing and directly imitate him. I think he would listen to find out what the other player is playing that he cannot play, and then he would try to work that expansion of capacity into his own playing. Occasionally, a particular way of playing a thing may occur in a musician's improvisation; if this is actually a line that he is known to play all the time, then it may be an active imitation if it occurs in someone else's music. However, if one listens to all the Coltrane improvisations that he played down through the years, one is hard-pressed to find—except occasionally—another person's music. So, in an individual like Trane, an influence would be an unconscious departure from what was continuously evolving in his music.

Coltrane synthesized his influences and laid them out, almost automatically. For him, the *magic* of his sound came through the process of making his own music. His own music sought out the influences of sound—the magic of sound—that aspect which takes people to another level. Of course, throughout the history of Western man those people who profess to practice magic have been castigated; but magic is a real process to the traditional man. It is seen throughout his legends and his mythology, and it is the process of magic through sound that enables him to bridge the gap between the invisible and visible worlds. This was the quest of John Coltrane. We are talking now not about a process that has not been perceived (because magic has been perceived through the ages), but about the process that Trane used, especially after his transformation, to attempt to bring beauty and harmony to the commonplace. It was a stoic obedience to practicing that got him from the local bars of Philadelphia to the Miles Davis Quintet. Even during the period of his drug problem he was able to sustain and maintain an ongoing practicing discipline. This practicing discipline was beginning to allow Trane to express his ideas and give birth to the new musical images that he found himself playing. This was a style period known as hard bop, and Trane was, through diligence, becoming its master.

Coltrane first listened to his elders, gained proficiency on his instrument, and then brought that proficiency to his art. He saw the nuances of others' styles and fused them into what would become his own style. Even as late as the middle fifties he was actively trying (as Charlie Parker had tried in the forties) to liberate sound from harmonic patterns and go back to the natural scale and linear music, melody and rhythm.

When he was first hired by Miles Davis in 1955, Trane's proficiency was formidable. He was cresting on a wave that was to carry him into one of the two basic functions of music in traditional African societies: to bridge the gap between the invisible and visible worlds, between the world of man and the world of the archetypes, and in doing this bring himself and the whole context of his being in direct contact with those forces which control the destinies of that being. Trane rode this wave for four years, peaking frequently in both the bands of Davis and Thelonious Monk, where he started to intensify his work on compound phrases.

On the improvisation of "Ah-Leu-Cha" (recorded, as I mentioned before, in October 1955), Trane's proficiency allows him to play a large number of cross-rhythms. It was this proficiency which erroneously led his critics to label him a vertical player. He found himself among those contemporaries who were exploring chord changes, and he completely scrutinized the style (hard bop) using melodic-rhythmic lines within the progression spaces. The solo begins with eight patterns of four eighth notes. Each pattern sounds different because of the melodic-rhythmic shapes. The first moves down from a' to e' in steps; the second goes from d' up to f# (whole step-half step-half step); the third begins at g' and moves down minor thirds to d'; the fourth, from e' down to f in major thirds; the fifth begins on B♭ and moves in F up to e'; the sixth shows the first turning statement, moving f' down a minor third to d', then up a minor second to E♭' and a major second to f'; the seventh descends from g' to E♭' for the first time beginning a pattern with a minor second, ironically ending in the reverse of the preceding pattern; in the eighth and last pattern, we see the movement of a fourth for the first time in a pattern. Rhythmically, laying aside his poor execution from the second note of the fifth pattern to the end of the sixth pattern, these total patterns sound very duple. This driving at the music, making it swing by changing accents

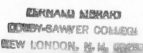

on rhythmic phrases, became a hallmark of Coltrane's improvisations throughout his life. His increasing proficiency compelled him more and more to summon up his source—Africa (Example 3). Concepts that Trane had been working out with Cal Massey and some of his earlier Philadelphia peers can be seen in this solo, especially the double diminished scale, which uses whole steps followed by half steps.

First Chorus

Example 3

The one other piece recorded on this day was "Budo," a piece written by the visionary pianist Bud Powell. Coltrane had played for a very short period with Bud Powell in the late forties, and he certainly knew this piece. His playing here, however, seems stiff and a little tight; so that, when Miles Davis produced his first album with Columbia, "Ah-Leu-Cha"—which was much better recorded overall—was kept, and "Budo" was released later.

The Miles Davis quintet included William Red Garland on piano, Paul Chambers on double bass, and Philly Joe Jones (Philly so he wouldn't be confused with Jo Jones) on percussion; a rollicking rhythm section which functioned with versatility as a unit, and with equal strength as individual soloists. Their influence can be seen in the final formation of Trane's sixties quartet, which included the rhythm section of McCoy Tyner on piano, James Garrison on double bass, and Elvin Jones on percussion. Garland's playing was sharp. Not only was he an outstanding harmonic player but his concept of space, coupled with his individual melodic style, made a mark upon Coltrane's musical thinking. Garland was very good at listening sensitively to the soloist, launching him, and providing him with a canvas to paint on. During the middle fifties he was considered, along with Horace Silver and John Lewis, one of *the* accompanists to work with, if available. His own solo playing included a "block chord" style. Instead of playing single lines during his solos—allowing his left hand to accompany his right—he would play harmonic lines. The chord was called "block" because when the phrase moved, the intervals would remain in the same relationship. The lowest and highest notes of the right hand were played at octaves while the inside voices were played at fourths or fifths. Sometimes the fourth would be raised, creating great tension in the chord. The chords were usually played in closed position and the harmonies he created were more than interesting. This style was a basic refinement of chord structures initiated by Erroll Garner. Garland had a superb ear and a sense of space that always had him in the right place doing the right thing. He, along with Bud Powell and Thelonious Monk, was among Tyner's early influences. In fact, during the infrequent moments when Garland and Tyner were able to get together, Red was very encouraging. Garland was thirty-two when he entered the Miles Davis Band. He had been a professional prize fighter when he was younger and was reputed to be one of the better persons to know. When Coltrane started to record under his own name in the second half of the fifties he used Garland almost exclusively. Garland had a firm hold on the rudiments, and his high level of musicianship is well documented. John Coltrane looked over his shoulder, plenty!

Garland had known Philly Joe from Philadelphia. They had played there together before entering the Davis band. Both were approximately the same age and Jones was a very revolutionary percussionist. He was virtually a one-man drumming ensemble. Each limb sounded as if it were autonomous; the balance of strength was so equalized. I remember Fela Sowande once mentioning that when he first saw Max Roach he thought he was listening to a whole ensemble. Jones was a descendant in that lineage which began with Chick Webb, Jo Jones, and Sid Catlett, then extended to Kenny Clarke, Art Blakey, and Max Roach, all of whom brought power and a dazzling solo proficiency to jazz. Philly Joe Jones was a virtuoso soloist and the aggressive driving force of the band. He was very fast and employed multiple rhythms as a rule rather than just occasionally. Very close in style to Roach, he was the first after Roach to use the tops and bottoms of the high-hat cymbal during his soloing. As Elvin Jones would later do in Coltrane's band, Philly Joe took complete control in this one. Philly Joe, however, often shared the drumming chair with Art Taylor, and Art Taylor figured in very heavily in the thinking of John Coltrane when he finally selected Elvin Jones. Art Taylor was a master at playing in tempo. The dominant quality that Philly Joe Jones had was that he was a great listening drummer. Similarly, the preeminent quality of Elvin Jones was certainly his ability to repeat on the drums the rhythmic lines that Coltrane would play during his improvisations. This was the calibre in drumming that Philly Joe brought, and that I'm certain Trane picked up on.

Paul Chambers, only twenty years old in 1955, was the youngest in the band. He was a nearly perfect synthesis of the syncopation of Charles Mingus and the strong tempo of Percy Heath, two of the more challenging bassists of the fifties. He had outstanding note selection and was especially devastating on the bottom end of the bass. Like all the members of this rhythm section, Chambers was exhilarating as a soloist as well as an accompanist. But it was the work he did in concert with Miles that was most impressive. He roamed all over the bass, and Davis was able to execute duos with Chambers at tempos equaling, and with insights surpassing, those achieved with Percy Heath in an earlier band. Chambers was a master of tempo, playing any combination of changes and syncopated lines, and when he applied his revolutionary technique to medium tempo blues pieces he was an *unbeatable* accompanist.[2] Added to his outstanding pizzicato style was a singing arco. His arco style was influenced by pianist Art Tatum's bassist, LeRoy Slam Stewart, who during his solos would play arco and hum at the unison or octave. The resonance of the two voices would create a very natural sound. Chambers achieved this same resonance by playing double stops at the fifth interval instead of singing. Often he would use his own voice as a third voice. "Still more revealing would be a history of musical instruments written, not (as it always is) from the technical standpoint of tone-production, but as a study of the deep spiritual bases of the tone-colours and tone-effects aimed at."[3]

The style called hard bop (1949 to 1959) was a crystallization of harmonic or vertical patterns. Chambers epitomized that style. He had an excellent ear, and his lines drove toward the progressions. He knew all the modulating possibilities and could leap to intervals like a Thomson's gazelle. In addition to the fact that his rhythms were always changing—by changing the accents, playing retard, accelerando, or playing on the beat—he always had great anticipation. He could move step-wise with great authority, beginning near the bridge on the G string, and using melodic and rhythmic sequences, moving down to the E in one long swoop. His sound was unique, containing almost no vibrato. He played low in tonality, giving the feeling that he was playing flat, but his sound buzzed.

When I first started listening to the Miles Davis Band in this period, I know that Paul Chambers was the first person my ear picked up. He played so beautifully low on the bass and he really expanded the parameters of the tone. Unquestionably, the tempered system had an influence on jazz in that the players, especially those who brought innovation to jazz, have always tried to bend this temperedness of tone back into its real natural state; and Chambers playing a natural instrument would not have the same problems that Trane, Miles Davis, or Garland would have. So his tones—that is, where he played his stops on the bass—had tremendous parameters. It also gave him a unique sound, a unique quality in his bass playing, even though my feeling is that Chambers did this so naturally that he himself didn't recognize what he was doing and the deep influence that he would have on Trane. "For the traditional African uses the natural scale, while the five lines and four spaces of Western Europe notational system are adequate only for the contemporary 'tempered' scale of Europe."[4]

The Miles Davis Band was a honed rhythm section, schooled by the masters and themselves "speaking well" to the people. All were excellent accompanists—versatile, flexible, and consistently on the mark. Chambers executed the tempi with visionary imagination, and his fixed rhythms allowed Jones to range unrestricted. Being able to count on Chambers, Philly Joe paced himself beautifully, laying out when Miles and Chambers played duo, or even when John played solo with Chambers, but always making his presence known upon reentering. In all of this, Garland felt his way, providing an extra rhythm. So the soloist always had a rhythmic ensemble behind him. This intuitive sense propelled the band.

Being possessed by the *idea* of music, and having all this going on in the band already, allowed Coltrane to take as many liberties as he wanted to further explore the possibilities of his music. Looking again at "Ah-Leu-Cha" (Charlie Parker), right at the beginning of the second chorus Trane begins a new line, an eleven-note theme which begins in C, moves quickly to G, then to c minor, and back to G (Example 4). At the end of the line there are two rests. He then repeats

First and Second Choruses

Example 4

this line, with a slight variation which cancels out the rest and causes the new line to sound as if it is in double time. The first line is reinforced by the second line which in turn introduces the next line (Example 5). His music was very tightly knit: a statement (theme), a response (varia-

Second Chorus

Example 5

tion), then on to the next. Lines repeated verbatim were used for rhythmic patterns and became much more important in his later style. His music, while comprised of small fragments, possesses continuity as a whole, like a giant puzzle made up of extremely small pieces, each having its own shape.

3

Now we can approach traditional music in terms of its structure, aiming to pinpoint as many of its musical characteristics as we can, so that we can classify it, through analysis, correlation of derived facts, and so on and so forth. This is a valid approach, which has its place in the scheme of things. But apart from the fact it would be of real interest only to professional musicians, I have always thought that its value was greatly overrated. For an analytical approach can give us, at best, only the anatomy and physiology of the music considered; it can tell us nothing about the informing life of the music, nothing about its essence, nothing of what it meant to its creators and why, and at the end we are left with the mere skeleton of what was a living art.

But we can also approach traditional music in terms of its function rather than of its structure; its content, rather than its form; its purpose and meaningfulness, rather than its size and shape, always aiming to relate it to the tradition from which it sprang, and to the day-to-day life of the people who gave it birth. At once we find ourselves facing a vast canvas, full of symbols; some of these are relatively easy to decipher; others are not so easy; still others appear to be weird hieroglyphics which may well defy all our efforts to fathom.[1]

—Fela Sowande

Elvin Jones — 1961, Newport Jazz Festival. The master drummer.

Charlie (Bird) Parker died in 1955. His death had a tremendous impact on the whole community of people who loved jazz. Throughout the country people wore black armbands to indicate their emotional attachment to this pioneering musician. He was the most dominant musician of his time and Trane's indebtedness to him can partially be seen in a photograph from Simpkins's book.[2] While Parker is soloing, Trane—then a member in the Jimmy Heath Band—is staring up at him, not with amazement, but as if he were mesmerized by Parker's sound. Parker himself comments:

> I remember one night I was jamming in a chili house (Dan Wall's) on 7th Avenue between 139th and 140th. It was December, 1939 . . . I'd been getting bored with the stereotyped changes that were being used all the time, and I kept thinking there's bound to be something else. I could hear it sometimes but I couldn't play it. Well, that night, I was working over "Cherokee" and, as I did, I found that by using the higher intervals of a chord as a melody line and backing them with appropriately-related changes I could play the thing I'd been hearing. I came alive.[3]

This use of the higher intervals for the melody line completely revolutionized jazz. It brought it to the end of a cycle. That is, if one starts on middle C and goes up seven intervals of a third (C—E—G—B♭—D—F—A—C; the B♭ allows the player to move into the flat keys), one will arrive at C again. It was this innovation on the part of Parker that brought about the whole examination of chord possibilities that happened throughout the fifties. In this period every alternate, inversion, and upper interval possibility was used.

Even more important than the use of different chords, and what Parker saw in that, was his ability to execute his ideas on his instrument. He played faster than any saxophonist before him, so from each chord change he developed many entering and exiting patterns. In the latter half of the fifties Trane had to have been among the fastest-playing tenor saxophonists around, and, as Parker had done before him, when Trane moved from one chord change to another, he used different patterns.

Parker, in spite of the fact that the music he developed seemed in its quick pace and syncopated lines almost the antithesis of lyricism, was a great lyrical player. You only have to listen to the music that he played with strings to see how beautiful and moving his ballad playing was. Yet he was a man who had a great sense of phrases—when to play a note longer than another note, when to accelerate, and when to retard the pace—and it seems an ironic coincidence that he died in the very year that Coltrane began to get national notice.

That year—1955—was also the year in which Coltrane married his first wife, Naima, who was Islamic. Marriage, in the thinking of traditional man, is of course an extremely important episode in life: it is the metaphysical, symbolic meeting of the masculine and feminine minds. Naima brought into Trane's life the great discipline—especially as it is applied in day-to-day life—of Islamic people. Trane saw this discipline, and he knew that he had to have it in his life in order to get over his drinking and drug problem. Naima saw Trane through his most dependent period—a period in which many times he started to give up music. It really seems inconceivable that a man of Trane's potential, even at this point, would have to give up music for any reason.

Coltrane made an exhaustive study of bebop (1939 to 1949), a period of African-American music which its negative critics might call chaotic, but a period, nonetheless, in which jazz as a valid art form began to emerge and examine itself. Jazz was evolving at this time both melodically and harmonically, with changes and lines that brought skepticism from its own ranks. Louis Armstrong had this to say in 1948:

> They want to carve everyone else because they're full of malice, and all they want to do is show you up, and any old way will do as long as it's different from the way you played it before. So you get all them weird chords which don't mean nothing, and first people get curious about it just because it's new, but soon they get tired of it because it's really no good and you got no melody to remember and no beat to dance to. So they're all poor again and nobody is working, and that's what that modern malice done for you.[4]

More important than anything else, it was Armstrong's comment about dance that is important. The swing period was a dance music period, and because the music had accelerated in its tempo it became no longer a music to physically dance to but a music to move to in one's head. It was an exhausting challenge to harmony, coupled with new "rhythmic" ways to use melody, and developing what Father A. M. Jones called "rhythmic harmony" when describing African music. Involved in this total context were Charlie Parker and Dizzy Gillespie. The music which developed in the after-hours of Minton's Playhouse and Monroe's Uptown House in Harlem was essentially their music. With Gillespie and Parker were Thelonious Monk, Kenny Clarke, and a handful of other revolutionary musicians who saw the increasing interest in African-American music and the possibilities inherent in that *primary* African source.

At the same time, Gillespie incorporated his advanced harmonies in a complex melodic line, a melody played with dazzling technical facility. To the advanced harmony and complex melody, Gillespie added a sense of timing which indicated a clear comprehension of Afro-Cuban rhythms—one of his early interests. . . . It was Gillespie who hired the greatest of all Cuban drummers, Chano Pozo, for his big band in 1947.[5]

Coltrane didn't play in that 1947 band but in 1949 he and Jimmy Heath joined together as altoists in Gillespie's band when Pozo's cousin, Francisco Pozo, was playing bongos and conga. Chano's playing drew a direct line to Africa. When he was in Havana, he had belonged to the Abakwa, a secret society that provided the rhythmic impetus for the Mardi Gras each year. That particular society originated in the Niger River area of Nigeria.

A couple years ago when I sat on a panel with Dizzy Gillespie he spoke of Chano Pozo and the tremendous influence that Pozo had on his thinking. However, what was most relevant in his comments at that time was the fact that Pozo would always sing rhythms to Gillespie before he would play them on the drum.[6] Coltrane sensed the primary source of Chano's playing just as he had sensed the strength and energy coming from Jimmy Heath and his other early musical associates from Philadelphia:

> As far as musical influences, aside from saxophonists, are concerned, I think I was first awakened to musical exploration by Dizzy Gillespie and Bird. It was through their work that I began to learn about musical structures and the more theoretical aspects of music.
>
> Also, I had met Jimmy Heath, who, besides being a wonderful saxophonist, understood a lot about musical construction. I joined his group in Philadelphia in 1948. We were very much alike in our feeling, phrasing, and a whole lot of ways. Our musical appetites were the same. We used to practice together, and he would write out some of the things we were interested in. We would take things from records and digest them. In this way we learned about the techniques being used by writers and arrangers.
>
> Another friend and I learned together in Philly—Calvin Massey, a trumpeter and composer. . . . His musical ideas and mine often run parallel, and we've collaborated quite often. We helped each other advance musically by exchanging knowledge and ideas.[7]

"Ah-Leu-Cha" and "Budo" were only two of several pieces that Coltrane recorded during his first stay with Miles Davis, who was beginning to record for Columbia. Miles still had a few dates to complete with Prestige, and these two dates produced some of the best records that Miles put together in this period. It also demonstrated Miles's unique way of using standard pieces. Music that one would think no jazz musician would play—like "Diane," "Surrey With The Fringe On Top," and "Just Squeeze Me"—were interspersed with pieces that have now become jazz standards, "Stablemates" and "Salt Peanuts" among them. This quintet could play anything, but Davis's affinity for little-used standards was certainly impressed upon Coltrane's mind.

When he wasn't recording with Miles Davis, Trane was often in the studio with others of his contemporaries. One of the most dynamic exchanges to happen was his one and only collaboration with Sonny Rollins. As is so often the case with jazz musicians, it was a rather spontaneous occurrence. Rollins had a record date and wanted to use the rhythm section of Miles Davis's quintet (as did so many performers at this time). Coltrane had gone along just to listen but was persuaded to play on one of the tracks. As Sowande says, "Now, whatever African music may or may not be, one thing about it is that it communicates. It is for this reason that we find, on the *social* levels, that we do not have performers and listeners, but performers and participants; we do not fix time date and place for making music, it 'happens' when the spirit moves us."[8] Trane and Rollins were the two most influential tenor players around, especially among the younger set. This one cut showed the differences in their sounds but also the closeness in both of their needs to make music.

The piece they played was called "Tenor Madness" but the line is clearly from a rhythmic pattern known as Oop-Bop-Sh'Bam, a twelve-bar blues which they play here in B♭, tailor-made for the tenor saxophone. It seems here that these two saxophonists would have been competitive in their playing. But what resulted was the antithesis of this. Extremely complementary throughout, exchanging lines, it was literally a communication through the language of music. I remember, when Sonny Rollins retired for the first time in 1959, how many people were saying he couldn't take the competition of John Coltrane. This 1956 recording demonstrates that when two great jazz musicians play together, the ultimate in positive creation can happen. There are points in their playing where their exchanges almost sound like one line; they were so in tune with one another that they would go on exchanging lines for several choruses before reaching the climax of a specific thought. This is especially true between the thirty-first and thirty-eighth chorus. Trane plays—as he did throughout his early recording period—mostly in the high register. Rollins, on the other hand, was adept in the middle and lower ranges of the tenor saxophone.

Even at this time Coltrane was a very aggressive player, bellowing the instrument, seeking more from it. Rollins was a lay-back performer, making every note in every line important. Where Coltrane would double-time his improvisations, Rollins would halve the tempo, especially when it was up. Rollins played with a distinctive vibrato which was really noticeable in his ballad playing. Although only twenty-seven, Rollins was one of the more formidable ballad players in this period. Two of his own pieces, "Oleo" and "Airegin," had already become jazz classics. "Tenor Madness" was Trane's longest recorded solo up until this date: including the trading of solos, he took forty-two choruses. The piece was a real *tour de force* in the hands of these superb musicians. Later in the year, Rollins would replace Trane in the Davis band.

As dynamic as this band was, work—as it usually is for jazz musicians—was not that plentiful. Miles was not that dependable when it came to keeping engagements either. I remember once personally anticipating his coming to Pittsburgh and then finding out later that he canceled his engagement. Several times I traveled to cities as far away as Cleveland, Columbus, and Cincinnati just to see him play, only to be disappointed by his "no show." So due to the financial hazard that it takes to keep a band together, Miles had to disband this one; and Trane found himself back again in Philadelphia.

Just before being fired by Miles, Trane participated in a recording session led by Paul Chambers (September 21, 1956). He contributed two compositions to the date—"Nita" and "Just For The Love." Both pieces were stamped bebop. Both had that notched melodic style which hallmarked the earlier music. The melodic lines were a combination of definitive rhythmic fragments, in an antilyrical linear form, with exploratory harmonic changes. "Just For The Love" used the five members of the band almost as a drumming ensemble.[9] Because the line was a series of rhythmic fragments, it acted—as each drum acts in the drum ensembles of Africa—as another rhythmic force. The two horns played the line in unison, allowing the timbre of each to produce its own sound. Chambers, a very disciplined bassist, holds the tempo steadfastly, almost as if his life depended on it. So the center of the music was maintained. This was Jones's kind of line; he sometimes played its rhythm, at other times a different one, meanwhile sustaining these rhythms, along with the tempo, on the high-hat cymbal. Horace Silver, a very solid pianist of this period, was especially sensitive to inner, closed-position harmony, interspersed with chords throughout. Four different rhythmic lines occurring at the same time result in multidirectional rhythms.

"Just For The Love" was a further drive towards linear, rhythmic music. The mixed rhythms of the three voices and the ostinato of the bass tempo created a percussive ensemble, especially if one listens to the brisk pace and the acceleration of the band once the line gets started. The structure of the melody is in six bars with a repeat, making it a twelve-bar blues. Harmonically, the line moves through all of the flat keys, and Coltrane, during his solo, correspondingly outlines these keys, either by arpeggios or scale fragments (Example 6). Harmony was becoming an exercise in pursuing tonal directions, and as this exercise became more familiar, the pursuit became more intensified. So a piece with essentially six measures had the equivalent number of harmonic changes. This was the very thing that Trane would eventually pull away from, giving himself much more space in which to build an improvisation. One of his contributions to jazz was a liberation of vertical sounds and a movement closer to the rhythmic/melodic foundations of African music. "It is this urge to be a participant and yet to contribute something new to whatever is already afoot, that is to some extent responsible for the multiple-rhythms of Africa."[10]

Example 6

Although "Nita," Trane's second composition for the date, was a thirty-one bar melodic line, its execution and feeling place it in the same bebop context as the previous composition. It has tremendous vertical movement, although the same "multiple-rhythmic" process occurs in the juxtaposition of the voices. Interestingly enough, during Trane's improvisation there was a five-bar rest right in the middle, something unusual for him: most of the time he was pushing the music, driving it. This particular piece has a twenty-three bar line which changes tempo for six bars, followed by a two-bar break. Perhaps so much activity in such a short space left too little room for Trane to sustain his kind of improvisation.

Trane's use of rests is essential in understanding his stylistic evolution. Since music does move through space and time the use of rests is as important as the actual sounds heard. Trane's use of rests in this period was a way that he regrouped his ideas. So often the rests occurred not as part of the ongoing improvisation, but as a distinct stopping point. His use of rests in his later period evolved into a whole continuum of sound. At this point the rests were used at breaks and later as part of the integrated effort of his improvisation.

When I first saw him in the fall of 1955 in Miles's band he was almost unknown. He would step into the foreground when he and Miles played the line of a piece and then during Miles's improvisation he would stand far off to the side, in the background, usually watching the chords and scrutinizing the space that Garland was using in music. He wore, as he did throughout most of his life, inconspicuous clothes—usually a dark or gray suit. He looked worn and thin and his clothes almost hung on him. But Trane was inconspicuous only until he picked up his horn and started to play. He was a tremendous contrast to Miles in the band, and they were certainly complementary to each other.

When Miles regrouped the band in late 1956 without Trane it was a crushing blow to him. However, as would be true throughout his life, he realized what he would have to do to get over this setback and to go on with his music.

4

He must first have sacrificed his individuality at the altar of what Jung terms "individuation," through which "he becomes not only an individual but also a member of a collectivity, and the wholeness he has achieved is in contact, through consciousness and the unconscious, with the whole world. The accent is not on his supposed individuality as opposed to his collective obligations, but... on the fulfillment of his own nature as it is related to the whole." How he does this, he must find out, for he is his own initiator; no one can help him; no one will ever know the price he has to pay for achievement; but equally, no one can filch from him the peace which passeth understanding that comes with achievement. But he will not travel in an air-conditioned car on tarred roads; it is not a journey to be undertaken, and perhaps only a sense of compulsion that drives one on regardless of aught else will ensure success.[1]

—Fela Sowande

John Coltrane — December, 1961, Jazz Gallery, New York City.
Every artist has a certain number of breaths.

To properly understand Trane it is necessary to see him both as an American and as a person of African descent. From his American context he picked up its song forms and the tenor saxophone (an instrument of European origin), and he explored the harmonic system to which a tempered instrument adheres. But his ancestral heritage, his primary source, was African. "One thing is certain, an artist does not stand a chance of becoming truly creative—a man with a vision and a spiritual awareness of life and the purposes of life—unless and until he has first reconciled himself with his traditional prehistoric past."[2]

In order to present the most accurate picture of Coltrane as an artist one must examine certain aspects of his African cultural heritage, looking beyond the propaganda which has been circulated concerning that heritage. That propaganda has essentially given no credence to its oral tradition with the "legends and myths which support it" and has rejected outright the notion that African-Americans have and have had a distinct culture. In music the course has been to investigate the structural manifestations of jazz and to put importance on *that* far exceeding its worth and to call *that* scholarship. "In the structural [mode of analysis], where form is held to determine content, its value is inflated beyond all reason, with the result that an analysis of how a thing is shaped or done is virtually now regarded as supplying the key to the essence of its being. . . ."[3]

Looking at just the *form* of Coltrane's music, while ignoring its content, and assuming that his American birthright, rather than his African cultural heritage, nurtured his music, creates a misconception about John Coltrane. That Trane was of African descent should always be taken into account, because it is in this connection that Trane could be said to have found the true sources of his inspiration. And Trane was able to realize his potential by giving up and throwing off those excesses which stifled and cut off his connection with his ancestors.

Creative energy is blocked when a person has a psychological problem, and drugs and drinking can be that. Coltrane had not been rehired in Miles's band because he had found a formula to cure his drug problem—drinking. This only compounded his difficulties by creating problems of articulation. Having to leave the band was a tremendous blow to Trane. He had received his first real public notice there, even though it was not always favorable. Miles had provided a forum that was relaxed and flexible. Miles himself was an ongoing musical inspiration, providing ideas to jump off from, constantly setting up his other horn, and developing a concept of space and duration with which Trane saw himself united. Coltrane was a different voice, and, just as Miles had been a different voice in Charlie Parker's band, he was perfect in this situation. His embellishing provided a contrast to Miles, who was conservative with space, using it judiciously. Trane was very supportive in the band, and his emerging extended view of music had allowed Miles to "hunt and peck" comfortably. Perhaps above all, Miles had provided steady employment in a very creative situation, and a musician has to work.[4]

In my conversations with Fela Sowande we dealt with the question of drugs and alcohol and the effects they might have on a figure like Coltrane:

> I think that for Coltrane [music] was "an exalted mood"; and if he found this via drugs, that is a commentary on the social conditions under which he had to function, not on Coltrane. In other words, I believe that if the dice had not been so loaded against him—as they were also for Charlie Parker—he might well have adopted the life-style of a monk. In any case, the character of the artist does not begin to matter. In the visionary mode, the artist does not handle ideas; he becomes possessed by an Idea, which heightens his consciousness far beyond that of ordinary mortal man, but then there is always a reaction when that artist returns to normal, and how he lives is often as far from that of the accepted norms. It could not be otherwise. . . .[5]

It was the "visionary mode" of artistic expression that Trane was slowly moving towards. He had one obstacle, and that was to break the cycle of escapism through alcohol and drugs. At this time Trane and Naima were living in Trane's mother's house, a place in the Germantown section of Philadelphia that Trane had bought for her a few years earlier. He was already a legend in that town. Tenor saxophonist Archie Shepp remembers Jimmy Heath speaking a few years earlier about Trane and comparing him favorably to Rollins. Shepp had been particularly impressed to hear this coming from Heath, who was himself a tremendous saxophonist. While in Philadelphia, Trane began practicing with his old friend of the late forties, Calvin Massey. One evening Massey took Trane around to the Red Rooster, a now defunct nightclub. They had gone to see the young pianist McCoy Tyner, and while there the owner offered Trane a week's engagement, which he accepted. Two very significant things took place during that week. First, he hired for that job two-thirds of his sixties rhythm section— Tyner and bassist Jimmy Garrison. The percussionist was Albert Heath, the youngest of the Heath brothers.

Music saturated the Heath household, and their contributions to the music of African-American people are inestimable. The family itself was musically very prominent in Philadelphia, exercising the kind of natural control that comes from a great musical family. Of all the outstanding musicians who came out of Philadelphia during this period, the Heath family provided the largest number.

McCoy Tyner was only seventeen at this time but had been involved in the study of music from his preschool days. He had been writing music from the time he was in primary school and had started studying not only piano but conga drumming as well, which developed his highly sophisticated rhythmic concepts. Garrison was twenty and another strong musician among what seemed to be a multitude of dynamite musicians coming from Philadelphia. Trane had been working on "Giant Steps," and he and McCoy would go to Jimmy's house to work on the new changes.

The second and most important occurrence of the week was Trane's decision to give up drinking. During the early part of the week Trane was still hitting the bottle hard, and it clearly showed up in his articulations. Suddenly he stopped drinking and by the end of the week was completely clean. Tyner was puzzled by this and asked Trane how this could have happened. It seems that Reggie Workman, another fine Philadelphia bassist, had mentioned to Trane how disappointed he was to see one of his idols in such bad shape—and that did it! This direct confrontation, combined with his losing the Davis job, convinced him that music had to be uppermost in his mind and all deterrents eliminated.

Tyner remembers that week well: "It must have been somewhat of a forecast to the band itself. You know, to that band that was to come later. During the first part of the week Trane wasn't articulating that well, but I still could hear his sound. His sound was different from any other saxophonist's I ever heard—his tone, his approach to chords. His approach to music was different. . . . There was something in his playing that was just different. It was very, you know . . . drew you to it, drew your attention."[6]

Trane was experiencing a metamorphosis, one which had been forecast by the brilliant trumpeter Clifford Brown. Brown was one of the first post—Charlie Parker musicians to signal a new direction in a personal life-style, one that excluded drugs and alcohol. Although originally from Wilmington, Delaware, he experienced his early playing in and around Philadelphia and undoubtedly knew Trane; he perhaps even played with him on occasion.[7] Now, quite dramatically, Trane began to travel the route of sobriety and abstinence, and his commitment to a more spiritual life became clear.

It seems that the influence of a musician like Clifford Brown, who refused to be pulled into the excessive life that often accompanies playing jazz, can never be overdramatized. Parker had left this legacy of drugs; and Clifford Brown's complete rejection brought a new thinking to not only the people who played jazz, but also to the younger people who idolized the players so much. My one brief encounter with this totally gentle person is something that I'll remember for the rest of my life. And again, it seems more than just a coincidence that in the very year that Clifford Brown had his fatal car accident, John Coltrane would break the cycle of physical degradation that had haunted him from the late forties.

Trane's metamorphosis had an immediate impact on other musicians around him, especially the younger players—the ones who were most vulnerable to the excesses that are available to musicians.

Breaking the cycle of drink and drugs, a cycle which is not only physical but psychological in its implications, was extremely arduous. Unless a person has experienced this transformation—which is most debilitating—it is hard to realize what it means and how very difficult it is.

The first band that Miles Davis had was known in the streets as the "D and D Band," the drunk and dope band. Although Miles had made the transformation, the other four members of the band hadn't. Being an addict was so commonplace during this period that any individual who was a musician and had not tried some dope or who did not drink a lot was the exception rather than the rule.

So three factors brought Trane into 1957: the ongoing musical support of his mother and now his wife; his breaking the cycle of deprivation that alcohol and drugs bring; and his spiritual awakening, that is, the beginnings in him of a philosophy of life that would be with him until he died ten years later.

5

During the year 1957, I experienced, by the grace of God, a spiritual awakening which was to lead me to a richer, fuller, more productive life. At that time, in gratitude, I humbly asked to be given the means and privilege to make others happy through music. I feel this has been granted through His grace. ALL PRAISE TO GOD."[1]

—John Coltrane

Art Davis — 1961, Newport Jazz Festival.

The year 1957 was a productive one for Trane. It was the first time he led a band into the studio under his own name, although he had co-led several dates before. Even more important, it was the year that brought about his collaboration with Thelonious Monk. They played together for six months, and the fruits of their relationship can never be overestimated.

> Working with Monk brought me close to a musical architect of the highest order. I felt I learned from him in every way—through the senses, theoretically, technically. I would talk to Monk about musical problems, and he would sit at the piano and show me the answers just by playing them. I could watch him play and find out the things I wanted to know. Also, I could see a lot of things that I didn't know about at all.[2]

With Monk, music had a magical quality. To him space and its intrusion meant more than just the handling of chords. Monk's accompaniment was not an ongoing, systematic spacing of chords, but rather the placing of "sounds" in just the right spots at the right times. Many times he would lay out for whole choruses or here and there remind the soloist of the melody. In this context, Trane projected and experimented, making broad use of phrases with thirty-second and sixty-fourth notes.

> About this time, I was trying for a sweeping sound. I started experimenting because I was striving for more individual development. . . . But actually I was beginning to apply the three-on-one chord approach, and at that time the tendency was to play the entire scale of each chord. Therefore, they were usually played fast and sometimes sounded like glisses.
>
> I found there were a certain number of chord progressions to play in a given time, and sometimes what I played didn't work out in eighth notes, 16th notes, or triplets. I had to put the notes in uneven groups like fives and sevens in order to get them all in.
>
> I thought in groups of notes, not of one note at a time. I tried to place these groups on the accents and emphasize the strong beats— maybe on 2 here and on 4 over at the end. I would set up the line and drop groups of notes—a long line with accents dropped as I moved along. . . .[3]

There are only four documents of the work of Monk and Trane together but they stand as a testament to their efforts. All of the pieces were Monk's compositions. "Trinkle Tinkle," "Ruby My Dear," and "Nutty" were recorded April 16, 1957. The last, "Epistrophy," was recorded June 27, 1957. During Trane's improvisations in the first three pieces, fifty-four compound statements occur with numerous triplet figures (Example 7). I mean by compound statements long lines

Ruby, My Dear /First Chorus

Nutty / Second Chorus

Trinkle Tinkle / First Chorus

Example 7

that can only be spelled out in unorthodox groupings; these compound statements are executed with amazing ease of articulation.

Ideas have no material reality until they are materialized by the persons who bring them into existence. The clear and clean articulation of compound phrases is only possible because Trane, through years and years of practicing, was reaching closer to spelling out through his music exactly what was in his mind. As Coltrane developed, both musically and spiritually, so did the complexities of his ideas. In looking at Trane's development from a "psychological mode" player to a "visionary" player, it seems important for us to be concerned not only with *how* Trane brought material existence to his ideas but *why*.

Trane's improvisation on "Trinkle Tinkle," which includes three choruses of thirty-two bars each, is a good example of Trane's conceptualization. In the seventh measure of the third chorus he plays a beautiful example of his three-on-one approach, using eleven notes to go an octave in two beats. The line is moving down and up, almost simultaneously, going from E♭ to D to C to E♭(Example 8). His proficiency was probably best described by Miles in the following words:

> I always liked Coltrane. . . . When he was with me the first time, people used to tell me to fire him. They said he wasn't playing anything. They also used to tell me to get rid of Philly Joe Jones. I know what I want though. I also don't understand this talk of Coltrane being difficult to understand. What he does, for example, is to play five notes of a chord and then keep changing it around, trying to see how many different ways it can sound. It's like explaining something five different ways. And

Third Chorus

Example 8

> that sound of his is connected with what he's doing with the chords at any given time.[4]

It is his precise articulation which allows him to execute these rhythmic patterns on one beat. In the ninth measure of his third chorus Trane executes a ten-note phrase in a beat and a half, in E♭, but using half-step intervals to give a feeling of chromaticism (Example 9). You can definitely hear the e♭', d', and c' accented but the overall effect sounds like a glissando. He is constantly extending the melodic line and doing it rhythmically. The tempo is medium fast (♪ =168 MM) with bassist Wilbur Ware only syncopating fourteen times during Trane's entire solo. The importance of this is that Ware kept a steady pulse, a steady pace. Monk accompanies throughout the whole first chorus of Trane's solo very aggressively, playing part of the line. During the second chorus he plays only in bars eleven and twelve, and in the third chorus he doesn't play at all. "I always had to be alert with Monk" Trane once said, "because if you didn't keep aware all the time of what was going on, you'd suddenly feel as if you'd stepped into an empty elevator shaft."[5]

Third Chorus

Example 9

Look at what Trane was doing with lines in a piece like "Trinkle Tinkle"—beginning by almost methodically emphasizing the key of E♭ (Example 10), hitting the e♭ at the beginning of each chorus (Example 11), then using melodic patterns to reinforce rhythmic phrases (Example 12) and turning them into different melodic/rhythmic lines. Increasingly, he was getting away from the diatonic scale per se, playing larger and smaller scales in rhythmic ways.

> I feel like I can't hear but so much in the ordinary chords we usually have going in the accompaniment. I just have to have more of a blueprint. It

First Chorus

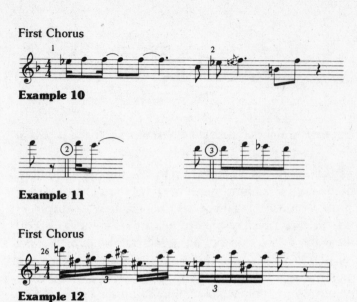

Example 10

Example 11

First Chorus

Example 12

> may be that sometimes I've been trying to force all those extra pro-
> gressions into a structure where they don't fit, but this is all something I
> have to keep working on. I think too that my rhythmic approach has
> changed unconsciously during all this, and in time, it too should get as
> flexible as I'm trying to make my harmonic thinking.[6]

The two things were happening together, only the harmonic structure,
that is, the tight space between the changes, was keeping him from
sustaining rhythms.

Bassist Ware's tempo is very steady and his articulation sharp,
allowing drummer Shadow Wilson to mix the rhythms somewhat.
Monk intersperses his accompaniment mainly in the first chorus, as in
"Nutty," where he accompanies only briefly in Trane's first chorus,
always playing part of the line. McCoy Tyner has said that when he
studied with him, Monk taught him about the "magic in sound." Tyner
remembers that from the time he was young he had always liked the
way Monk's lines sounded, in spite of the fact that many others
thought they were "funny." The numerous sounds he gets from the
piano are coupled with his brilliant use of rhythm. Monk places his
rhythmic figures in such a way that nothing in his playing seems superfluous. He knows exactly when to play a chord, a melodic line, or even
a single note. He hears multiple rhythms and cross rhythms constantly;
thus, the intervals he plays and the sounds he hears inside the chords
are also different. His touch on the piano, and his fantastic control

between the pedals and the keys, allow him to make whatever sounds he wants at any given time. No one has ever copied Monk, as others have been copied, even though he hasn't changed much from the forties, because he is extraordinary at what he plays.

Trane's solo in "Nutty" is really a duo between himself and Ware. Here again the things that Trane was talking about doing can be heard. An uneven group of notes is started immediately at the bar which precedes his first chorus (Example 13) and compound statements are heard constantly throughout his solo (Example 14). The triplet figure is also heard throughout the piece (Example 15).

Example 13

First Chorus

Example 14

Second Chorus

Example 15

No one in his senses would be rash enough to attempt to specify this or that scale as being "typical" of Ibo or Yoruba music, traditional or otherwise. But there is, in both areas, an important group of vocal music characterized by: (a) the use of triple time, i.e., three beats, or multiples of three beats in each bar; and (b) the use of the pentatonic scale, i.e., the five-note scale of doh, ray, me soh, and lah. And so we may suggest that, in certain cases, the use of triple time, and of the pentatonic scale would lend an air of "authenticity" to the music written to accompany Ibo or Yoruba words.[7]

The compound statements are not only in uneven groups, but in "Nutty" many are in groups of six notes (Example 16). Interestingly enough, as Monk always does in his solos, Trane brings back bits and pieces of the melodic line of "Nutty" throughout his solo. He does this for many different reasons: sometimes to pause before starting a line, to remember exactly where he is in the improvisation and to reaffirm this in the minds of the others who are accompanying, or just as part of the line he is building (the last two mechanisms being interchangeable) (Example 17).

Example 17

As in "Ah-Leu-Cha," he was still working in small areas, developing them, giving them length through an increasing concern with rhythmic structures. On "Nutty" he adds a beautifully articulated triplet in the middle of a tremendously long line of sixteenth notes, spelling out an f-minor chord with a doubled fifth, thus changing the line's sound (Example 18). The range of this phrase is only a minor eleventh

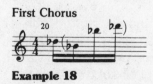

Example 18

but in that space there are fifty-three notes. So it moves up and down and all around, moving in octaves, flatted sevenths, sixths, fifths, fourths, major and minor thirds, plus major and minor intervals (Example 19).

"Ruby My Dear" is taken at a slow tempo (it opens with the same number of notes as syllables in the title—four). Trane uses this slower tempo to develop longer, compound lines with nine, thirteen, and fourteen notes to a beat. These long, intricate statements are used to

Example 19

Example 20

get from one note to the next in the melodic line of the piece (Example 20). All of the compound statements are ascending, and most of them spell out a tonality. Trane's fascination with rhythmic information comes across, even in the one chorus of this solo.

Monk's and Trane's six-month collaboration was widely cele-brated, with some comparing it to the work of Gillespie and Parker during the forties. Trane played with great confidence, and the music of Monk helped him to realize and explore his developing melodic-rhythmic lines. Monk had been without his cabaret card for a long time in New York. This card was necessary for a musician to play in the liquor-licensed clubs. So this event helped to reestablish Monk as an important link in the history of jazz. In "Coltrane on Coltrane" Trane said about him:

> I think Monk is one of the true greats of all time. He's a real musical thinker—there're not many like him. I felt fortunate to have had the opportunity to work with him. If a guy needs a little spark, a boost, he can just be around Monk, and Monk will give it to him.

Also of importance for Trane was that near the end of his tenure in the band Ahmed Abdul-Malik replaced bassist Wilbur Ware. Abdul-Malik was one of the early African-American musicians to show serious interest in the music of the East. His association with Trane continued Trane's own interest in Eastern music, an interest that would carry Trane into an involvement with various musical cultures of the world.

6

For the artist is a strange kind of human animal, and the creative artist a queer bird. Individualism is his keynote, and so the experiences of any one creative artist cannot be used as source references for generalizations about the type. Every creative artist goes as it is written of him, and you might as well try to push an express train back with an umbrella as stop him in his course, if he is in fact a creative artist and not merely fooling himself and others. He is a law unto himself, often just as utterly insensitive to the feelings of others as he is ultra-sensitive to his own where his art is concerned. He is often stubborn, to the point of being pigheaded; furthermore, it is the rule, rather than the exception, that he is highly sexed, with his own codes of "morality."

All this means, of course, that he can be likened to a tight-rope walker; for as long as he is devoted to his art, and dedicated to his calling, all is well. But let him but swerve from the path of duty; let him but mistake means for ends; let him but remove his Muse from her pedestal and install himself there; let him but fail to control the surge of life forces which course through him as he struggles—like a woman in child-bearing—to give shape, form, life, meaning and purpose to things which he himself can but dimly intuit; let him make any of these false moves, and the creative spirit of life abandons him as a broken vessel, of no further use. He is left, a slave to his own passions, perhaps a deft musical carpenter, but no longer in possession of that magic of creation, through which even stone becomes a sentient living thing under the hands of an inspired sculptor. Having once scaled the heights, he cannot now return to walk in the middle of the road. Either he becomes a colorless, crafty bore, or he degenerates into a boorish, cruel and coarse person.[1]

—Fela Sowande

Reggie Workman — 1961, Newport Jazz Festival. A natural instrument in a sea of temperedness.

In 1957 Trane and his wife Naima, along with her child Saida, moved to New York. They finally settled on Central Park West after spending a couple of months in cramped hotel rooms. Trane always had long periods of practicing, but it was in this year that he began bringing systematic order to that practice—beginning with holding long tones and then going to his scale and arpeggio work. He also was beginning to develop an increasingly strong world music view. That is, instead of having separate views of the world's music, he began to see the connecting factors in all of the world's music and applied it to what he was doing. From the time he was a child and had watched his father play the violin and the ukulele he had had a strong interest in string instruments. This interest began to materialize into actually listening to as many different string players as he could in a whole host of different musical situations.

Being in New York now marked the second time, however, that he found himself geographically away from his mother, but her strength and devotion to him as an artist was ever-present in his mind. Trane knew that his mother's church commitment was still active. She was in church every Sunday, but now it was a storefront gospel church just down the street from where she lived. That was really the only church that continued the traditions that she had experienced in her own father's church. The storefront black churches throughout America have always kept up the participating, ritualistic practice of religion, and that was the kind of religion Trane's mother was used to.

It wasn't just Trane's work in Monk's band that was becoming noticed as fresh and new. All of his work seemed energized with his demanding proficiency on the instrument, combined with his sound. His sound contained many voices. And he was quick to utilize the different registers of his instrument. This utilization of the registers is most profoundly articulated in Trane's playing of the blues. The blues offered the kind of structure that Trane loved to work in. The simple I—IV—V—I form provided great viability for Trane's artistry. Trane's sound especially communicated to people in the blues; it was an intuitive form for Coltrane, embodying as it does one of the very traditional aspects of African-American music. He had repeatedly played blues forms in his work in Earl Bostic's band in the early fifties and in Eddie Cleanhead Vinson's band in the late forties. In fact, in his first big job with Joe Webb, the blues were played continuously.

Trane's knowledge of the blues brings us to another aspect of Trane's artistic evolution:

Knowledge is to consciousness what the signpost is to the traveler: just an indication of the way which has been traveled before. Knowledge is not even in direct proportion to being. . . .

The supreme lesson of human consciousness is to learn how *not to know*. That is, how not to *interfere*. That is, how to live dynamically, from the great Source, and not statically, like machines driven by ideas and principles from the head, or automatically, from one fixed desire. . . .

Education means leading out the individual nature in each man and woman to its true fullness. You can't do that by stimulating the mind. To pump education into the mind is fatal. That which sublimates from the dynamic consciousness into the mental consciousness has alone any value.[2]

So the execution of the blues that Trane learned from these early bands indicated a direction he would take, but it was by no means the exact road he would follow. Education was to this great man a mechanism in which he brought out his total being. And in the blues he exposes himself completely. The blues was the first secular form developed by African-American people (other than the work songs). It is one of our primary connecting sources and every great African-American musician was and is a "dangerous" blues player. Here the music is played with great emotion and the simplicity in the form allows for elastic improvisations. Ultimately it moves into the realm described again by Sowande: "By far the most important single factor in African music is the full recognition and practical endorsement and use of the metaphysical powers of Sound."[3]

It was the transference of that idea which created the blues. How this idea evolves, that is, what shape it will take, becomes complicated by the nature of an artist. The artist described in the beginning of this chapter is in fact an entity, but Trane belonged to a different milieu, and it was in the playing of the blues that this is best seen. It was here that Trane sacrificed his individuality and connected up with what Jung called "central energy."

When Trane recorded blues pieces that were in B♭ his whole connecting force with the instrument and what a blues means emerged. Pieces like "All Morning Long" (recorded November 15, 1957) and "Bass Blues" (recorded August 23, 1957) are perfect examples of this. Both pieces are very simple in the form and melodies that they take, but Trane's improvisation brings a whole different perspective to their meaning. This perspective was clearly delineated in Zita Carno's celebrated analysis of Trane's work during this year. If anyone is sincerely interested in a study of John Coltrane, he should certainly look up the issues of the *Jazz Review* in which she wrote this analysis. Time after time, Trane brings about the unexpected in music, and that is the substance of Ms. Carno's analysis.

Yet, these blues pieces had other qualities. Occasionally (and specifically on the piece "Mary's Blues") he would insert patterns used by his teachers. "Mary's Blues" uses a series of chord sequences that Bud Powell first used in the piece "Bouncing With Bud" in the late forties. In fact, just listening to this piece, one can almost see Bud Powell emerge from it.

"Mary's Blues" was written for his beloved cousin Mary, and it points out another use that Trane brought to his compositions. If one goes back to the first two pieces that he recorded, "Nita" and "Just For The Love," one can feel the strong association that he uses in naming the pieces. "Nita," was of course named after Naima, and "Just For The Love" obviously was in her behalf. Using compositions in this way was one of the many ways that Trane demonstrated his love for the people who were close to him.

Nineteen fifty-seven was the first year that Trane signed a record contract. This was with Prestige, and he would record with them on and off for about two years. Ironically, although the work that he did with this company was very strong, perhaps his best work from this year comes from a recording he made on the Blue Note label.

This was in the fall of 1957, and the band was a sextet, instead of his usual quintet or quartet. The other two horns were played by trumpeter Lee Morgan and trombonist Curtis Fuller, both young Philadelphians. In his work with them on "Blue Train," he was beginning to realize the space he would need in order to further develop his melodic-rhythmic communication. "Blue Train," Coltrane's own piece (recorded on September 15, 1957), is a twelve bar blues in E♭ taken at a medium tempo (♩ = 144 MM).

Coltrane's solo on "Blue Train" is evocative. He plays eight choruses with the ensemble (Lee Morgan, trumpet; Curtis Fuller, trombone; Kenny Drew, piano; Paul Chambers, bass; Philly Joe Jones, drums), entering at the sixth and playing through to the end of the seventh. There is a tempo change initiated by Trane two bars before the beginning of the fourth chorus and percussionist Jones holds double time until the end of the fifth chorus. Of the eight choruses, three are in tempo, two at double time, two are with ensemble accompaniment, and the last ends the piece. Trane's playing is mostly in tempo, although it is predominated by groups of four six-teenth notes. There are only five uneven compounds, three at five notes and two at three, so he isn't playing as fast as he might be.

His source emerges when one looks beyond the surface of the arrangement of the piece. There are numerous triplets, causing one to be constantly aware of Sowande's observation of the importance of the triple figure in Yoruba music and language. That is, the triple figure can either be set alone or incorporated within the quadruple mea-sure. This triplet figure is called by the Yoruba people the konkolo rhythm; like the triple figure of African-American music, it is found everywhere, and is a dominant force in the music of all African-American people. Its dominance is expressed clearly because a tonal language usually comes in a triplet sign (pitched high-middle-low).

The language pattern can be seen in the numerous triplet figures using neighboring notes, in the use of a figure moving down a third and up a minor second, and in a beautiful phrase in the eighth chorus where there are four triplets in a row (Example 21). The first moves down a fourth and back, to a major third, down a major third and back, to a minor third, down a minor third and back, to a minor third, down a minor third and back, outlining a seventh chord. This is a stunning use of a sequence which in its essence moves to delineate the inflections of a tone language. His quadruple statement, in many cases, uses the rest to play an imitating line so that a pattern is re-peated (Example 22). Many times the pattern is repeated verbatim.

Eighth Chorus

Example 21

It is when Trane plays the blues that he comes in contact with his "central energy." He plays certain notes during the improvisation as if his life forces are right there in his breath (Example 23). The tone is so round, yet it is approached with such incredible force that it sounds like a shout. When the ensemble is accompanying between the sixth chorus and the end of the seventh a polymetric pattern occurs. The ensemble plays for two measures, rests for two measures throughout the two choruses. This is preceded by the combination of the percus-sionist double timing while bassist Chambers keeps the tempo—another polymetric source. Trane uses the ensemble's playing beauti-

Fourth Chorus

Eighth Chorus

Example 22

fully, not as a call and response, but more as an antiphonal motif. His articulation is stellar, with every note clearly played, and new mixtures constantly heard. *Industry* was connecting with *will,* which was, to say the least, impressive.

First Chorus   **Sixth Chorus**

Fifth Chorus

Example 23

What is this central energy? What is this life force that is so predominant in Trane's music? The concept of central energy was expressed by C. G. Jung in these terms:

The central energy runs through all subsequent differentiations; it lives in them all and cuts across them to the individual psyche; it is the only factor that remains unchanged in every stratum. Above the "unfathomable ground" lies the deposit of the experience of all our animal ancestors, and next that of our oldest human ancestors. Each segment stands for a further differentiation of the collective psyche, until, in the development from ethnic groups to national groups, from tribe to family, the summit, in individual human psyche, is attained.[4]

The central energy, then, is the connecting mechanism between Trane and his ancestors. Central energy is the force that connects up all unifying processes; and it was this force that Trane so clearly recognized after his transformation and dedication to a more spiritual life.

In his solo on "Blue Train," Trane, as he did with Monk, was playing faster, not just to play faster but to execute rhythmic patterns with that assured sound of his. He was still playing faster than anyone had before, and with pinpoint articulation. He was doing this while developing rhythmic-melodic lines. Now he needed the space in which to sustain these lines. This didn't necessarily mean more playing time, but rather stretching out the space in changing harmonies, in order to further sustain his rhythms. Even in the tight space he was working in now, he was demonstrating that he was a visionary musician.

All his work on this particular date was like a never-ending well of ideas. The thirty-two bar "Lazy Bird," played at an up-tempo ($\flat$ = 208 MM), is played with that driving to the changes that really marked this period of his music. Through the constant changing of accents he increased the acceleration towards the distinctive harmonic separations in the chorus. The symmetry with which he was playing at this point is really incredible. At the beginning of the twenty-fifth bar of the first chorus of Trane's solo there is a phrase that goes for two bars which he later repeats at the beginning of the seventeenth bar in the second chorus. After the first time it is played there is a rest, followed by the start of another line. However, after the second time it is played, a beautifully syncopated line unwinds (Example 24). Yet at the beginning of the seventeenth bar in the first chorus he begins with an eighth followed by an accented dotted-quarter, by an eighth and another accented dotted-quarter; the next measure *begins* with an accented dotted-quarter followed by an eighth, two eighths connected and a quarter rest. This phrase is repeated nowhere in his solo and the two measures sound very different. He plays the dotted-quarters with that stretched tonality which his forced playing seems to do to a tone. This only further emphasizes the accented notes. One is immediately reminded of what Trane said about his own music at this time: "I would

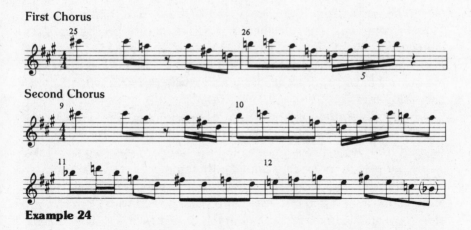

First Chorus

Second Chorus

Example 24

set up the line and drop groups of notes—a long line with accents dropped as I moved along. Sometimes what I was doing clashed harmonically with the piano—especially if the pianist wasn't familiar with what I was doing—so a lot of times I just strolled with bass and drums."[5] This was his ability to handle accents and use them to accelerate or decelerate lines. His mentioning the harmonic clashes with the piano must have been made at a humble moment because he was quite remarkable at knowing where he was in any given composition. I suspect that hearing how the changes were moving, irrespective of their activity, was very elementary for Trane at this time. Just looking at "Lazy Bird" one can see his amazing symmetry and his knowledge of what he wanted to do where (Example 25). Technical difficulties were to a large extent behind him; he was now primarily concerned with the source of his music, a concern that would run throughout his life. More and more he was striving to establish real meaning in his music: he was looking more to his central energy.

During 1957, Trane recorded with a lot of different people in a lot of different situations (see listing of recording sessions). The band with

First Chorus

Third Chorus

Example 25

which he recorded "Blue Train" and "Lazy Bird" included Lee Morgan, who was nineteen then. He was a man of prodigious skills who even at that young age sounded better than most. His ideas were fresh and alive, but he was at an age where the business can rip one to the quick. He was shot to death by his ex-wife in 1972, when he was only thirty-four.

Morgan's sound was clear and his execution of the double time on "Blue Train" was amazingly dexterous. The notes bounced and skipped from his instrument, pushing the tempo, never lagging. Like Trane, he played interesting, moving rhythmic-melodic lines. And he could jump to any interval on the trumpet. One could talk about Morgan day in and day out. Although Trane played with Donald Byrd almost constantly in his recordings at this time, this one session that he made with Morgan demonstrated that, of all the horn players that Trane was involved with, Morgan had without question the greatest potential.

I have already spoken of my admiration for Philly Joe Jones and Paul Chambers, the percussionist and bassist on this date. Their playing was certainly up to par, always providing great support. The trombonist was Curtis Fuller, at twenty-three pretty much dealing with the instrument, but playing very interesting lines. The pianist was Kenny Drew, twenty-nine, a man with great vision whose proficiency caught him up in lines. Drew fired out lines, making great use of the minor second interval and the sequential minor third. He was an excellent, driving accompanist, doing different things, building off the soloist, playing constantly interesting chords with close harmonies. His accompaniment was very much like that of Horace Silver. His improvisations were intense because he would send out lines at uneven spacings, but he had—as Art Tatum had had—a great gift for making it all sound right when it came out.

7

But surely research which does not as a direct result take what is new and reshape it into a familiar form is no more than a sterile intellectual exercise. Surely it is obvious (a) that in order to reshape what is new into a familiar form you have first to discover what is new—which is the Theory side of Research, and the reshaping being the Method side; (b) that for this discovery of what is new one needs to have that type of mind which will attract to itself high-level Ideas; (c) that in the reshaping of what is new [into] a familiar form, only that greater mind which bears the stamp of the feminine alone will yield results that are both meaningful and profitable; (d) that the purely intellectual masculine mind is but an adjunct to the foregoing factors—an irreplaceable and vital adjunct but all the same an adjunct; and (e) that it is only this aspect of research that can to some extent be examined, análysed, discussed, and taught. [1]

—Fela Sowande

John Coltrane — 1963, Newport Jazz Festival. Long fingers flashing over the instrument.

During 1957 Trane also played in large bands, quartets, quintets, and in an interesting trio with bassist Earl May and percussionist Art Taylor. They recorded two standard tunes and a blues piece. Trane loved to play the standards. In my many conversations with McCoy Tyner I can recall his telling me how much Trane loved to sing— particularly when he played ballads. And he always played ballads as if they were the blues. Trane had a definitive lyricism in his voice, but it was open and embracing, almost bold, in its honesty.

It is obvious that his being possessed by the idea of music would encompass a total view of music, not only a view from what Sowande calls the "masculine level of mind," where proficiency and specialization are gods.

Trane was deep into musical research. He was constantly talking about what he was doing and what directions he wanted to pursue. When he spoke about his association with Johnny Hodges and the tremendous spirit he carried from that band, he mentioned that it was "firsthand information about things that happened way before my time."[2] Hodges and his unbelievably wonderful lyricism made a pronounced mark on Trane's musical mind.

Trane's playing of the ballads, his way of interpreting the standard melodies, illustrates just another aspect of the depth of his mind. Both his ability to research and his proficiency were of the highest order; he played everything at least as well as it had ever been played, if not better. His improvisations are textbook examples of scaler modulations, arpeggioed modulations, and at tempos which begin to defy transcription. He used a blistering sound on the blues, one that pulled and stuck like a magnet, and another more passionate voice for the ballads, a voice that sang more—still with a stark naked sound, but slightly lighter than his sound in the blues. In his ballads, he had a way of lengthening the notes, giving the feeling of moving off. He operated in all styles with absolute fluency.

The pianoless trio was not a new innovation. Sonny Rollins had begun working in that format during 1957 after working without a piano in the Max Roach band. It seemed consistent with the nature of Coltrane's mind to continually feel new working situations. In the trio with Earl May and Art Taylor (August 16, 1957), he recorded for the first time with only the string bass and percussion, but he sounded very relaxed and solidly supportive. May, best known for his work with singer Gloria Lynne in the sixties, was perfect in this forum, which is a further testament to Trane's unique sense of knowing what he wanted in any given situation. He always took the opportunity to play in all situations, whenever he could, so he knew a lot of musicians.

In a rather flippant observation, a comparison of Rollins and Coltrane was made by Mark Gardner in 1969:

> Oddly enough, Rollins has rarely indulged in this sort of exchange. His tenor battles have been confined, on record at least, to confrontations with Coleman Hawkins, Charlie Parker and Sonny Stitt plus Coltrane. Which suggests that he selects only the toughest "opponents."
>
> Coltrane, on the other hand, was always ready to meet new partners like Hank Mobley, Johnny Griffin, Al Cohn, Zoot Sims, Gene Ammons, Paul Quinichette, Frank Hess, Hawkins, Bobby Jaspar and, in later years, Archie Shepp and Pharaoh Sanders.[3]

If one rejects everything that is said about Rollins and strikes out the words "opponents" and "confrontations," some validity might be found here. The other musicians were just reed players, and Trane was also in touch with many musicians who played a variety of instruments and who were themselves in contact with others. Thus Trane had a tremendous reservoir which he welcomed.

May was a wonderful example of the depth of that reservoir. He had a beautiful sound coming from the bass, a big sound, bouncing off Trane's tenor. He knew exactly when to repeat a note, when to move in minor steps, and—although he played mostly in tempo—when to play syncopated lines, all with skill and finesse. His sensitivity to Trane is illustrated in "Trane's Slo Blues" where he retards the tempo at the beginning when Trane enters, because Trane hears it there. It's funny because May increases the speed slightly after having retarded it, but Trane keeps his pace so May retards again. On the ballad "Like Someone in Love," May retards the tempo after they get started. There was a conscious effort to be the perfect accompanist for Trane, who was meanwhile ranging all over the tenor. May also moves decidedly with Trane, and, like Wilbur Ware and Paul Chambers, he anticipated Trane's every move, especially harmonic moves. He made this a *tour de force* for Trane because of his steadfastness, and Trane consolidated all the information he had at that time, putting it right out there. As always, percussionist Art Taylor kept excellent time. In the middle of the fourth chorus Taylor and Trane execute a beautiful roll phrase simultaneously.

Ballads, old standards, and Broadway melodies were always part of Trane's repertoire. "In terms of writing as well, John feels he's learned from Miles to make sure that a song is 'in the right tempo to be its most effective'."[4] Certainly this was true, but Trane often applied those directions in unexpected ways. His tempos on standards were often faster than usual, and many, such as "I Love You," moved from 6/8 into 4/4 time. He was reshaping, seeing what was new in the familiar and making from it his own form.

Trane's compositions during this year were all marked with either his early influences or the influence of his Philadelphia associates. On his first album as a leader for Prestige (May 31, 1957), two of his own pieces occur and one by his very close musical associate at this time, Cal Massey. Cal's piece was called "Bakai," and its form demonstrates Massey's intrigue with stacking rhythms on top of tempo. Incidentally, Trane's piece "Straight Street" uses this same device. What could be more African than having rhythmic phrases stacked on top of a specific tempo? Not only that, but having these rhythms enter at different times in the composition, a device constantly used by African master drummers.

During these early, prolific recording years, Trane often found himself working with people who just could not handle their own end. A clear example of this is the bass playing of George Joyner on the piece "All Morning Long." Although Joyner keeps tempo very well, he was assuredly uncertain of where the stops are on the bass and plays out of tune throughout the entire piece. To a player like Trane this certainly would have had a disconcerting effect. Throughout Trane's life, he would pull along with him individuals who were unfortunately less talented than he was. Just as certain was that throughout his entire life he had not only a dedication to Charlie Parker's music, but was decidedly under the influence of Duke Ellington. Many of the pieces that he recorded during this year were pieces arranged for low horns like the baritone saxophone. Unquestionably, Ellington loved the low-register instruments.

Trane reentered the Davis band in December 1957 and stayed until the beginning of 1960, winding down on a long apprenticeship that had lasted a decade and a half.

Trane loved playing with Monk, but Thelonious was notorious for just wanting to play in New York City, and after their Five Spot engagement was over work was becoming scarce. So Trane jumped at the chance to get back into the Miles Davis band.

> After leaving Monk, I went back to another great musical artist, Miles.
>
> On returning, this time to stay until I formed my own group a few months ago, I found Miles in the midst of another stage of his musical development. There was one time in his past that he devoted to multichorded structures. He was interested in chords for their own sake. But

now it seemed that he was moving in the opposite direction to the use of fewer and fewer chord changes in songs. He used tunes with free-flowing lines and chordal direction. This approach allowed the soloist the choice of playing chordally (vertically) or melodically (horizontally).

In fact, due to the direct and free-flowing lines in his music, I found it easy to apply the harmonic ideas that I had. I could stack up chords—say, on a C7, I sometimes superimposed an E♭7, up to an F♯7, down to an F. That way I could play three chords on one. But on the other hand, if I wanted to, I could play melodically. Miles' music gave me plenty of freedom. It's a beautiful approach.[5]

It was Miles who made me want to be a much better musician. He gave me some of the most listenable moments I've had in music, and he also gave me an appreciation for simplicity. He influenced me quite a bit in music in every way. I used to want to play tenor the way he played trumpet when I used to listen to his records. But when I joined him I realized I could never play like that, and I think that's what made me go the opposite way.[6]

Between the time Trane left in 1956 and reentered, several horn sidemen had marched through Miles's band. His current sideman was Julian Cannonball Adderley. Adderley, like Trane, was a Southerner, having been born and raised in Tampa, Florida. He had really been a smash hit when he first came to New York around 1955, playing in the band of Oscar Pettiford. Many were comparing him—as so many alto players were compared at that time—to Charlie Parker. But Adderley was his own player, clearly and distinctly.

This band was easily the most influential band of the late fifties, and Trane's contributions were immense. He really appreciated the opportunity to work steadily while finishing his own introspection, and playing beside two persons of the stature of Adderley and Davis was a great thrill. Adderley was in complete command of his technique and provided Trane with inspiration every time they played. The old rhythm section was still intact, at least for a brief moment, and played with almost abandoned assuredness. But Coltrane was their heartbeat from the time he reentered until he left. He was the man digging for source material, studying, constantly looking for and talking about music. It was in this band that he demonstrated his mastery of hard bop. Even on the first record date after his reentering the band, his improvisations were masterworks: Trane, perhaps more than any other musician at that time, was *the* great exponent of the hard bop style.

Hard bop (1949 to 1959) was the natural evolutionary successor to bebop. It had an East Coast stamp of hard blues playing juxtaposed with the melodic inventiveness of Charlie Parker. Hard bop established certain quartets and quintets which came to dominate the period. The Modern Jazz Quartet (M.J.Q.) was organized in 1952, and Art Blakey's Jazz Messengers was reorganized in 1955. (Blakey first developed his Messengers band in the late forties; but this band— starring Hank Mobley on tenor saxophone, Kenny Dorham on trumpet, Horace Silver on piano, Doug Watkins on bass, and Blakey on drums—was the first to get really serious public notice.) From the Messengers band sprang the Horace Silver Quintet and, of course, Silver with his many, many compositions. Also, the Clifford Brown/ Max Roach Quintet established their dominance during this period. In addition, hard bop was well known for the many organ trios that emerged out of this period. Especially well known was Jimmy Smith, whom Trane had played with just before entering Miles's band in 1955. There were many individual great players who came out of hard bop; and it signaled the last time that harmony would have a great influence on jazz.

In hard bop, Trane was the master teacher on the tenor saxophone, and his improvisations provided a thesis of examples on moving through arpeggios, down or up scales, and the many usages of scales, especially the non-Western scales which were not predominantly used by other players.

During his improvisation on "Milestones" (April 2, 1958—also known as "Miles"), in the measure before his second chorus, he begins a series of nine arpeggios moving in groups of four notes, from F to f", moving in the key of F. The first chord is a Dominant 7 followed by an M7, m7, Dominant 7, M7, m7, m7, Dominant 7, and M7. The arpeggios are descending, with the fourth note moving in the scale and the seventh always accented (Example 26). There are thirty-six notes in two and a half measures, and all except the first four are clearly moving in sixteenth-note values.

On another piece recorded that day, "Straight, No Chaser,"

First and Second Choruses

Example 26

Trane executes his three-on-one approach. At the end of his second chorus, he goes through e♭″ —d″ —d♭″, using thirteen notes in four beats, one of those beats being a rest. There are three groups of notes in a 5-4-4 pattern, with the e♭″— d″ — d♭″ getting the accents (Example 27). Another phrase which was then becoming a motif for his playing is the line that occurs at the end of the third chorus, a line moving from g to g′ in nine different notes, with the fifth (in G) being repeated three times (Example 28). The line begins as a scale in g,

Second Chorus

Example 27

Third Chorus

Example 28

then at the third step moves up a minor third, then down to c′ (a major second), from c′ in steps to e′, then down a major third to c′, up a fourth to f′ and down a minor third to d′, then up a major third to f#′, then down a major third to d′, and then up a fourth to g′. The line ends off spelling a CM7. From g to g′, the d′ (fourth note), e (seventh note), and f′ (ninth note) are accented. (The notes in the parentheses represent the order in which they are heard, not the order in which they appear in the scale.) Trane uses triplet figures to change the rhythmic direction—attempting, sometimes, to expand the tonality as well. His intrigue with rhythm is very apparent here. He begins the fifth chorus with three groups of sixteenth notes, ending on an eighth and a beat and an eighth rest. This is repeated and then repeated again, except that the groups of sixteenths continue instead of being followed by an eighth, a beat and an eighth rest. There are six sets of sixteenth notes leading into a beautiful triplet which breaks that rhythmic pattern and starts another one (Example 29).

Two forces seem to have been propelling Trane at the same time. First, Trane was compelled to practice, to continue to work out his research within the existing style of the period, and to study the history

Fifth Chorus

Example 29

of jazz—not only his own music, but any music that he could possibly find theoretical works on:

> I'm very interested in the past, and even though there's a lot I don't know about it, I intend to go back and find out. I'm back to Sidney Bechet already.
>
> Take Art Tatum, for instance. When I was coming up, the musicians I ran around with were listening to Bud Powell, and I didn't listen too much to Tatum. That is, until one night I happened to run into him in Cleveland. There were Art and Slam Stewart and Oscar Peterson and Ray Brown at a private session in some lady's attic. They played from 2:30 in the morning to 8:30—just whatever they felt like playing. I've never heard so much music.[7]

Trane himself had played in a varying number of bands, and his great love for and interest in Ellington came from playing in the Hodges band and before.

> Then I worked with one of my first loves, Johnny Hodges. I really enjoyed that job. I liked every tune in the book. Nothing was superficial. It all had meaning, and it all swung. And the confidence with which Rabbit plays! I wish I could play with the confidence that he does.[8]

Trane listened, really listened to his employers. In fact, it was part of his nature to listen to everyone he played with. Before playing with Hodges, he had toured for awhile with the rhythm and blues band of Earl Bostic.

I went with Earl Bostic, who I consider a very gifted musician. He showed me a lot of things on my horn. He has fabulous technical facilities on his instrument and knows many a trick.[9]

I remember Tyner's relating to me that once he and Trane played on the same bill as blues singer Lightnin' Hopkins. When Lightnin' played, he would move to the dominant whenever he felt like it and not at any particular bar. Trane realized that, in his own work, form had taken precedence over content, and what was also of importance, was the use of the five-note (pentatonic) scale in all its derivations and the fact that the "blues scale" had emerged with the secular music arising from spirituals and early work-songs, *not* the subdivision into specific categories. It was an intense realization, one which became immediately apparent in his music.

Second, Trane was going through a spiritual awakening which began, by his own admission, at the beginning of 1957. He had been exposed to Christianity as a child, and to Islam during the early years of his association with musicians in Philadelphia. Later, his wife Naima reintroduced him to Islam. He had, of course, been aware of the religion from the late forties. His cousin Mary's first husband, Charles Greenlee, had been a devout disciple; so Trane was aware of, and in fact into, Islam before he met Naima. However, he never converted to Islam, although it had a profound, positive effect on him.

8

Black Experience of Religion must obviously consider the blackman within the context of the traditional religion of his African forefathers, the integrity both of the blackman as well as of Africa being maintained. Most of us know only too well that such terms like "African Traditional Religion" are often used to identify an ersatz system assembled from the questionable findings of even more questionable authorities, and that a great show of seriously considering this perversion is made, while in fact it is being used as a foil to highlight the virtues of "Christianity" or "Islam" over all traditional beliefs of Africa. [1]

The Way of Life of the Blacks of Africa, as for Peoples of African Descent anywhere, is firmly rooted in the UNITY of GOD-MAN-NATURE, and its study, or the study of any aspect of that Way of Life whatever, must be undertaken within the context of this Unity. In the final analysis, it is the Intuition that must be brought into play, not the Intellect. For the Intellect cannot cope with the Archetypes which are neither good nor evil but both in an undifferentiated state, and the World of the Blackman is an Archetypal World. [2]

—Fela Sowande

Jimmy Garrison — 1963, Newport Jazz Festival. Digging deep for the total dimension of the sound.

Religion to Trane was not a creed, not a group of selected dogmas which so many religions have become today—dogmas by which life itself is split into camps of sacred and profane. To Trane, all of life was sacred. He was, and he knew he was, a man experiencing the end of one zodiac period (Pisces) and moving into another (Aquarian). The Aquarian age is predicted to be the age of man, the age of brotherhood, where man would be ideally striving for a more spiritual life. In the zodiac signs, when one is passing from one age to another, there is considerable chaos and disorder brought about by the essential movement from one sign to the next. He knew, and not only knew but predicted through his music, where this specific sign would take us. Trane was possessed by music—and more specifically, by the music of African-American people—and the spirit communicated through his music is rooted in the traditional black experience of religion.

Religion had certainly become an "inner awareness of a . . . dynamic relationship between the individual on one hand, and the cosmos and the world of Nature on the other" for Coltrane. And music was the art through which he manifested the "meaningful expression of that relationship." It doesn't seem inconceivable to begin to relate the use of the triplet in his music to the symbolism of either the Trinity or the God-Man-Nature UNITY.

The Trinity is clearly spelled out in the traditional religion of the Yoruba people of Nigeria. Olorun is the god-symbol; Eleda is the root form, the form from which all other forms are derived; and Ori is the communicator with the life-spirits on earth. So this cycle of the triplet so prevalent in Yoruba traditional music and also in the tonal language of Yoruba people, and the triplet as Trane so consistently applied it throughout his whole life—its application most often coming in breaking one phrase from another or in many, many different uses—is undeniable.

This spiritual awareness had a great bearing on all aspects of his life, and is even apparent in the titles of many of his later works: "Dahomey Dance," "Spiritual," "Africa," 1961; "Tunji," 1962; "The Promise," 1963; "Wise One," A Love Supreme, 1964; "Song of Praise," "Dearly Beloved," "Amen," "Attaining," "Ascent," "Ascension," "The Father and the Son and the Holy Ghost," "Compassion," "Suite: Prayer and Meditation: Day, Peace and After, Prayer and Meditation: Evening, Affirmation, Prayer and Meditation: 4 A.M.," "Dear Lord," 1965.

By the time Trane reentered Miles's band he had fully merged a complete technical proficiency with a religious devotion to his music.

He was reaching the end of a long examination of harmony, which exploded on the dates which made up his album *Giant Steps* (May 4—5, 1959). Zita Carno, a great admirer of Coltrane, one of his transcribers, and a pianist herself, analyzed his music. She commented that his range "is something to marvel at: a full three octaves upward from the lowest note obtainable on the horn (concert A-flat). . . . There are a good many tenor players who have an extensive range, but what sets Coltrane apart from the rest of them is the equality of strength in all registers, which he has been able to obtain through long, hard practice. His sound is just as clear, full and unforced in the topmost notes as it is down in the bottom." She describes his tone as "a result of the particular combination of mouthpiece and reed he uses plus an extremely tight embouchure" and calls it "an incredibly powerful, resonant and sharply penetrating sound with a spine-chilling quality."[3]

He was playing in the third octave when he first entered Miles's band in 1955, but he really began to operate with fluency when he was hired by Monk in 1957. (In the eighteenth bar of his third chorus in "Nutty" he plays a♭" in the third octave [Example 30]). Though most people first became aware of his playing high harmonics in the piece "Harmonique" (December 2, 1959), he had been playing them with Monk and probably earlier (Example 31).

Third Chorus

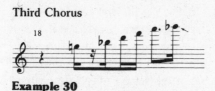

Example 30

Trinkle Tinkle / Second Chorus

Example 31

Coltrane had reentered the Davis band because he was not yet quite ready financially to take on the responsibility of his own band, and he felt he still had much to learn. Miles's format was different after Garland and Philly Joe Jones left, but he found an outstanding alto player in Adderley. On their first recording in 1958, Trane played in "Milestones," a piece which has forty bars. The piece itself was in G minor using its Dorian and natural minor. This gave Trane much more room to play rhythmic lines and thus his improvisation became longer (Example 32). The music was relating more to tonal centers which were consistent with Trane's new awareness of the music of India and especially the raga.

Second Chorus

Example 32

Playing in the band with Adderley was a very reciprocal experience for Trane. Being an ex-alto player himself, he saw the wizardry in Adderley's technique, and they borrowed and traded often during their many improvisational exchanges. Adderley was a lighter voice, a very different voice from Trane. Cannonball liked to play low in the horn, and, of course, Trane was always reaching for a higher note, so many times their voices crossed. Adderley played as well as he has ever played in this band. The most significant interplay between Adderley and Trane can best be seen in live recordings made in 1958. The first was at the Plaza Hotel in New York City in the spring of 1958, and the second at the Newport Jazz Festival in Newport, Rhode Island in the summer of 1958.

The recording session that comes from the Plaza demonstrates concretely the dichotomy between playing before a live audience and playing in the studio. I have never really been able to understand why those persons who produce dates don't see this. Of all the conflicting critical views that were emerging concerning John Coltrane's playing, the one thing that I think all critics would agree on was that he certainly played different live than he did on his records.

A quartet of pieces—"My Funny Valentine," "If I Were a Bell," "Oleo," and "Jazz at the Plaza" ("Straight, No Chaser")—were the most dynamic evidence of Trane's playing at this time and his most creative work on record up until his next live recording in 1961. Again, as always, it's symmetry that constantly holds forth in Trane's playing. For instance, if one listens to his solo on "If I Were a Bell" it becomes apparent immediately that this Trane is playing faster, and that the lines that he's playing hold more interest because they are all whole melodic lines; and he ranges throughout and beyond the instrument.

At moments, he begins phrases that are operating four times faster than the tempo of the piece. Consequently, one gets the feeling that he's not going to be able to execute this or that particular line, but he always does; and it is always executed with great precision. He starts his solo near the end of the melodic line which immediately puts him in a strange place in terms of the chord changes. But he always knows where he is and, therefore, executes flawlessly.

In the many studies that will follow this one, people will again and again find that when Trane played in front of an audience, his mastery, not only of the form but of the content of the music that he was trying to express, is exquisite. That was one of the things that he revolutionized; that is, he revolutionized playing time. He played longer with more definitive ideas coming out, consistently challenging himself and the other musicians that were around him. And this is most dynamically put forth in the live recordings.

Adderley, although a different voice from Trane's, was just as dynamic in this situation. Cannon, as he was to be known by his musical contemporaries, was just as fluent and remarkable in his solos as Trane. He only played on two of the pieces at Plaza—"Oleo" and "Jazz at the Plaza"—and one would have to go very far and hunt very deep to find his playing at any other time more energized, more intuitive, than it was in this session with John Coltrane.

The situation was exactly the same at the Newport Jazz Festival in the summer of 1958. "Straight, No Chaser," Monk's composition, is played here as a twelve-bar blues in 4/4, but in the middle of Miles's second chorus the band breaks into a 6/8 which it holds for a chorus and a half. Then Miles breaks back into the 4/4. When Trane takes his solo it begins in 6/8 and goes for two choruses before it breaks into a 4/4. In his last chorus, beginning at the end of the eighth bar and going to the end of the solo, he plays a series of thirteen eighth-note triplets. Unlike most of his improvisations, this one is comparatively sparse of triplet figures. At the very end Trane gives a figure which is completely different in feeling and sound from anything he had previously played in the solo (Example 33). The triplets are organized after a beginnning of three notes of a major third, then six notes outlining d' — f' — a' — c', moving to c' — e' — g' — bb', then b —d' — f' — a, then a departure, ab — b — eb' — gb' (ab minor), then to g— bb — d' — f', ending at g—bb—c'—e'. The triplets are heard in pairs and the top line of each pair spells out a' — c" — bb' — a' — gb' — f' — e', up a minor third, down a major second, down a minor second, down a minor second, down a minor second, down a minor second. All of this provides an introduction to Adderley. Members of the band constantly set one another up, playing off each other's lines. Sowande's description of the "hierarchy of ideas" would certainly relate this band to the "Ideas that deal with the profound levels of Being, and with the esoteric side of manifesting Life."[4]

Sixth Chorus

Example 33

Even in this very stimulating company, Coltrane was unquestionably impeccable. Hard bop was a period where form was truly taking command over content. In Miles's band form was becoming elastic but the tempos were high, and Coltrane was the bellwether in that context. He played comfortably in the highest tempo that the percussionist and bassist could manage. The symmetry flowing from these lines supports Carno's assertion that "Coltrane, for all he's trying to express in any given solo, has a remarkable sense of form."[5] The sound produced by this combination comes across clearly on "Two Bass Hit," performed at the Newport Festival on July 3, 1958.

"Two Bass Hit" was a bebop tune written by John Lewis and Dizzy Gillespie in the late forties. Trane had played it countless times so he knew the line in all its manifestations. The tempo is very high (♪ = 208 MM ca.), but this is no deterrent whatsoever for Trane. Trane is the only soloist, not an unusual occurrence in this band. The form was in twelve bars. Trane plays seventeen choruses, with the piano accompanying on the first two choruses, leaving until the second measure of the eleventh chorus, then accompanying until the beginning of the thirteenth chorus. Miles and Adderley enter at the beginning of the sixteenth chorus and accompany until the end of Trane's solo. He plays mostly in eighth and sixteenth notes, playing the notes at longer values rather than bellowing out. The highest note he plays in the improvisation is a♭″ in the top of the third octave, which sounds like a shout, almost as if he had belched at the same time. It's a dotted-quarter played as if something deep down below hurt. It occurs at the end of the fifth measure, fourth chorus. The db' that he hits at the end of the fourth measure, sixteenth chorus, has a three and 1/8th-beat value, and is played almost lyrically and low on the tone. He uses that note to spring to the third octave which is held for a two and 1/16th-beat value. This begins at the end of the fifth measure of the sixteenth chorus (Example 34). The long values and statements, begin statements, break rhythmic phrases, connect them, and are used for turns (like the above db').

Sixteenth Chorus

Example 34

His rhythmic phrases are inventive and communicative, with many at close intervals. Moving into the ninth chorus of his solo, at the second beat of the measure before the ninth chorus, Trane begins a repeat phrase of four measures, two plus two, using thirty-second notes but only traveling a fifth in its parameters (Example 35).

Eighth and Ninth Choruses

Example 35

Trane can operate in small areas, pulling up, uttering a repeated phrase that is really different from what has preceded and what will follow. He uses accents in this phrase as if he were speaking instead of playing music. And the statement comes right after a seven-measure mixture of eighth and sixteenth notes (Example 36). Just listening to the solo, and seeing how it is built, shows that nothing is superfluous. At the beginning of his second chorus on "Two Bass Hit" he plays a line going from db' to db" using five notes (db' — eb' — e' — ab' — db"), the first four being eighth notes and the fifth a half-note value.

92

Example 36

This line is followed by three quarter notes (ab' — ab' — eb"), and suddenly the Ab becomes very pivotal—the middle, the fifth in Db' and the fourth in Eb. The Eb becomes the fifth in Ab, and Db the fourth in Ab. The fact that Trane played in all three octaves is not really important per se. But how he used them, playing mostly in the upper octaves, playing one rhythmic phrase after another, and, as in the above line, using many five note fragments, is amazing.

He had a beautiful way of either building from a small fragment or making a larger one smaller. As the beginning of the third chorus is moving up, the lowest note he plays is a'. The whole chorus seems to be ascending; then in the last two measures, there is a descent. He doesn't move up to the high d", he begins there and moves into the fourth chorus, in db", which is moving down. So the choruses themselves shape into patterns of interest both harmonically and rhythmically (Example 37). He uses rests to separate patterns and to distinguish parts within rhythmic phrases (Example 38). He was beginning to solidify patterns which would become a part of his style that, once perfected, he would discard. His solos are saturated with movements using motif sequences or merely imitation (Example 39). He begins lines in one scale, then dips a third, moving in the same direction but in a different scale, then dips again to return to the original scale, lengthening the melodic line (Example 40). There is an expanded use of the pentatonic scale. There is no question that the increase in tempo just spurred on his ability to turn and to make sounds buzz. This was especially true once he got started at turning figures (Example 41). His sense of tempo and harmonic movement never allowed him to get lost or caught in a weird situation. These statements are round and

93

Third Chorus

Example 37

polished gems, true records of his spirit on earth. Trane had set new guidelines for musical accomplishments in this style period. In 1958, he was the master musician among master musicians.

The recording of "Two Bass Hit" produced live at the Newport Jazz Festival further points out a significant aspect of Trane: his live recordings represented his true musical state at any given time; and this was only his second issued live date. Trane commented on the value of a listening audience when he said:

> It seems to me that the audience, in listening, is in an act of participation, you know. And when you know that somebody is maybe moved the same way you are, to such a degree or approaching the degree, it's just like having another member in the group.[6]

My personal recollection of Trane in the Davis band, at this stage, was that he often played just with the rhythm section, playing many choruses, getting away from the structure. By playing the same rhythmic phrase, in tempo, he created polymeter. In another situation, Jimmy Garrison once recalled seeing Trane in this band playing a solo that was so "dangerous" that Cannonball turned to Miles and asked what was he going to play now, after Trane had played it all. In playing

Sixth Chorus

Fifteenth Chorus

Example 38

Seventh and Eighth Choruses

Example 39

Second Chorus

Sixth Chorus

Example 40

Fifth Chorus

Tenth Chorus

Example 41

time alone, Trane's solos in the Davis band were extremely long, but most of the recorded improvisations from the studio just gave Trane enough time to warm up. This contradiction between the live performances and the studio recordings, with a few exceptions, remained a problem throughout his career.

There is a spirit that jumps out at you from both the July 3, 1958 recording at Newport and the recording at the Plaza. Trane sings, bellows, shouts, speaks, and dances out lines with a consistency that demonstrates that it isn't just an everyday occurrence.

It was not only Trane and Cannonball; Miles and the other players were equally stimulating. In the Plaza recording Trane follows Miles in solo sequence, and each time before launching into his own solo, Trane connects onto the end of Miles's playing. Miles's playing here is so incredible, so inventive; his use of the mute in that unique piercing, penetrating way of his shows what Trane learned from this great musician. Philly Joe on drums also accompanies with great sensitivity—listening to what the pianist is doing in terms of his accompanying, listening to what the soloist is playing, and constantly urging him on to play deeper and with more feeling.

In this situation, outside of Trane himself, Paul Chambers offers as much as anyone. He and Trane had been friends—not only friends but brothers—since 1955. When Trane and his wife first moved to New York, Chambers's wife and Naima became very close friends, especially when Paul and Trane were on the road. In his first stint with Miles, Chambers had been his roommate, and a couple of times they had been stranded when they showed up to play but Miles failed to show. There is a solo at the end of "My Funny Valentine" on the Plaza recording which sums up everything that Chambers was about. As he takes his solo he hums quietly in unison. The information that these two people shared could probably fill a hundred books on music.

The year 1958 had been a really good one for Trane. He had continued his studies of Eastern thinkers; he had been involved in yoga; and he was trying to get on a no-meat diet, but he really wasn't too successful at the latter. Besides the music that he was playing in Miles's band, he had made several significant recordings for Prestige and he was becoming financially more and more independent.

Trane was still playing ballad pieces with the great distinctive style that brought new meaning to any song form. His rendition of "Come Rain or Come Shine" (recorded January 10, 1958), and especially his use of the registers, is amazing. Perhaps his most significant recording in 1958—outside of the Miles Davis situation—was "Little Melonae," the lovely minor blues by Jackie McLean. It's interesting that this piece was not released by Prestige until the early sixties. And, though it is generally unknown, it is one of Trane's most fluent creative improvisations in the studio up to this date. It first of all demonstrates how well he was able to work with Red Garland, Paul Chambers, and Art Taylor. On his improvisation there are several choruses in which he plays without piano accompaniment, and he and Paul Chambers reach a synchronized communicating level that very few musicians are able to reach in concert with one another.

Jackie McLean was another so-called extension of Charlie Parker; but nothing could be more of a misnomer than that. He was always a unique player, playing the alto saxophone in a very, very hard style and always low in the horn. He sounded as unique in tone as Coltrane did. However, for years McLean battled the drug situation, which must undoubtedly have drained his energy.

Of course, not all of Trane's records during this period were exceptional. He continued to play with artists who were far less equipped technically than he was, and even though where they might have wanted to take the music was correct, the actual document itself was not up to his standard. This was true of the pieces that he recorded with Wilbur Harden ("Dial Africa," "Domba," "Gold Coast," and "Tanganika Strut") and, ironically, true of the date that he did with Cecil Taylor (October 13, 1958). Of the two, the Cecil Taylor is perhaps the more disappointing—mostly because here was the meeting of two geniuses whose styles and accompanying players threw off the significance of the event. Chuck Israels, the bassist for this date, played very slow tempo; and Cecil seems to place chords and sounds at places which don't connect up at all. As I think about this record more and more, I clearly recall seeing Cecil Taylor at this time in New York. He was playing in his usual trio context of drum, alto sax, and piano (Sonny Murray, drums; and Jimmy Lyons, alto), and he was so dynamic I could not bear to listen to anyone else that evening after I had heard him. He is one of those persons whom one literally has to see and watch and hear simultaneously in order to truly appreciate the immenseness of his creative ability. Yet his collaboration with John Coltrane was decidedly unsatisfactory.

9

The "organization of the raw material of Sound into formal and structural patterns" occurs at several levels in African traditional society. We can, I think, properly recognize five categories as: Ritual, Ceremonial, Social, Functional, and Recreational.

    1: The Ritual Level involves the contemporary members of society (or the group) as a corporate unit with its concept of the Creative Forces of Life at their most potent and directly affective of the group. Here the group stands naked and unashamed as it were before its gods and goddesses, its ancestors and heroes on the one hand, and on the other, Mother Earth and the Elemental Forces of Nature. Material at this level relates to the group at the most profound levels of its being, but at no time in the long history of mankind has such material been accessible to the non-initiate, or available for "study and analysis" and Africa is no exception.

    2: The Ceremonial Level consists of (a) public ceremonies which are required in some cases to follow secret rites and thus complete the ritual; and also, (b) those ceremonies which have as their focal center the high-ranking spiritual and temporal leaders of the group, in their positions as the accredited human representatives and human Regents of Psychic Forces that control the destinies of the group. Here we have the type of material often referred to as "Praise Songs," but they are more than that. The purpose here is to re-activate and re-energize the psyche links which connect the human representatives with the Psychic Forces of which they are the Regents. Such ceremonies are mostly public, but some have secret rites attached to them as a result of which they are more properly classified under Rituals, insofar as the secret rites are concerned.

    3: The Social Level is concerned with (a) the four major life-stations of each member of the group, namely birth, puberty, marriage, and death; (b) the moral and social education and integration of young and old members of the group alike; here we have those functions at which it is permissible to sing abusive songs about named members of the group, whose conduct is deemed unsatisfactory, as well as poetry and wise sayings in which the element of music is very close to the surface; and (c) all other activities that are conducive to the continued moral, mental, and social health of the group.

    4: The Functional Level produces Work Songs and such material.

    5: The Recreational Level covers all music-making purely for the purpose of enjoyment or personal satisfaction.

    Only a small proportion of this material—and even then mostly at levels 4 and 5 above—lend themselves to some form of transcription.[1]

—Fela Sowande

Eric Dolphy — December, 1961, Jazz Gallery, New York City. They were brothers.

From the beginning of 1959 until May of 1960 Trane went through a long transitional period. In fact, jazz itself was going through the end of one cycle and into the beginning of another, from the overwhelming preoccupation with harmony and modulating techniques developed through the use of tempered instruments to a concern with the rhythmic-melodic connecting elements of the music—those that deal with melody and rhythm moving along together and expanding.

Trane was also beginning his last year and a half of playing in someone else's band, that is, being in a situation where he had no control over the music except indirectly, by his contribution to the whole. He had thought about having his own group from 1957 on, and he had discussed it quite often with Naima, and also with Cal Massey and other musical friends. But he had not yet made the break, and this year would put an end to his indecisiveness.

Having one's own band, and especially being a national performing figure, is not as easy as it may seem. Beside all the musical responsibilities, there is the awesome, time-consuming job of making sure that the other people in the band are working consistently so that the group will hold together. When he was in Miles's band Trane had seen personnel walking in and out, as though through a revolving door; so even with a person of the musical stature of Miles Davis there was the continuous problem of holding talented musicians together.

Trane made his last recording for Prestige in December 1958, and that in itself was significant because Trane and almost all his associates had at one time or another recorded for either Blue Note or Prestige. In the beginning of 1959 he was able to secure a record contract with Atlantic Records, and, although their association was a short one, it produced many significant albums. However, his contract with Atlantic only called for three albums per year, which was a great underestimation of Coltrane's creative ability.

To illustrate this cutdown on recorded work: in 1958 Trane played on over twenty record dates; in 1959 he played only seven. In May 1959 Trane had an eight-tooth upper front bridge put in, a result of what heroin had done to his body. Even though Trane had not dealt with the drug for four years, he was still experiencing its unfortunate after-effects. This alone must have had some effect on his playing, as it does with any musician—especially a reed player—when he has to get dental work. Some people say that Sonny Rollins never really sounded the same after his permanent teeth were removed. It certainly has a great effect on a player's embouchure (the embouchure is the position of the lips in producing a musical tone on a wind instrument).

But more essential than anything else for Trane was the movement of jazz, and the fact that he knew there were different things going on; and for him not to recognize and further examine these different things would be untrue to his own personal calling. This was the first year he was to meet Sun Ra. And if there is anyone whose significance and importance in the development of jazz has been lost, it was Sun Ra. His bands had from the mid-fifties been ongoing musical institutions, and his philosophies—especially those concerning the universality of life—affected all those musicians who at one time or other played in his band. He was a strict disciplinarian, constantly rehearsing his bands, always prodding his colleagues to play things that were unfamiliar.

But more than anything else, it was the year of Ornette Coleman, emerging from the West, creating great controversy with his style of playing without chord changes. For the first time in twenty years the major changes in jazz were coming from outside New York. Sun Ra was doing his work in Chicago, and Coleman, along with Sonny King (altoist), Dewey Redman (tenor sax), and Sonny Simmons (altoist), came from California. More directly related to Trane, of course, was Eric Dolphy, who was from Los Angeles.

Aside from the changes that Coleman and others were bringing to jazz there was also a style developing called "third stream" music. This was vanguarded by pianist John Lewis and composer Gunther Schuller; it was an attempt to merge European "classical" music with jazz, but it did not work out because the improvised nature of jazz became subservient to complicated written-out parts.

Trane was now making more money than he ever had, and he moved to Manhattan to Queens and bought his first house. He had a wonderful relationship with Naima and her child, but he still had no child of his own and the business that he was in kept him almost constantly on the road. And moving from his apartment in Manhattan had its bad side too, because it had been a place where many of his old and new friends showed up frequently, either to talk or to practice. His most ardent musical admirer, Zita Carno, came by quite often, and she was known to wait for hours just to get a chance to talk and play with Trane. But it was also the stop-off place for many, many other people who came to New York—especially his friends from Philadelphia.

Three of us were driving back from a date in Washington in 1959. Two of us were in the front seat and the other guy, a sax player, in the back. He was being very quiet. At Baltimore we made a rest stop, then got back in the car, and thirty minutes later realized that the guy in the back wasn't there. We hoped he had some money with him and drove on. I

> took his horn and suitcase to my apartment in New York. I opened the case and found a soprano sax. I started fooling around with it and was fascinated. That is how I discovered the instrument.[2]

That's how he latched onto the soprano saxophone and what was to become not only a second instrument but another voice for him to produce his sound on. And this voice directly affected how he played the tenor saxophone. In fact, the two instruments so beautifully complemented each other that they opened up Trane to more and more space vistas.

His first date for Atlantic was a real disaster. Again, as producers so often did, Trane was put in the company of players with whom he was generally unaccustomed to playing; and they played pieces more to accommodate the record company than to express their real artistic creativity. This date was on January 15, 1959 and it included Milt Jackson, vibes; Hank Jones, piano; Chambers on bass; and Connie Kay, drums. Kay is unbelievable on the date; he just lays back and hits the cymbal and keeps the time and nothing else. He is one of those truly lucky persons who happened to be in the right place at the right time. Although he was perfect in the Modern Jazz Quartet, he was merely a liability in this situation.

This was a beginning and ending period though—a beginning of greater emphasis on melody and rhythm, and an ending of harmonic concern for itself. And the pieces that Trane recorded later for Atlantic were to bring much more productive fruit.

On May 4 and 5, 1959, Trane recorded the following pieces: "Cousin Mary," "Giant Steps," "Countdown," "Spiral," "Syeeda's Flute Song," and "Mr. P.C." ("Naima" was recorded on December 12, 1959 but released on the *Giant Steps* collection.) Significantly, all of the compositions were his, and several were named after personal relatives—his wife, Naima; his stepdaughter, Saida; and his favorite friend and childhood cousin, Mary. Mary's relationship goes back to High Point, North Carolina, and, beside his mother, she was one of his last blood relatives. Throughout his whole life he had great love and affection for her.

"Mr. P.C." was named after Trane's almost exclusive bassist of the preceding four years, Paul Chambers. To appreciate the closeness of these two men—especially musically—one only has to see that in the sixty-seven record dates that Trane made between 1955 and 1960 Chambers played on thirty-seven—and on all of the most significant dates. Trane, perhaps better than anyone else, gave a vivid description of the greatness of this man:

. . . one of the greatest bass players in jazz. His playing is beyond what I could say about it. The bass is such an important instrument, and has much to do with how a group and a soloist can best function that I feel very fortunate to have had him on this date and to have been able to work with him in Miles' band so long.[3]

One of the first things recognized by McCoy Tyner about Trane's work at this time was his new way of working progressions. When he was talking about numbers of progressions in a given time, Trane mentioned using faster note values to execute this space: "I haven't completely abandoned this approach, but it wasn't broad enough. I'm trying to play progressions in a more flexible manner now."[4] This new flexible manner involved using changes at the half measures. "Countdown" moves E — F — B♭ — D♭ — G♭ — A — D (a measure), E♭ — A♭ — B — E — G — C (a measure), D♭ — G♭ — A — D — F — B♭ — E — F — B♭ — E♭ (the last five are measures) and they read as follows: minor second, fourth, minor third, fourth, minor second, fourth, minor second, fourth, minor second, fourth, minor third, etc. This piece is most notable in that it begins as a duo between Trane and percussionist Art Taylor, forecasting the work of Trane and Elvin Jones in the sixties. Taylor was the ideal percussionist in this situation. He was excellent at keeping the tempo, never retarding or accelerating. He had worked with Trane from the middle fifties and knew his style very well. "Countdown" is the piece that Zita Carno refers to when she talks about Trane's symmetry. Trane plays it almost like an exercise—nine choruses of sixteen bars, almost completely in eighth and quarter notes with a three and 1/8th-beat value appearing at the thirteenth measure of the eighth chorus. The piece begins with a thirty-six—bar solo by Taylor. Then Trane enters and plays with him until the beginning of his fifth chorus, at which time pianist Tommy Flanagan enters, interspersing chords until the ninth measure (Trane's last), when bassist Chambers enters. The whole arrangement is reminiscent of a West African ensemble, with the bell beginning, followed by the entry of different parts. The bell set the pace, like the gong in Indonesian music.

Trane enters playing a series of fifteen groups of four eighth notes, ending this series with a half-rest at the fourth beat of the eighth measure. The first note of each group is accented, and the last two eighth notes that end this phrase are accented (Example 42). The new phrase begins with the second half of the above half-measure rest, again running in eighths, only this time being broken after the fifth with a quarter note. Then another group is started, this time broken after

First Chorus

Example 42

three, with a phrase which is decidedly different in accents (Example 43). Where, in the other phrases, he was hitting accents on one and three for the most part, this phrase hits decidedly on two and four, and then on the second half of the second beat, on three C's. This occurs in the thirteenth measure of the first chorus and continues through the end of the fifteenth. Parts of the above example appear again at the thirteenth measure of the fourth chorus (Example 44), then again on the three and 1/8th-beat value beginning at the thirteenth measure of the eighth chorus. (I might add that the ninth chorus is a tag or coda) (Example 45). The highest note in the solo is an e♭", approached from the c" and played three times. His solo is remarkably free of triplets, because it is mostly played in tempo. They occur only three times: twice in the third chorus—the most fragmented chorus of the solo—

First Chorus

Example 43

and once in the last measure of the eighth chorus. Yet, the prevalence of the number three, whether used throughout a piece or to end on, becomes more and more meaningful, especially when viewed in the light of the concept of UNITY embracing GOD-MAN-NATURE. "All a musician can do is to get closer to the sources of nature, and so feel that he is interpreting them to the best of his ability and try to convey that to others."[5]

Fourth Chorus

Example 44

Eighth Chorus

Example 45

"Countdown" was played at a very high tempo (♪ = 184 MM). It and "Giant Steps," or at least sketches for the two pieces, had been worked on as early as 1956; the modulating patterns moving from the minor third to the fourth would become part of Trane's style and can be seen in the duet that he and Rashied Ali recorded in February 1967. (The piece "Mars" especially uses this pattern.) Coltrane once told McCoy Tyner that recording these two pieces in this style had liberated him harmonically. Following this liberation he was able to pursue other commitments:

> I've been devoting quite a bit of my time to harmonic studies on my own, in libraries and places like that. I've found you've got to look back at the old things and see them in a new light. I'm not finished with these

studies because I haven't assimilated everything into my playing. I want to progress, but I don't want to go so far out that I can't see what others are doing.

I want to broaden my outlook in order to come out with a fuller means of expression. I want to be more flexible where rhythm is concerned. I feel I have to study rhythm some more. I haven't experimented too much with time; most of my experimenting has been in a harmonic form. I put time and rhythms to one side, in the past.

But I've got to keep experimenting. I feel that I'm just beginning. I have part of what I'm looking for in my grasp but not all.

I'm very happy devoting all my time to music, and I'm glad to be one of the many who are striving for fuller development as musicians. Considering the great heritage in music that we have, the work of giants of the past, the present, and the promise of those who are to come, I feel that we have every reason to face the future optimistically.[6]

"Giant Steps" was more flexible than "Countdown," perhaps because it was taken at a slower tempo. But for whatever reason, it turned out to be a remarkable example of just how fluent Trane could be, bouncing and moving through the European harmonic system which he had mastered so well. He could have articulated rhythmic phrases which would have been more easily sustained, but his major concern was with keeping the tonality always moving. There were still sustained rhythmic figures, but the melodic twisting and turning to accommodate the harmonic changes somewhat camouflages them. The very first chorus begins as "Countdown" began, only much slower in tempo (medium-fast), with twelve groups of four eighth notes. The first note in each group is accented. This is broken by a quarter note, two eighth notes, and a half-beat rest; followed by nine groups of four eighth notes broken by an eighth rest, then three groups (the rest acts as a connector and can thus be used on both parts) of four eighth notes ended by a quarter note. In the last three measures a line is developed around the c'', which is the highest note played in the solo. These last three measures also tie off the first chorus and lead into the second. Therefore, the rests follow the pattern: quarter rest; four eighths followed by two eighths; an eighth rest; an eighth followed by two eighths; a half measure rest. The line then moves into the second chorus, which is made much more flexible by the mixing of shorter with longer patterns (Example 46). But all of this is hidden by the predominating sound of the harmonic patterns, which are decidedly pounced on by Trane.

Typical of the form which emerges from all of Trane's works, "Giant Steps" communicates through its symmetry. It certainly repre-

Second Chorus

Example 46

sents more of a merging of the masculine and feminine elements of Trane's mind than "Countdown," which sounds more like a product of the analytic masculine mind. "Giant Steps" makes greater use of imitation and contains a greater variety of rhythms and lines having more rests combined with short note phrases as their components (like the last three measures of the first chorus). There is a recurrence of melodic material, mainly to remind the listener of where the piece is harmonically. These pieces are exercises left by a master musician, containing modulating material moving in both arpeggios and scale lines, beginning new lines with rests or jumps in the improvisations, usually over a fourth. Any student of the tenor saxophone would be greatly served by studying these pieces (Example 47).

The piece "Cousin Mary" is best described by Trane: "She's a very earthy, folksy, swinging person. The figure is riff-like and although

Sixth Chorus

Eleventh Chorus

Example 47

the changes are not conventional blues progressions, I tried to retain the flavor of the blues."[7] The progressions move as follows: tonic for four measures, sub-dominant for two, tonic for two, raised fourth for a measure, sub-dominant for a measure, then tonic for two. Given Trane's propensity for examination and recall, the results are again useful material for the student. The execution of that line embodies something which will remain a basic part of his music—the loping fourth/third, where he starts moving down a fourth, then back, and up a third—an interlocking, attached triplet (Example 48).

Seventh Chorus

Example 48

There is a beautiful phrase which begins at the first measure of the eighth chorus and goes through to the eighth measure. The phrase moves from g♭" to e♭', then from b' to a♭', then back to g♭" and e♭', with the top note always accented (Example 49). In the second measure of the eighth chorus, the g♭ gets accented four times; in the third measure it gets accented six times; the b' gets accented three times in the fifth measure and five times in the sixth; the g♭' gets accented six times in the seventh measure and twice in the eighth. This presents a problem for Trane's decipherer but certainly not for him.

Where "Countdown" and "Giant Steps" marked a point of

Eighth Chorus

Example 49

liberation from harmony, "Naima" is indicative of a new direction. By this time Trane had maintained a long interest in non-Western music, first African and now Indian and all the others he could find.

> From a technical viewpoint, I have certain things I'd like to present in my solos. To do this, I have to get the right material. It has to swing, and it has to be varied. (I'm inclined not to be too varied.) I want it to cover as many forms of music as I can put into a jazz context and play on my instruments. I like Eastern music; Yusef Lateef has been using this in his playing for some time. And Ornette Coleman sometimes plays music with a Spanish content as well as other exotic-flavored music. In these approaches there's something I can draw on and use in the way I like to play.[8]

He saw the viability of the space in the new modal directions of his playing with Miles. In modality, Miles's pieces seem to have lost their vitality with the departure of Garland and Jones and the arrival of Bill Evans on piano and Jimmy Cobbs on percussion. Although Evans brought a heavy lyricism to the band, it pulled energy from its vitality. However, Evans did introduce Trane to the works of Krishnamurti, a South Indian spiritual teacher and philosopher.

During Trane's second tenure in the Davis band Evans was replaced by Wynton Kelly, an old friend from Philadelphia. Kelly, although he was known professionally as a pianist, also played tenor saxophone. He had perfect pitch. Furthermore, his playing style on piano was very relaxed and consistent with the kind of piano energy that Miles Davis always had in his band. So, as always in Trane's working situations, he took what he could use, altered it and applied it to his music.

"Naima" was one of Trane's first well-known works, and it is still part of McCoy Tyner's repertoire. If the other pieces on the earlier date signify the end of Trane's long harmonic period, this piece demonstrated the direction that he was about to embark on with his own band. This was Trane's description of the structure of the piece: "The tune is built . . . on suspended chords over an E♭ pedal tone on the outside. On the inside—the channel—the chords are suspended over a B♭ pedal tone."[9] The tonic and dominant are used in the drone from which improvisations are developed, just as in the music of India. Also, the music of India is rhythmically very complex and compelling.

> Rhythm is popularly supposed to be the prerogative of the African, his own special field in which he excels. But on two separate occasions, I have heard Indian solo drummers playing Indian music on the Indian drums on a London stage, and while my eyes tell me that I am in London, and that I see before me an Indian master-drummer playing

Indian drum music on an Indian drum, when I shut my eyes my ears tell me that I am really in Nigeria, and that I am listening to a Nigerian master-drummer playing Nigerian drum music impeccably on a Nigerian drum.[10]

My first experience of seeing a South Indian Nadaswaram troupe occurred during the fall of 1973, when a troupe performed at Amherst College. (The nadaswaram is a double-reed wind instrument.) The drummer for that troupe played the thavil, a drum made in this case from the wood of an Indian fruit tree and the membranes from goatskin. The drum was played at both ends, tuned to the drone. The master-drummer used a stick at one end and the middle joints of his fingers at the other. His fingers had been individually wrapped with adhesive. During the concert the drummer not only continually changed rhythms but also changed tempo. Trane had certainly seen this flexibility and its potential application to his own music. "Naima," with its tonic-dominant structure, represents one aspect of Trane's "world view" as applied to his music.

The December 2, 1959 date also provided one other piece of note. This piece was "Harmonique." It seems funny now, but in the live recording that he made with Miles Davis in 1958 he began to demonstrate his emerging control over the harmonics of his instrument. The harmonic is actually the tone or tones connected in the overtone series of any specific note. That is, if a person strikes an A on a tuning fork, the sound that is produced is not only just A but all of the sounds that are connected above that specific pitch. So what Trane was putting together for himself was a further extension of his instrument, now not only playing the fundamental but also all the other tones of that specific pitch. So, as in all of nature, there is in the playing of John Coltrane an end and a beginning: I think this year—1959— marks the end of his harmonic studies and the beginning of an all out, flexible way of using his music to communicate his emotional feelings.

10

The archetypal creativeness of inner vision is the true source of all art, and it is here that the ways of art and those of meditation meet, though it may appear as if these ways were moving in different directions; that of art towards the realm of sense-impressions, that of meditation towards a realm in which sense-impressions and forms are transcended. However, this difference pertains more to accidentals than to the essential nature of both. Because meditation does not mean pure abstraction or negation of form—except in its ultimate stages of complete integration and liberation in the experience of the boundlessness of our true nature—but rather the complete onepointedness of our mind and the elimination of all inessential features of the subject in question, until we are fully conscious of it and are able to experience it as an aspect of a deeper reality. . . .

Art proceeds in a similar way: even if it uses the forms derived from sense-impressions of the external world, it does not try to imitate nature, but to make it the exponent of a higher reality by omitting all accidentals, thus raising the visible form to the value of a symbol, expressing a direct experience of life.

The same experience may be gained by the process of meditation. But instead of creating an objectively existing result (like an artist in his work of art) of formal expression, it leaves a subjectively acting impression in the mediator, a character-forming, consciousness-building force. . . .

An artist who, on the other hand, has attained this state, crystallizes or objectivates his inner vision or experience into the visible or audible form of a work of art by reversing the meditative process into a process of materialization. It is irrelevant in which way the artist arrives at this state of creative intuition, whether through inner or outer stimuli, be it the beauty or nature or the impression of a human face, be it an illuminating thought or an exalted mood; in each case the pre-condition is the same as in the case of meditation, namely receptivity (renunciation of "self"-assertion) and concentration. Only through conscious concentration upon this stimulus or experience, i.e., through elimination of all accidentals, all non-essential elements, can this living experience crystalize into form and materialize into a work of art.[1]

—Lama Anagarika Govinda

Johnny Hartman and McCoy Tyner — March, 1963.

When I saw Trane in 1958 and again in 1960, his demeanor seemed to be different. I remember mentioning this once to percussionist Warren Smith and he corroborated the fact that Trane seemed to be someplace else when he wasn't actually playing. Warren related to me that when he saw Trane with Miles Davis, he would stay on the bandstand, even between sets, seemingly preoccupied with his own thoughts. I can recall him being the same way and in fact not even noticing where he was between times that the band actually played. I know now that he was in a deep process of meditation, probably about many things, but mostly about his music, his family, and the composition of his band.

Trane entered the sixties prepared to organize *his* band. He was a well-experienced man, mature and committed to music. He had been an addict and knew the people who populated that dreadful world. He had been a heavy drinker and knew the people who were into that. He had played everywhere in this country, in Europe—where he was not at first acclaimed—and with Miles Davis and Thelonious Monk. He had played with many different musicians and in many different forums during this apprenticeship period. Trumpeter Donald Byrd was his frequent recording partner, and, in the open recording studios of Prestige and Blue Note, they produced some of Trane's most outstanding recorded music.[2] Donald Byrd was one of the many musicians who came out of Detroit at this time. All of those persons seemed to be good friends of Trane. They included Chambers, bassist Doug Watkins, guitarist Kenny Burrell, and last but not least, Elvin Jones. Byrd, although often said to have been highly influenced by Miles Davis, had a very individual sound. He had been one of the early African-American musicians to earn advanced academic degrees and practice his profession simultaneously. He had a great sense of duration and always knew where the progressions were. He and Trane exchanged much information.

Trane had many outings in his documented works during the second half of the fifties that just didn't come off well. Perhaps one of the most disappointing ones was the only occasion on which he recorded with the extraordinarily gifted pianist Cecil Taylor. The whole activity was clearly a mistake that even Taylor's dynamic endeavor could not rectify. Trane had been in even more disastrous sessions. His recording with trumpeter Wilbur Harden was important more because of their unified interest in African music than their actual playing.

For his own group, Trane chose a quartet with no side horn, only rhythm. The above mistakes may have been the reasoning for this. But

I think it was mostly because he wanted to work or to improvise in an ensemble. He had a wealth of players from which to draw a composite of the sound he wanted to support him. He was clearly *the* improviser of his time. In February 1960 he bought a soprano saxophone, and by the time he made his debut with his first new band at the Village Gate in May 1960 his improvement on that instrument was such that he opened with it.

> Last February, I bought a soprano saxophone. I like the sound of it, but I'm not playing with the body, the bigness of tone, that I want yet. I haven't had too much trouble playing it in tune, but I've had a lot of trouble getting a good quality of tone in the upper register. It comes out sort of puny sometimes. I've had to adopt a slightly different approach than the one I use for tenor, but it helps me get away—lets me take another look at improvisation. It's like having another hand.[3]

He was not the first jazz musician to be serious about the use of the soprano. Sidney Bechet and Johnny Hodges were extremely fluent on the instrument, and Steve Lacy had been using it as his first instrument in his work with Thelonious Monk.

Coltrane was armed with two instruments, one mastered in its present context, the other about to be mastered. He was truly a creative artist, an artist who felt he was just touching his potential at the time he organized his own band, but one who was acknowledged by his peers as the master of his instrument. He loved to play long:

> There's a story told by Cannonball Adderley who worked with Coltrane in the Miles Davis group. "Once in a while," Cannonball says, "Miles might say, 'Why you play so long, man?' and John would say, 'It took that long to get it all in.' "[4]

Trane was possessed by the *idea* of music. In his discussions he makes no doubt about his desire: "I'm very happy devoting all my time to music. . . ."[5] A man who thinks like this would only want to bring in material which would be essential to his music. Coltrane should also be seen in the following context:

> The point here is that cultural material must necessarily be viewed and examined and evaluated, only in terms of those primary assumptions from which they have arisen, and from which they have acquired validity and meaningfulness. Perhaps more importantly, we have to realize that in handling cultural material, we are not handling archaeological artifacts, but that which we mean when we speak of man in general, which is: his psychic world, his state of consciousness and his mode of life. Obviously we are, not in the world of logic, but of psychology; one that demands the utilization, not of the logical but of the psychological mind for perception, for examination, for reflection, and for the drawing of conclusions, if the process is to have any relevance or meaning at all.[6]

Coltrane's state of mind was one of disciplined concentration, and his mode of life was visionary. And since he was of African descent, many of his "primary assumptions" could be said to have sprung from the traditional mechanisms of that society.

The soprano saxophone really was the liberating force in Trane's changing style. He always played high in the tenor, using the bottom of the horn to spring lines, reaching and always leading to the highest note he could play, always emphasizing and preparing for that high note.

Changing over from one instrument to another, even if those instruments are in the same family, is a big move. But the soprano was another place where Trane heard music, so much so that the soprano became almost more of a favorite instrument than the tenor. However, for Trane the tenor and soprano were complementary instruments. It was clear that Trane rarely utilized the lower register of the tenor saxophone up until the time he started playing the soprano. Actually, I should not say rarely, but that he didn't use it as much as he used the upper part of the horn. The soprano saxophone, being an overlapping instrument, allowed him to think more concretely about how he could better utilize the lower half of the tenor saxophone, because he was now sure that he had the upper part of what he heard in his mind covered by the soprano.

The first instrument that Trane had played was a clarinet—a straight reed instrument. Now he found himself back with another straight instrument and this in itself (that is, how one holds an instrument) would naturally give a person a different concept of how to play it. So instead of being saddled with another instrument he was provided with an extension, a greater color spectrum of his own mind.

The rhythm section that performed with Trane up until a year before he died was not formulated immediately. Trane first employed pianist Steve Kuhn, on a temporary basis, for the two weeks when Tyner was unavailable. Benny Golson, the Philadelphia composer and tenor saxophonist and Trane's long-time friend, had hired McCoy for his Jazz-Tet, co-led by trumpeter Art Farmer, but as soon as their short tour was over, McCoy entered Trane's band.

Tyner was twenty-one and had been Trane's student since the early fifties. He was the synthesis of Garland, Monk, and Wynton Kelly. He is left-handed, and he showed strength very early in his ability to accompany with very imaginative harmonies. I was fortunate enough to have seen him in the Jazz-Tet just before he joined Trane's band. He was glowing during that whole week, and all the younger musicians looked up to him because everyone knew he was going to be in Trane's band and that he was Islamic. Being selected as part of the quartet gave Tyner a big boost in his confidence. He had been Trane's choice for the piano since the Red Rooster days. Whenever Trane had a break from his traveling and would go home, Tyner would play with him in any local Philadelphia gig they could get. Tyner always considered himself Trane's student. They were very close in spirit and McCoy was very dedicated to Trane's music. Tyner clearly described his role in the band in an interview with Stanley Dance:

A rhythm section is supposed to support and inspire a soloist, and it is a very sensitive thing . . . sometimes when John is soloing I lay out completely. Something important is involved here, I think. The pianist tends to play chords that the soloist knows are coming up anyway. Normally all the pianist does is try to give him a little extra push in the accompaniment and possibly to suggest some new ideas. When the piano isn't there, the soloist can concentrate purely on what he has in mind with pure limitations and boundaries. Otherwise, what the pianist plays can attract his attention away from his original thought. So it is all a manner of giving the soloist more freedom to explore harmonically.[7]

Tyner was also Monk's student, and Monk taught him the magic "in" sound. It was in Thelonious Monk's band that Coltrane's potential was first really exhibited, so the linkage here was very strong. Tyner brought great harmonic strength to the band plus a perfect student's temperament. His sense of space and sound application helped Coltrane rise to new heights. Tyner also brought the discipline that accompanies many Islamic people, and this discipline can be heard throughout all of his music.

Pete LaRoca was Trane's first percussionist. He was soon followed by Billy Higgins; but Elvin Jones, who was at that time playing with Harry Sweets Edison, was Trane's selection. As I look back and think about it now, it's clear that both LaRoca and Higgins were too young and inexperienced to handle the awesome responsibility of accompanying John Coltrane. Jones was a master musician when he entered Trane's band and had played in a host of different situations. He had been playing in jam sessions with Trane off and on since the beginning of 1959. When I saw him with Bud Powell he was extremely sensitive to Powell's playing. I remember that there was great consternation over Trane's selection of Jones, but, whatever anybody's opinion of him, I feel that even in the mid-fifties he was an extremely aware player. He was just a year younger than Trane, and brought the musical maturity which he inherited from a great musical family: his brothers are the pianist Hank Jones, and Thad Jones, fluegelhorn and trumpet player, most known for his beautiful arrangements for the bands he and drummer Mel Lewis lead.

Elvin Jones is a magnificent tempo player, a player with a great sense of space and with the proficiency, unequalled in the early sixties, to mix and combine rhythms within any tempo. He is very fast, and played with power and self-assurance in this band. In his interview with Frank Kofsky, Trane compared Elvin's readiness upon entering his band to his own potential readiness in Miles's band:

> He was there, Elvin was there for a couple of years—although Elvin was ready from the first time I heard him, you know, I could hear the genius there—but he had to start playing steadily, steadily, every night. . . . With Miles it took me around two and a half years, I think, before it started developing, taking the shape that it was going to take.[8]

Jones, more than anyone who played in Coltrane's bands, provided the foundations for Coltrane's improvisations. Elvin drove, propelled, spurred on, and generally provided the spring from which Trane launched his "visionary mode of artistic creation." With Jones, Trane was able to move beyond the psychological mode—the mode which deals with the lessons of life and its emotional shocks, ranging from high passion to the depths of human despair. But this mode deals with an individual's present life and can neither call up from past experiences nor prophesy the future. The horrors of what has already happened and the promises of a more ordered destiny can only be expressed in the visionary mode. It is, however, in the visionary mode that the artist is the most naked; his information lies in the most sacred hidden parts of his own mind. It is in the understanding of Trane's visionary expression that one begins to see and really to understand what he was trying to communicate.

Coltrane's ventures lay in the visionary mode, and it was Jones who sustained him, kept him bouncing into this realm of art. He was the complete accompanist for Coltrane, and provided the strength and stamina that Trane needed to allow himself "a glimpse into the unfathomed abyss of what has not yet become." Except for a brief period in 1963 when he was unavailable, Elvin Jones was Trane's drummer until almost the end of 1965 when he was joined by a friend, percussionist Frank Butler, in California. Butler left the band and Trane hired Rashied Ali as an additional percussionist. Not too long after, Jones left the band.

Art Davis was Trane's first selection on bass. Art had worked with Trane on numerous occasions when Trane was trying to realize the sound of the Indian water drum, and together they hit upon the idea of using two basses for the sound. But he was generally not available, so Trane selected Steve Davis, a fellow Philadelphian who is a cousin of Tyner.

The first time I saw the quartet was when Steve Davis was playing. This was around the fall of 1960. Even though I had seen Art Davis before (and I believe that of the four bass players that Trane used in his band Art Davis was the strongest in terms of technique), Steve Davis had the greatest potential from my point of view. He was very disciplined, and it was discipline that Trane needed more than anything else from his bass players. Even though this tonic-dominant bass concept was liberating for himself, it seemed to hold problems for the bass players who used it, especially when Trane used two bass players at one time.

Steve Davis was with Trane when he recorded his most lasting works with Atlantic, including the album of blues pieces (October 24, 1960) in which Trane first recorded the tenor saxophone and soprano saxophone on the same piece. The name of the composition was "26-2." But most important, Steve Davis was with Trane when he recorded the piece "My Favorite Things"; and it was that piece that literally launched Trane into the public prominence that had eluded him up until that time.

It was in this period, just before the beginning of 1961, that I was first able to get a glimpse of John Coltrane the person. As I mentioned in the Introduction, my friend Kenny had asked Trane if they could practice together, and Trane arranged for my friend to meet with him early one morning. Kenny was kind enough to take me along, and there we were, about 8:00 in the morning—my friend getting ready to practice with the master musician.

Where I grew up, a musician was every bit as big a hero as a baseball player or any athlete. The things that I can recall from this visit were the things that are most at the forefront of my mind and had the most indelible form. I remember Trane was a very humble person; he greeted us not as if we were youngsters but as if we were peers. He was also very businesslike. He immediately went to his instrument, and for the first hour or so he and my friend never played a note but simply operated the stops. This was the first technique that he showed us, and I would say that from then on everything he did during that period was brand-new. He mentioned that he didn't want to play too early because they might get phone calls from the manager of the hotel. So for the very first part of their practice time they just fingered the keys. After that they moved to playing long tones and then to scales. Occasionally

Trane would stop and then play purely solo, launching through all kinds of different scale and rhythmic patterns. He showed Kenny how to get harmonics, and the amount of space that can be derived from the saxophone between actually getting the harmonic sound and the fundamental. Everything that he could think of teaching my friend he did.

I mostly sat in the corner watching them go through their ritual and looking around his hotel room. I was amazed at the number of books that he carried with him, despite the fact that this was a short trip and they would immediately be on the way back to New York. He had three or four different Bibles, and he showed us a copy of the two-volume Negro Spirituals Book which he said he read through numerous times. He talked to my friend Kenny about meditation, but I can't remember him talking at all about religion or any specific creed. With one question he could go on for an hour, demonstrating through the instrument and talking about that specific angle of using the instrument. They talked about reeds, and he showed Kenny how to clean out the mouthpiece and the necessity for keeping the mouthpiece constantly clean.

He also had sheets of music in a book which he described as a "fake book," and I believe that that was the first time I had heard that specific term. He mentioned that almost all the musicians he knew kept a book of their own pieces and pieces from other people, and that this was only one of several books that he had. I think that Trane got off as much on having us there with him as we did being there with him. No words can really describe the immenseness of this individual as a human being. The other thing that I remember, and I think it's one of the things that was most pronounced in my mind, was that every time they played he used the tape recorder. He told us that he kept a tape recorder with him all the time so that he could listen to his practicing, especially the times when he just practiced improvisational parts rather than some specific method. He made it plain to us that he felt that jazz had developed from a listening point of view, and that one should always be aware of his own music and be as objectively critical as possible.

Every time that I saw Trane after this first meeting he always spoke to me. Sometimes he was surrounded by people asking him questions, and if he spotted me he always stopped and came over and shook my hand and asked how I was doing.

He was named "#1 Tenor Saxophonist" by the readers' poll of *Down Beat* in 1960. Irrespective of how one feels about that poll, it should be made clear that a musician gets a tremendous boost when this happens. His music for Atlantic, except for the date he made with Don Cherry in the very beginning of 1960, was mostly very successful. Today that company is still selling the records that he made for them.

That date with Cherry came at a time when Atlantic seemed to be more than anxious to pull together their leading avant-garde musicians. So it might have seemed, on paper, that Trane playing together with Don Cherry, Charlie Haden (bass) and Ed Blackwell (drums) would be a natural. But, as was so often the case, it came out very unsynchronized; and although Trane and Cherry play very, very well and hard, Haden seems to be stuck (unusual for him) in a retarded tempo, and Blackwell is almost a nonentity except for his solos.

11

Three Psychological Verities (and to the traditional African they are no less and are nothing else) are major factors in the attempt to establish and maintain this ideal condition, and they are:

1: SYMBOLS—as the transformers of psychic energy, vehicles of manifestation for the thing symbolized, (usually a spiritual force).

2: SOUND—as a metaphysical agent, potent in its own right and as itself as a Creative Force, which operates effectively according to the laws of its own nature, with or without the awareness or consent or approval of man.

3: SEX—in its role as the SACRED FIRE, in which role it has always been the very core of every religion that is alive, dynamic, and meaningful with reference to man—the universe—and the relationship between the two. It is not for nothing that, in all African traditional societies, sexual misdemeanors constitute a "god-palaver," and the society made haste to "amputate" the offending members before the avenging gods visited their wrath on the entire group without mercy and without compassion.

These three Psychological Verities together constitute the foundation on which every traditional art is based, and from which it has emanated as a logical extension in a particular direction. Music—far from being an exception—is perhaps the art most thoroughly conditioned, resting as it does on the use of Sound.[1]

—Fela Sowande

Roy Haynes and Jimmy Garrison—1963, Newport Jazz Festival. Roy Haynes: "Trane just kills me . . . He doesn't sound different to me today; he's probably playing a lot of different things, but the feeling is still the same."

Nineteen sixty-one was Trane's first really super year, and if one looks at the end of 1960, especially with the amount of music that he was beginning to turn out, one can get a glimpse of what 1961 would bring to him. It was the first time that he had won the critics' poll of *Down Beat*. It was the year that he would finally come to a conclusion about the kind of bass player that he wanted in his band. At this time, Trane was formulating the reality of the musical composite in his mind. Davis had made some definitive contributions to the band, but the double bass was not really fixed until December 1961 when Jimmy Garrison joined and stayed until Trane's death. In between Davis and Garrison was Reggie Workman who, although he was in the band for only a very short period, participated in Trane's first experiments using two bassists; coupled with this, Workman also was present at Trane's musically successful concert in Copenhagen at the end of 1961.

In addition, this was the year that Trane first collaborated with the man who perhaps most influenced him theoretically about music— Eric Dolphy. Dolphy played flute, bass clarinet, and alto saxophone. He had been Trane's friend since the early fifties; and Trane had made very few big musical decisions without first consulting with him. How they played together and made music is another example of the partnership of two superior and complementary musicians. While Trane was a very fluid player, using arpeggios, sequences, and scale fragments to work through the instrument, Dolphy was constantly jumping from register to register of whatever instrument he happened to be playing at that specific time. When they played in unison it was almost as if there was only one voice. They weren't perfect, because I think Trane could play with a lot of different musicians; but they did have that spark, and each was so profoundly fluent on his instrument that whatever one played it would just take the other to a higher musical level.

This was also the last year that Trane would work with Miles Davis and with his good friend, bassist Paul Chambers. But that activity in the early part of 1961 really is distinct from all of Trane's other efforts.

Trane first used two basses in May 1961. He used them on his last record for Atlantic, on May 25, 1961. An interesting thought is that he used the two bassists on the pieces "Olé," "Africa," and "Dahomey Dance." And I think that if one matches up the fact that Trane used two basses to get the effect of what he called the "Indian water drum" one can see his world view materializing.

"Africa," "Greensleeves," "Underground Railroad," and "Blues Minor" were Trane's first large orchestra works on record. They were orchestrated by Dolphy. The personnel in the orchestra, and its instruments, are certainly worth mentioning. There was one trumpet, manned by Dolphy's musical associate Booker Little. Little was a dynamic musician who had been invited to join the quartet but had to decline because ill health kept him from working every night. He died in October 1961 of a rare disease, uremia. He was just twenty-three and, like Clifford Brown, the great trumpet player of the fifties, he had been taken from us just as his potential was beginning to be realized. Alongside of Little were one trombone, one euphonium, *four* French horns, a tuba, Dolphy, Coltrane, Laurdine (Pat) Patrick on reeds, and the two bassists, Tyner and Jones (see listing of recordings for complete personnel).

Two takes of "Greensleeves" and "Underground Railroad" were the first things that Trane did for Impulse Records, and it was his recordings that took Impulse off the ground and kept them buoyant during the critical time that all new record companies have to undergo in order to sustain themselves. Impulse was a subsidiary of ABC Records and it was this company's first effort to develop a jazz line. Having just had a very good media year (1960) Trane was obviously an excellent choice to help launch this new jazz program.

Both "Greensleeves" and "Underground Railroad" were melodies that Trane borrowed from traditional materials. Two takes of "Greensleeves" have been released: one was on Trane's original release of *Africa/Brass* and the other has just been released along with the one take of "Underground Railroad." Although—as was so often the case in his studio work—Trane does not take a long solo on either piece, he demonstrates, especially on "Greensleeves," how fluent he had become on soprano saxophone. He plays the tenor on "Underground Railroad," and here he goes far beyond just moving through progressions; he has now reached a point where he practically transforms sound into colors. Elvin Jones, who was firmly in the band by this time, accompanies in his usual aggressive but sensitive style: there was only one drummer—at least during this period—for John Coltrane, and that was Elvin Jones.

"Africa" was a significant work of this period, so significant that it won a major recording prize in France for ABC's French affiliate, Vega Records. Trane said about the album, "I had a sound that I wanted to hear . . . and what resulted was about it. I wanted the band to have a drone. We used two basses. The main line carries all the way through the tune. One bass plays almost all the way through. The other has rhythmic lines around it."[2] Trane had been listening to African music for quite some time and had associated with Wilbur Harden on an earlier date which produced the songs "Dial Africa," "Domba," "Gold Coast," and "Tanganika Strut" (August 18, 1958). The piece he recorded on October 26, 1960, "Liberia," was dedicated to a group of Liberians he had met in the late fifties. However, "Africa" and "Dahomey Dance" were his first real efforts to put indigenous African material in his music.

"Dahomey Dance" was a line taken from a drumming piece he and Tyner heard on an African music record. He had begun looking more into the possibilities of 4/4 time because he had been using both 4/4 and 3/4, and finding the latter to be somewhat of a hindrance:

> On *My Favorite Things* my solo has been following a general path. I don't want it to be that way because the free part in there, I wanted it to be just something where we could improvise on just the minor chord and the major chord, but it seems like it gets harder and harder to really find something different on it. But it usually goes almost the same way every night. I think that the 3/4 has something to do with this particular thing. I find that it's much easier for me to change and be different in a solo on 4/4 tunes because I can play some tunes I've been playing for five years and might hear something different, but it seems like that 3/4 has kind of got a straight jacket on us there.[3]

So Trane looked for source material to attempt to find new ways of dealing with 4/4 and began to shape melodies from rhythms. The mere fact that Trane had gone across the bar line for years, and that now it was a characteristic of the music of African-American people, made this attempt at seeing the flexibility in 4/4 successful. "It's the first time I've done any tune with that kind of rhythmic background. I've done things in 3/4 and 4/4. On the whole, I'm quite pleased with 'Africa.'"[4]

This was the first time that Trane had organized a large band. Working in Miles's large band, in addition to the other large-sized bands he had been associated with during his career, had given him a wealth of experience. There was plenty of space to operate in, although many orchestra parts were moving in and out. Coltrane had given the line (melody) of "Africa" to Tyner, who worked out harmonies which he gave to Dolphy to orchestrate. All of the lines have their rhythmic statements within 4/4, and the piece moves from D to E. So a strong feeling of polymeter is established from the beginning and is held throughout.

> There has been an influence of African rhythms in American jazz. It seems there are some things jazz can borrow harmonically, but I've been knocking myself out seeking something rhythmic. But nothing swings like 4/4. These implied rhythms give variety.[5]

The overall feeling of the piece reminds me of a tape of music which Professor Sowande once played at a meeting. The music was from the Waters Province of Nigeria. It was sung by fishermen, and part of the piece had a very metric sound which gave one the impression of paddles moving through water. In "Africa," there are different effects—the glissando by the bass, the steady accentuation of the first and second beats, the trills by the piano and horns, the ascending lines shouted by the trumpets, and the movement of the voices in and out—all creating a strong foundation for Trane's improvisation. From all of this spring many symbols and much imagery.

Here, more than any place else, Dolphy and Coltrane's minds meet. Dolphy was extremely aware of the sounds of animals, especially birds, and he, more dramatically than any other jazz player of his time, was trying to incorporate those sounds into his music. So coming from "Africa" is more than just moving through progressions or at a certain tempo or some specific rhythmic parts; it is an attempt to give the listener the whole spectrum of what Africa meant to Dolphy and Coltrane.

Trane's playing on "Africa," as well as on "Underground Railroad," masterfully transcends the traditional European parameters of the tenor saxophone. The piece lasts almost sixteen and a half minutes. If anything is disappointing, it is the relatively short time he solos—on both takes. On the take from Impulse A-6, "Africa" begins with the two basses, then percussion, piano, the high-register horns followed by the lower horns, then Trane playing the line. The band fades when Trane finishes the line, and he plays with the rhythm. The band reenters, playing for a chorus, then leaves while Trane takes the longest part of his improvisation. It comes in again for a chorus, and then Trane takes his improvisation out. Tyner then improvises, followed by the basses playing pizzicato and arco. Again Tyner solos, while the band enters and exits. Elvin Jones then solos, and the piece ends with Trane and the band taking it out. Jones's solo is interesting because, at the end, he accents the first two beats and rolls and plays different rhythms on the next two. The steadiness of the accompaniment allows Trane to bellow.

The first thing that hits me is how powerful Trane is during the parts when the ensemble accompanying him moves off. He takes a really incredible amount of energy from them as they play together. His rate of growth from the Miles Davis band to now, in his own band, was meteoric.

I've been going to the piano and working things out, but now I think I'm going to move away from that. When I was working on those sequences which I ran across on the piano, I was trying to give all the instruments the sequences to play and I was playing them too. I was advised to try to keep the rhythm section as free and uncluttered as possible and if I wanted to play the sequences or run a whole string of chords, do it myself but leave them free. So I thought about that and I've tried that some, and I think that's about the way we're going to have to do it. I won't go to the piano any more. I think I'm going to write for the horn from now on, just play around the horn and see what I can hear. All the time I was with Miles I didn't have anything to think about but myself so I stayed at the piano and chords, chords, chords! I ended up playing them on my horn.[6]

Because he didn't have to worry about chords in "Africa," the amount of space he had to work in was huge. He ranges throughout the tenor, exploiting much more of the lower register, growling and spinning out like a cyclone. When Trane spoke about how Monk taught him to play two or three notes at one time, he mentioned another player: "John Glenn, a tenor man in Philly, also showed me how to do this. He can play a triad and move notes inside it—like passing tones!"[7] Trane was doing that now, holding the root and moving the upper note up a fourth and back. Then he would do it the other way. Not only that, he was beginning to do it metrically, playing for four beats and resting for four. His triplets are not charging towards progressions. Many are played in place at varying speeds, with much more concern placed on how they are unfolding rhythmically. The move to another key is much more emphatic, rolling like a snowball going downhill, gathering weight and momentum. He feels a tremendous empathy with "Africa," and many times he hits the top notes on his tenor like a scream. It is obvious that he does not play the moving chord for its own sake, but in order to emphasize his point. This point is that sound in its own right is creative and effective. This sound is best used in its functional capacity as a bridge between the visible and invisible worlds and unity is only achieved within the alignment of God, Nature, and Man; and Trane's quartet will ultimately express a total unity of mood. With his proficiency second to none, Trane's playing became more searching. As he continued to organize his ideas, the form of his personnel came to its final shape.

"Olé" and "Dahomey Dance" were recorded on Trane's last date for Atlantic (May 25, 1961). These pieces not only demonstrated his use of the two bassists but also demonstrated his wanting more and more to work in and out of the 6/8-4/4 time signature. One can see this developing not only with these two pieces but with much of the music that was going to become part of Trane for the next couple of years. So the idea that he was just beginning to develop and work on at this time would be part of his whole band repertoire for the next two or three years. Also, the piece "Africa" was recorded the same year that Miles Davis's *Sketches of Spain* and Stan Getz's *Focus* were recorded. All three have their genuine merits and each will go down as profound works in the history of jazz. But Coltrane's "Africa" seems to be reaching more profoundly to the point that jazz must rely on as its fundamental basis—melody/rhythm.

12

The six musical requirements of Yoruba as a tone-language . . . are:

1. There must be Inflexional Correspondence between words and music, whereby the normal (tonal) inflexion of each Yoruba word is retained, its intended meaning being thereby preserved.

2. There must be proper observation of the "interval-period" of Yoruba words, whereby the interval-range within which the word has the intended meaning is neither diminished nor exceeded, as this would result in a change of meaning of the word, even though the music has risen or fallen or remained parallel with the direction of the tonal inflexion of the word.

3. There must be "unity of mood" between words and music, so that the emotional import of the words is heightened, reinforced as it were, and not lessened or destroyed by the music.

4. There must be Inflexional Correspondence between the verses, so that corresponding lines of each verse follow the same tone-curve, thereby allowing the same person of the same melody to be used for the corresponding lines in each verse, without injury to the normal meaning of any word in the line of any verse. . . .

5. There must be observation of the principles of meter, as they apply to Yoruba as a tone-language. The music may not displace the "normal accentuation pattern" of Yoruba words, and must take into account such specific features of the language as the use of certain tone-patterns to convey certain emotional ideas.

6. The use of the appropriate scales and pulse-measures must be observed. Here we are concerned solely with Yoruba hymns, not with Yoruba music (traditional or otherwise) as a type, With this proviso, it is an observable fact that, for reasons which have not yet been satisfactorily given, or convincingly explained, the vast majority of Yoruba traditional melodies which have been used, or lend themselves to being used, as hymn-tunes with but slight though important scalic and modal modifications . . . use the pentatonic scale and are in triple measure.[1]

—Fela Sowande

McCoy Tyner and John Coltrane — March, 1963, recording session.

Reggie Workman was on notice from the draft, so it was uncertain whether he could stay in the band or not. By the time this situation had straightened itself out, Trane had decided to use Jimmy Garrison. Garrison and Workman had played together in the band at times, but Trane went with Garrison. Garrison was a great fundamental bassist, excelling in the blues forms, as did his hero Paul Chambers.

If one puts Steve Davis, Reggie Workman, and Paul Chambers together, one sees clearly the kind of bassist that Trane wanted. First of all, all three were from Philadelphia and had known Trane from the days when he was really struggling. Each had a similarity in style, although I believe Steve Davis to have been a little stronger in terms of his rhythmic discipline: he therefore held patterns very well. So what Trane did here was to formulate what he wanted the bass to do, who he felt was the epitome of that style (Art Davis) and when he couldn't get the specific person he wanted he went back home and selected from his center.

Garrison's link with Trane went back to the mid-fifties and it was at his mother's house that Trane, Tyner and Garrison began the study for *Giant Steps*. He had also worked with the formidable alto saxophonist, Ornette Coleman. Although he was flexible, his greatest asset was his ability to keep time. His tone wasn't that strong, and sometimes he would disappear between the power of Jones and Coltrane; but he droned and moved very well in time. He and Elvin Jones played exceptionally well together, and their spirits were extremely compatible. Garrison came into the band with a great hearing potential which was developed through his working with the ever-moving Coltrane night after night.

To get a better understanding of Trane's influence over Garrison, I think a specific incident that I watched unfold will give a lucid view. When I was doing my Ph.D. academic work at Wesleyan University, Jimmy Garrison was one of the part-time visiting artists in African-American Music there. As a teaching assistant I had to teach one class a term and in the fall of 1971 I was teaching a course on Miles Davis. At the university there was an excellent South Indian violinist named L. Shankar (of late playing with guitarist John McLaughlin). One evening for my class, Garrison and Shankar played a beautiful duet which must have gone on for at least two hours. Here were two men who, although coming from truly distinct and different lands, were able to improvise for this length simply because they were both great listening musicians. Most of all, they both loved making music—their common denominator.

These weren't just four individuals in Trane's band, but a unit led by a matured spirit best described by the traditional philosophy of the Ibos of Nigeria, which states that the soul incarnates seven times. First come the "young souls" who often do wrong things because they don't know better. Then at the end of the cycle are the "old souls" who have gained wisdom through the experiences of their past lives. However, there are also the "perverse souls" who have not learned through the mistakes of their past lives and who have in fact gotten more perverse in each lifetime. At the end of this period of reincarnation the perverse souls are said to become inanimate objects. So here the young and old souls relates to the spiritual maturity of an individual; and in my lifetime I have seen few persons who were more spiritually mature than Trane.

Coltrane was a "traditional" man and his primary assumptions, his education, his being, were derived from a greater awareness of the "factual dynamic relationship between the individual on one hand, and the Cosmos and the World of Nature on the other."[2] Trane belonged to the traditional stream of thought, the premises of which include: (a) the invisible world as the world of causes, that in fact this world is only invisible to the eyes of the flesh and that this is the world of reality; (b) that the visible world is the world of effects; (c) that the visible world can be understood, analyzed, studied, and picked apart but that it is only the reflection or shadow of the content; (d) that the invisible world is the world of the gods and goddesses; (e) that these individuals were the humans of yesterday and that the humans of today will be the gods and goddesses of tomorrow; (f) that God, nature, and man are an unbroken continuum, each world distinguishable but inseparable; (g) that the human history of the gods provides the only reliable guidelines for positive action for the humans of today; (h) ingress into the minds of gods can be attained through intuition, while access to the visibility of the gods can be had through rituals; (i) that there is but one energy endowing each thing in life with its *own* life-force, which can be tapped and used through necessary training; (j) for the traditional man the universe is immersed in sacredness; (k) that God and the devil are *complementary,* each on the other side of the same coin; (l) that equality is determined by an individual's spiritual maturity, his soul age; (m) that hierarchy is a natural phenomenon, first positioned by the gods, and is the order of all beings; (n) that the world of effects is the school of life and we continue to return until we graduate, hence reincarnation; and (o) that the debts we incur in any one life must be accounted for, and that the gods see that they are accounted for, if not in that life, then in one of the subsequent lives. This is the law of karma in Indian thought, which, together with the law of reincarnation, forms what one may perhaps term the coordinates of mundane existence, to which everything is subject.

When one follows Trane's life, one can see these concepts emerge: his visionary contacts with Charlie Parker which Simpkins claims developed his looking into new patterns of progressions beginning about 1955—56; his breaking the cycle of drugs and alcohol; his constant research into and preoccupation with music; and in 1958, the payoff of hard work manifesting itself through Trane's acknowledgement as the greatest tenor saxophonist alive. In 1961 Trane's music was not only masterful in its technical skill but was beginning to go far beyond just notes on lines and spaces; it was music that was beginning to investigate all the space that lies between C and C#.

13

Thus art does not move exclusively in the opposite direction of meditation—as it might have appeared to a superficial observer, who values art only as a finished product—but it moves in the direction of meditation as well, namely in the state of conception. Thus, art and meditation compensate and penetrate each other.

The relationship between art and meditation is, however, not yet exhausted with the aspect of creative intuition. The effect of a work of art, the experience to which it leads the beholder, is equally important. The artist himself may not care for the effect of the work. For him the process of creating is the only thing that really matters. But art as a factor in the cultural life of humanity should have the function to stimulate creativeness and inspiration. The enjoyment of art is an act or re-creation, or rather of creation in the reverse direction, towards the source of intuition, i.e., an act of absorption, in which we lose our small self in the experience of a greater, all-embracing life and a universal vision.

Thus art means the ever renewed concentric attack and the breaking through of selfhood toward infinity, *the complete extinction of limitation by endless and as such uninterrupted turns of radiations and inhalations,* it means the condensation of the universe to a microcosmic focus, *and ever again* the establishment of a magic balance between soul and universe. *The object of art is the condensation of all the inconceivable streams, forces and effects of the universe upon the plane of human understanding and experience; it is the projection of psychic emotion into the infinite. The self dissolved and transformed into the whole—in which case emptiness only signifies the complete non-resistance—means the integration of the one into the other, the passionless acceptance of the world into the other, the passionless acceptance of the world into the liberated, i.e., unlimited, soul.*

Here art and religious life meet in a sphere of consciousness where all distinctions between self and non-self have disappeared. Therefore, wherever religion is a living force, there it finds its natural expression in art; in fact, it becomes art itself—just as art in its highest attainments becomes religion, *namely* when it succeeds to re-establish "the magic balance between soul and universe."[1]

—Lama Anagarika Govinda

John Coltrane — 1963, Newport Jazz Festival. A decided difference between his live sound and his records.

Where religion is not a living force, the so-called art that emerges is, at best, no more than a mechanical contrivance which no matter how cleverly done can only succeed in substantially reducing the mind's affirmative resonance with nature. Its unrelieved dissonance is indicative of a disunified God-man-nature, an evil art. Hence, what is religion and how can it be made a living force is the first riddle the would-be artist must solve.

The fruits of the quartet's relationship began to manifest themselves from the moment Garrison stepped into the band. A recording made live at the Village Vanguard in New York on November 2, 3, and 5, 1961, is a testimony to this fact. The material used during these tapings had been worked on previously, but was spontaneous as well. The music was certainly in Coltrane's vein and of his dimensions—the length of his solos, the blues, "Impressions," a piece using two tonalities, and a spiritual. But this live date was more: it was the combined collective energies of the audience-participants and the musicians. "I like . . . the feeling of a club, especially one with an intimate atmosphere like the Vanguard. It's important to have that real contact with an audience because that's what we're trying to do—communicate."[2] Communication developed primarily through the unity of mood translated through the band and founded on Jung's principle of synchronicity: "which [takes] full account of that peculiar interdependence of objective events among themselves as well as with the objective (psychic) states of the observer or observers."[3]

The material itself had come to take on a specific meaning for Trane, even though it might have sometimes been seen in a different light by others. On the composition "Spiritual" he commented:

I like the way it worked out. . . . I feel we brought out the mood inherent in the tune. It's a piece we'd been working with for some time because I wanted to make sure before we recorded it that we would be able to get the original *emotional essence* of the spiritual.[4]

This piece was part of a whole series of new compositions that Trane developed in which he would use his two instruments in specific ways. "Spiritual" became a vehicle where he would begin a solo or exclaim the line on the tenor saxophone; then there would be an improvisation by another member of the group, either Dolphy or Tyner; then Trane would return playing soprano saxophone. He did this on an earlier piece, "26-2," but here on "Spiritual" he began to use a specific pattern: any time he played "Spiritual" he would begin on tenor and then, after a solo from one of the other members of the band, he would come back on soprano sax.

The piece "Spiritual" itself is taken at a very slow tempo, and Trane would simply emerge out of the line itself until all of a sudden he and Elvin Jones would become a kaleidoscope of sound. One of Jones's great attributes was his ability to help a soloist build on his solo by using tremendously diversified dynamics during the piece.

On "Chasin' the Trane," another piece played during these recordings at the Vanguard, Trane had these comments:

> Usually, I like to get familiar with a new piece before I record it, but you never have to *worry about the blues,* unless the line is very complicated. In this case, however, the melody not only wasn't written but it wasn't even conceived before we played it. We set the tempo, and in we went.[5]

"Chasin' the Trane" was a spontaneous piece created right on the spot. It should be made plain, if it hasn't been already, that Trane was a spontaneous player: the lines that he wrote were simply lines for him to jump off from. Even though he left a wealth of compositions for other musicians to use, he was essentially an improviser, and he mostly used lines or musical concepts to launch his improvisations. In "Chasin' the Trane" Trane demonstrates again not only his mastery over the fundamental aspects of the instrument, but his development of great control over the harmonics. So every tone becomes larger and he is able not only to jump registers but to move to the harmonic of any fundamental. And out comes a whole host of the total reflections of people. This recording—or "spontaneous occurrence"—is one of the earliest examples of Trane's simply "getting away" on the instrument. Now one can get visual aspects as well as sound effects from Trane's music. Garrison follows Trane during the whole solo beautifully. It becomes in the trio's hand a new concept of how to deal with a traditional form, the blues.

Two of the oldest forms of African-American music are the spiritual and the blues. I'm reminded that, in traditional African societies, nothing is profane. For Trane, every aspect of his work became a true condition of his existence. He took extraordinarily long solos on "Chasin' the Trane" and "Impressions," and when asked if this was an attempt to further draw his listener into the music by developing a hypnotic mood, his response was:

> That may be a secondary thing . . . but I haven't reached the stage yet where I'm trying consciously to produce effects of that kind. I'm still primarily looking into certain sounds, certain scales. The result can be long or short. I never know. It's always one thing leading into another. It keeps evolving, and sometimes it's longer than I actually thought it was while I was playing it. When things are constantly happening, the piece just doesn't feel that long.[6]

The listener was also losing sense of time, and there was a hypnotic effect—whether it was consciously or unconsciously intended. In this whole process of concentration, so much can be a result of the energies that are going back and forth. Trane's fantastic ability to concentrate made him unaware of the passage of time and the length of his solos. This ability to connect energies is developed through meditation. Clearly, that kind of process is the only way of finding the energy to express what Trane displays in his music.

Trane was always listening to other people, on his instrument and others. Eric Dolphy occasionally toured with the band during the first half of the sixties, and he opened Trane up to the many different sounds he was getting from his instrument. His jumping style had a tremendous effect on Trane, for it was at this time that Trane began playing patterns in the upper and lower registers simultaneously through the use of harmonics.

> For a long time . . . Eric Dolphy and I had been talking about all kinds of possibilities with regard to improvising, scale work, and techniques. Those discussions helped both of us to keep probing, and finally I decided that the band was here, after all, and it made sense for Eric to come on in and work. Having him here all the time is a constant stimulus to me.[7]

The new discoveries he made with Dolphy were incorporated into his style. And these were the forms that took shape in "Chasin' the Trane" and "Impressions," as well as many later pieces.

Trane's music was more than spacious enough for growth. The brilliant tenor saxophonist in the Sun Ra band, John Gilmore, impressed him. He spoke about Gilmore, and, indirectly, about the implications of the oral tradition, saying that it was *'like . . . a big reservoir, that we all dip out of. . . .* I listened to John Gilmore kind of closely before I made 'Chasin' the Trane,' too. So some of those things on there are really direct influences of listening to this cat, you see. But then I don't know who he'd been listening to. . . ."[8]

This collecting, reshaping, and extending the parameters of the lines of others has been a dominant aspect of jazz. Archie Shepp related to me that once when Trane was playing with Monk in 1957, he and Trane practiced together, and, at one point, Trane played the cycle in many ways in a twenty-minute time span. Archie had been one of those frequent visitors to Trane's apartment during the latter 1950s. After these visits Shepp had a lot to think about for a long time. This dipping into the reservoir is the process of the oral tradition. It was the storehouse of oral transmissions that Trane unleashed on his first live date as a leader. In this context, a live context, where jazz was heightened by the vitality of the whole, Trane's oral history and visionary reflections met fully.

The pace of "Impressions" and "Chasin' the Trane" and the manner in which the quartet played them (trio on "Chasin' the Trane") stand as positive proof of this energized communication. On "Impressions," which has a tonality move from D to E♭ and stays in the first for eight bars, moves to the second for eight, then moves back for eight, Trane has immense room to work in. Tyner accompanies through five choruses, then lays out until the very last chorus when he enters on a cue from Coltrane. There are thirty-three choruses, so the trio accompanies in the next twenty-six. On the numerous times I saw this band, Coltrane, Garrison, and Jones would play for another fifteen minutes and then Garrison would lay out. Coltrane and Jones would then play as long as they wanted to. I recall one occasion when Coltrane and Jones played for an hour and forty-five minutes.

During his whole solo on "Impressions," Trane never gropes except in the most difficult rhythmic situation (Example 50). Jones and Coltrane display a tremendous unity just by the number of times they accent the same rhythms together. Jones provided immense power to Trane and they seemed to be enveloped in one another's energy— spinning out lines like a spiral. Trane is still playing scale runs much less frequently, and the compound statements are down to the bare minimum. Now Trane is working with smaller rhythmic-melodic statements that increase and decrease in rhythmic size, all with incredible symmetry. Nothing is out of place, and even "mistakes" are capitalized on. The music that emerged from this playing spelled out

Tenth Chorus

Example 50

clearly that this was the last *new* thing that was ever going to be played in tempo.

Elvin Jones was the keeper of the tempo, a master of 4/4 and its constantly emerging rhythms. As mentioned earlier, he had amazing stamina. As long as Trane wanted to solo, he was prepared to take the weight as his accompanist. The communication exchanged between him and Trane during "Impressions" was unique to them. Trane would get into rhythmic patterns and repeat them, changing the accents, and Jones would immediately feel what was happening and either reinforce those accents or play another complementary rhythm as a crossing action. Backed by this strength, Trane produced different sounds—harmonics, partial harmonics, flatting and sharping notes to give the feeling of fluctuating tonality.

I spoke before about the amount of space between C and C♯. The immenseness of this space can be experienced if one listens to the music of Indonesia. There is a system called the cents system. This system is a way of analyzing the amount of space between one interval and another. Between C and C♯—that is, between a minor interval— there are one hundred cents. Almost all the traditionally-trained Indonesian singers can sing intervals as small as seventy cents and as large as one hundred twenty. And it was this space that Trane was beginning to utilize and operate in. Trane would use whole choruses to express one rhythmic idea.

The twenty-seventh chorus of "Impressions" shows Dolphy's influence on his playing. At the ninth measure of that chorus, he begins a three note figure which begins moving A to a' then to B to b'. The figure, using the same rhythmic three notes with different accents to give the phrase a different sound, then moves up a minor third in its jumps. This jumping through octaves was one of Dolphy's favorite devices. It is a particularly hard figure to execute because of the uniformity with which Trane is using rests and the three note figure (Example 51). It is the classic example of what Sowande called the "submerged triple measure" which suddenly appears inherent in a quadruple measure.

While all of this was going on between Trane and Jones, Garrison would change the tempo many times, thereby heightening the improvisations at that time, or turning the solo into the next chorus.

Eric Dolphy was a tremendous asset to the band. His ability to play the alto saxophone, bass clarinet, and flute brought another dimension to the band and complemented Trane's tenor and soprano. There has recently been available a bootleg two-record recording of a

Example 51

tape made in Copenhagen by the band that included Dolphy, Jones, Tyner, Workman, and Trane. To get a real estimate of not only Dolphy's playing but the tremendous impact that he had on Trane, one has to listen to this particular concert. From each piece emerges a style of playing which Trane would continue almost throughout his whole career.

I've already talked about how he handled the piece "Spiritual." Also, on the piece "I Want To Talk About You" by Billy Eckstine he plays absolutely solo. This is a piece that he first recorded in 1958 that he was working on in 1961 and continued to work on throughout his whole career. When he plays solo in this piece it's like he's breathing life, or reviving through breath a man thought to be dead.

Another piece on this tour, "Bessie's Blues," became a *tour de force* for McCoy Tyner. And Trane continued to record this piece as late as 1964. So from this specific year—working with Dolphy—all kinds of musical situations evolved.

Even in their playing in unison, there seems to be something about the connecting forces of Trane and Dolphy—whose styles of playing were really dramatically different but whose need to make music was absolutely on the same level. On this recording there is a rendition on bass clarinet by Eric Dolphy of "Naima" which is a must for any collector. I don't think Trane ever played this piece as well as Dolphy does here.

I don't want to give the illusion here that Trane had a fixed concept of who he wanted in the band. One of the frictional elements that arose during 1965 was the fact that the John Coltrane Quartet was always a revolving door band. In the fall of 1961, the guitarist Wes Montgomery not only played for a short time with Coltrane but was asked to be part of the group. But he refused because of other obligations. This wasn't just some idle gesture on Trane's part; this was an actual invitation which Trane regretted when Montgomery decided not to be part of the band.

Dolphy played at a time when Coltrane was taking heavy abuse from the critics about the length of his solos and the many different sounds, especially shrieks and shouts, that were emanating from his playing. Dolphy was closely associated with the "new music" musicians, and many critics used this as an opportunity to more devastatingly attack Coltrane. These attacks, because they were attacks coming from ignorance rather than any position of understanding, greatly concerned Coltrane. They finally culminated in Trane's attempting to bring all parties together; that never materialized however. There is an interview of Dolphy and Trane reprinted in Simpkins' book from *Down Beat* of April 12, 1962, which not only is a distinct explanation of what these two tremendous musicians were doing, but a statement to make it evident to everyone that they in fact *knew* what they were doing. It is when a musician seems to be turning the corner and really dealing with the music in his head that things, most often out of his control, become disguised time bombs. In his interview with Kofsky, Trane remarked several times about the ignorant response of the "taste-makers":

> *Kofsky:* That's what so annoyed me about all of that stuff they were saying about you in '61.
> *Coltrane:* Oh, that was terrible. I couldn't believe it, you know, it just seemed so preposterous. It was so ridiculous, man, that's what bugs me. It was absolutely ridiculous, because they made it appear that we didn't even know the first thing about music—the first thing. And there we were really trying to push things off.[9]

Earlier in the interview Trane acknowledged that the critics were relying too much on what they didn't know to support their assumptions about jazz:

> *Kofsky:* I think it frightened them. Bill Dixon and I talked about this at great length; and he said: "Well, these guys, it's taken them years to pick out *I Got Rhythm* on the piano," and now the new music comes along and undermines their entire career, which is built around understanding things based on those patterns.
> *Coltrane:* Yes, I dug it like that too. I said, "Well, this could be a real drag to a cat if he figures this is something that he won't be able to cope with and he won't be able to write about." If he can't write about it he can't make a living at this; and then I realized that, so I quieted down. I wouldn't allow myself to become too hostile in return. Although there was a time I kind of froze up on those people at *Down Beat*. I felt that there was something there that wasn't—I felt that . . . they were letting their weakness direct their actions, which I didn't feel they should have. The test, was for me. They could do what they wanted to do. The thing

was for me to remain firm in what I was doing. That was a funny period in my life, because I went through quite a few changes, you know, like home life—everything, man. I just went through so many . . . everything I was doing.[10]

Trane, at this time, was not only expanding the possibilities in forms, but was also utilizing knowledge that he had gained from fellow musicians. He was making use of the "turnback" or the coda, where he would extend a standard piece by adding a coda or cadenza onto part of the melody to launch his improvisation. Compositions like "My Favorite Things" or "Out Of This World" (June 29, 1962), "Summertime," "But Not For Me," and others, used this particular motif. His soprano playing had begun a trend that many other musicians took advantage of and followed. His use of the pedal point in "Naima" was carried over to his other compositions, and, more often than not, modality became ever present in his playing. His interest in the music of India became more profound. In the same year that he composed "Africa" he also composed "India," which served to honor both the country and the name of the daughter of his great friend Calvin Massey. The similarities of African and Indian music go beyond rhythmic and melodic compatibilities. As Professor Sowande observed: "The absence of Western concepts of harmony in large areas of the African continent is similarly matched by India where, as in Africa, Western harmony is conspicuous by its absence."[11]

Sometime during 1960 or 1961 Ravi Shankar heard Trane play in New York. There is some confusion as to whether or not the great Indian sitarist spoke to Trane, but there is no confusion about the fact that Trane was immensely interested in the playing of this master musician: Trane's second son, born in the mid-sixties, is named Ravi.

14

*If Yoruba or Ibo words are to retain their normal and intended meaning
in song as in speech, several things are necessary:*

*1. The music must rise and fall in the same way as the voice rises
and falls when the words are spoken. This we may call, "Inflexional Correspondence between words and tune."*

*2. The correct musical intervals must be observed for each word. But
the tonal interval of a Yoruba word is not a precise musical interval; it is
approximate. Hence each word has what we may call an "interval-period" within which it retains the same meaning. The Yoruba word for
"crown"—"Adé"—retains its meaning within the intervals of a major
second to perhaps a major third or, in certain musical contexts, even
slightly beyond a major third. Hence it is the "interval-periods" rather
than any precise musical interval that needs to be observed for each
word, and the musical interval that is used is determined by the musical
context.*

*3. There will have to be, obviously, a "unity of mood" between
music and words, so that the music heightens and enhances the general
sense of the words. A Yoruba verse on the Passion of Our Lord would,
for example, not benefit by a tune suggesting the glorious Resurrection of
Easter morning, even if all other requirements were met.*

*4. When we come to consider a Yoruba or Ibo hymn of several
verses, other considerations have to be met: (a) the importance of tone in
the language; (b) the special use of certain tone-patterns; (c) the presence
of the tone-pattern high-mid-low-mid in uncomplimentary words, and the
intensification of this by the reduplication of the tone pattern on low-low-mid-low; so that while pálà-pàlà on high-mid-low-mid signifies unseemly behavior, pálà-pàlà on high-mid-low-mid: low-low-mid-low
signifies really disgusting behavior; (d) the liberal use of onomatopoeic
words; and (e) the fact that whereas English poets make use of rhymes at
regular intervals, the Yoruba poet does not write down his poem for
people to read, he says them for poeple to hear; his aim is to produce
certain effects on his listeners and his arrangement of lines is therefore tonal. Probably the same holds good for Ibo poetry.[1]*

—Fela Sowande

Pharaoh Sanders — 1966, Newport Jazz Festival.

Dolphy left for Europe at the beginning of 1962, but he and Trane teamed up often until he died on June 29, 1964, in Germany. Trane's band remained unchanged until 1965, with occasional exceptions and the 1963 stint on drums of Roy Haynes. Between the beginning of 1962 and the end of 1964 Trane was going through a tremendous period of transition. Both he and Impulse were affected by criticism, so what occurred during this period, especially in his recorded work, seems to have been compromised. In spite of all the pros and cons about his music with vocalist Johnny Hartman and with Duke Ellington, without question Trane's attempts were deficient during this particular period, not only on these two efforts but also on his ballad albums. As beautiful as those ballads are played, they seem to be somewhat lacking in the strength and vitality that he had demonstrated in 1961. His sound is almost thin on these recordings. This seems to be a tremendous letdown from what I had seen in person on the numerous occasions that I had the opportunity to see him during this time.

Unquestionably, he was having problems with his reeds and his mouthpiece even as early as the fall of 1961:

> Well, I tell you, I had some trouble at that time. I did a foolish thing. I got dissatisfied with my mouthpiece and I had some work done on this thing, and instead of making it better, it ruined it. It really discouraged me a little bit, because there were certain aspects of playing—that certain fast thing that I was reaching for—that I couldn't get because I had damaged this thing, so I just had to curtail it. Actually, I never found another [mouthpiece], but after so much of this laying around and making these kinds of things, I said well what the hell, I might as well go ahead and do the best I can. But at that moment, it was so vivid in my mind— the difference in what I was getting on the horn—it was so vivid that I couldn't do it. Because as soon as I did, I'd hear it; and it just discouraged me. But after a year or so passed, well, I'd forgotten.[2]

But I think the criticism that he was receiving was the main rationale for the production decisions of Impulse.

There were other situations that caused him to be hesitant or seemed to prolong this transitional period for him. From April to October of 1963 Trane was without drummer Elvin Jones who had gotten himself in deep trouble with drugs. So for half of that year he used Roy Haynes instead. Haynes is an astonishing drummer, but no one had the stamina and the rhythmic genius that Elvin Jones had at this time, and his being out of the band must have been very disconcerting for Trane

A major factor in this whole transitional period was the fact that Trane was becoming further and further estranged from Naima; their relationship had grown more and more distant since 1961. For one thing, Trane was very concerned about the fact that in eight years of marriage he and Naima had not had children. Happily for Trane, this concern did not arise in his second marriage: in the four years that he was married to Alice Coltrane they had three sons.

However, to conclude that nothing came out of this period would be wrong, especially in regard to his association with Ellington. It was Ellington who pointed out to Trane that any spontaneous music is played only once: even if you play it again, it can never be the same. Trane had gotten into the habit of recording numerous takes on each piece, and Ellington broke him of this habit.

But even though this was in certain ways a disheartening period for Trane, in the records he made then there are genuine parts which further demonstrate the growth of his skills—the new high notes through altered fingering, and his sound, now broader and with more voice definition. More and more the anguish experienced by so many African-American people in the United States was coming through in his music.

The sixties were an even greater period of confrontation than usual in this country. When, in 1963, black children were killed in a bombing in Alabama, Trane wrote a composition in memoriam called "Alabama." The significance of the piece is even greater when one realizes that the melodic line of the piece was developed from the rhythmic inflections of a speech given by Dr. Martin Luther King. His recording of the piece is in one of the most melancholy moods I have ever heard him play—low in the horn, then moving into tempo but quickly resolving back into the down mood. The line itself is played in a very spoken way. It only goes into tempo for eighteen measures, then abruptly stops. Trane turns and tells the band to stop playing tempo. There is a pause, and they begin the line again. Of the many compositions Trane recorded, this one certainly exemplifies what Sowande considers necessary "to retain normal and intended meanings in songs as in speech."[3]

Every point in this chapter's opening statement pertains to much of Coltrane's playing throughout his career, and particularly to "Alabama." In this composition, each note has its own significance, and the melody rises and falls as the voice would. The correct musical intervals are present throughout the piece, especially at the very beginning of the tempo where he moves from a' to d♭' (Example 52). There is "unity of mood" and when it becomes obvious that playing in tempo is incorrect for this piece, Trane quickly changes and moves back into "free" time. Phrases are reinforced throughout by the use of imitation—as always with Trane. Not at all an isolated case, it does demonstrate that Trane was much more than a "barn burner" in his playing. His music was a calling to the people. Compositions like "Alabama" and "The Promise" were his attempt to articulate the plight of African-American people and all oppressed people throughout the world.

Example 52

The period between the beginning of 1963 and the end of 1964 was certainly not a total disaster. He had met Alice in July 1963, and the transition in his personal life was completed by the beginning of 1964. His public playing was still as dynamic as ever and, if anything, was becoming more and more a contradiction of what he was putting on records. But I'm reminded of a letter (fully quoted in Simpkins's book) which will give everyone an insight into where Trane was in the last quarter of 1963. He first of all believed that there was a positive and affirmative philosophy inherent in the music of African-American people and that this philosophy was defined in the phrasings and the sounds of this music: that the entire globe was in itself a community—another indication of his all-embracing world view. He had an ability to scrutinize material and to pull from it what he wanted; he felt that the creative urge is a positive affirmation in spite of the personal tragedies one has to experience; that the difficulty that people had in accepting change could be brought down microscopically to his own life as a musician; and that through the oral tradition, African-American people could have a lucid picture of their ancestry, and without music the many physical and psychological punishments that African-American people had to go through would be beyond enduring.

Between the middle of 1961 and 1963 I was involved in a record shop partnership with my mother, my brother, and a friend. It was called Musing Record and Card Shop and it was located in Pittsburgh, about three blocks from the Grill. We especially attempted to provide as many current jazz records as possible. It was at this time that I realized just how late some records were released, and especially how difficult most jazz performers' records were to obtain.

Since one of the ways of familiarizing oneself with the personnel of specific bands was to go to see them live, I spent almost every weekend for that two-year period going to the Grill and listening to people play. I think during those two years I must have seen Trane about five or six times. Each time—with the exception of the time I saw him with Dolphy where Reggie Workman was the bassist—he had Garrison, Tyner, and Jones.

On two separate occasions he was kind enough to stop into the shop and talk to some of the local musicians who came through town.

I remember that the first time he stopped in he asked me if I had any African music in the store. I don't believe in the whole two years that we owned the store that we ever got a call for African music. He then asked me if I had heard any music by a friend of his, Michael Olatunji. I told him that I'd heard the name but that I really was not that familiar with his music. He talked a long time about African music and especially about that great Nigerian drummer. Not too long after that the pieces from the recording date of mid-1962 were released by Impulse and there was "Tunji"; I really felt great being the first person to know that that particular piece was dedicated to Trane's friend.

The next time he came in was around the time that the free-jazz album by Ornette Coleman was released by Atlantic Records. We had just arrived at the store when in walked Trane. I remember it so distinctly because it was on a day when the people used to come down and get their food from the surplus food station at an elementary school across the street from our record shop. The line that day must have been almost two blocks long—people queuing up to get whatever food they could. Trane asked me what was happening, and I told him that this was always the situation twice a month. He remarked about the dehumanization and that people must really feel humiliated to be in that situation. He then saw the Ornette Coleman album and put it on the record player that we had in the store. He never really said anything about it; and after a little chit-chat he left. Playing free music, or playing music without either harmonic restrictions or tempo restrictions, was not new with this album. Back in the middle fifties Charlie Mingus was experimenting with free parts in his forms. I remember one piece called "Pithecanthropus Erectus," which was recorded with Jackie McLean on alto and J. R. Monterose on tenor saxophone, where there is a short, free part. As far back as Dizzy Gillespie and Charlie Parker at their concert recorded at Massey Hall in Toronto, there is a short, free part. However, this record using two quartets—both playing free—was really startling at that time.

More than anything else, though, Coltrane was concerned with the tremendous divisiveness present in the United States and how that divisiveness was not only manifested in the overt racism of white people but in the factionalism of the civil rights movement. Cecil Taylor's assessment that Coltrane had a real feeling for the hysteria of the times was correct. It was he, more than anyone I knew, who tried to show through his music the existence of real love.

15

[T]he Hindu "Philosophy of Music" recognized correspondences between musical sounds and colors: the planets, gods, seasons, emotions, etc. Each day was divided into three periods: (1) the day, ruled by the Sun; (2) the night, ruled by the moon; and (3) twilight, ruled by Fire. Each period had its appropriate music . . . the proper use [of which] brought man into direct contact with the gods, and produced phenomena. . . .

The ancient Chinese differed from the ancient Hindu in his approach to life, for whereas the Hindu turned his back on the mundane world and sought "union with the Absolute," the Chinese . . . sought to establish order and harmony right here on earth. . . . [T]he Chinese "Philosophy of Music" followed practically the same pattern as that of the Hindu, for it rested firmly on the basis that music represented and produced harmony between heaven and earth, between man and spirits.

"The physical laws of sound represent the social laws of hierarchy and union; they symbolize, prepare, and support good Government." . . .

[T]he Chinese, the Hindus, and the Greeks, saw in music "a perceptible representation of the relations by which the different elements of manifestation are connected . . . a translation of the moral forces which are also a part of the Universe, (which) comes from it, but regulates it in turn, (and) acts on the Universe, Heaven and Earth, and on all things contained therein." The Chinese musical system contained five fundamental plus two subsidiary notes, a seven-note scale which was known as "the seven beginnings," and corresponded to Heaven, Man, Earth, Spring, Summer, Autumn, Winter. But the five-note Chinese scale was the basic scale, the Pentatonic Scale, consisting of, roughly, doh:ray:me: soh:lah:. This five-note scale was in fact made up of a "center-note" (doh) and four other notes (ray:me:soh:lah:), which corresponded to the four directions of space, the four perceptible elements, the four seasons, etc. Furthermore, the center-note represented the Prince, corresponded to the center of the earth, and had yellow for its color. Similarly, the second note (ray) corresponded to the ministers of state, to metal and autumn, and the color white. The third note (me), to the people, to wood and spring, and the color green. The fourth note (soh) to public works, to water and winter, and the color red. And the fifth note (lah) to the products, to fire and summer, and the color black. . . . To alter the pitch of any note in any way was to "disturb" that note. Like the Hindu, the Chinese held that this had far-reaching effects extending beyond the merely physical. For instance, "disturb" the center-note, and the Prince becomes arrogant; disturb the second note and officials are corrupted; disturb the third note—there is anxiety, and the people are unhappy; disturb the fifth note, and there is danger, resources are lacking; disturb all the five notes—there is chaos, and the kingdom may be destroyed in less than a day.[1]

—Fela Sowande

John Coltrane — 1965, Newport Jazz Festival.

On New Year's Eve 1963, Trane played a concert at Philharmonic Hall with the quartet plus Eric Dolphy. He was still playing his usual repertoire of "My Favorite Things" and "Impressions," but also adding his new piece from 1963, "Alabama." Soon after, Dolphy left for Europe, this time to stay until his tragic death; and for this whole upcoming year, Trane mostly worked with the quartet.

They were one solid unit, led by Trane, directed by Elvin Jones, droned by Jimmy Garrison, and studied by McCoy Tyner. McCoy and Trane couldn't have been closer to the ideal of master teacher and student. Their characters and their personalities were extremely close. Both were very humble—in their introverted way. However, they always were accessible if approached and more than willing to talk about their art. Tyner loved Trane's music and was mesmerized by Trane's playing. The fact that Tyner was Islamic brought a great discipline to his life; and he brought this discipline to the piano.

I didn't take to Tyner's playing right away: but I have realized now after listening over and over again to the music that these four men made what an integral and crucial part he was and how his strict, disciplined life brought a meter and a sense of space to the music that was the embodiment of the quartet as a unit. He is and was a great accompanist, of course—having perhaps the strongest left hand of anyone I've known—and his music today has brought into it more of the world view concepts that Trane left than any of the other members.

Jones and Garrison were really two peas in a pod, two very excessive people who often caused Trane concern. However, there was never any fooling around on the bandstand, although many is the time I saw these two men bouncing through the Grill door, laughing and giggling as if they had been up to some devilment, chewing on some spareribs that they had just bought from the Silver Pig, a greasy-spoon joint across the street from the Grill. Once they got on the stand, though, it was business. But there was something else going on in the band and a story once told me by a friend gives a vivid idea of what this something else was: It seems that Trane was playing in Paris, and during their stay in one of the night clubs, Garrison and Jones had been drinking quite heavily. Between sets they strolled out into the street and, looking for mischief, broke a couple of plate glass windows. When they returned to the café they were laughing and giggling and Trane was standing at the door with tears in his eyes. I'm told that on the next set they played some of the most energized music ever heard.

Trane and Jones, of course, were equal partners in crime. They were like Narcissus and Goldmund in the story by Herman Hesse: a positive and a negative pole which sparked a fire every time they got on the bandstand. During the years that Jones was in the band, he and Trane produced a music that may well be listened to even a hundred years from now.

That was the quartet, and during 1964 Trane seemed more and more eager to allow each member to express himself musically. The dates which brought forth these greater contributions from each member of the quartet were April 27 and June 1, 1964, when "Crescent," "Lonnie's Lament," "Wise One," "The Drum Thing," and "Bessie's Blues" (the old piece from 1961) were recorded.

In the second half of 1964 great tragedy came into Trane's life with the death of Eric Dolphy. Trane's recording output is an emotional commentary. There were only three dates and none between the time Dolphy died and the time Trane made A Love Supreme. So close was their relationship that Dolphy's mother gave Trane Eric's bass clarinet and flute because she claims that she had nightmares about Eric's playing the instruments. There is a beautiful analogy here: in one tribe on the western coast of Africa, when the master drummer dies he is placed in his chair and, through a ceremony known only to that drumming association, his drum is passed from his dead body to his apprentice. In a similar way, Trane received the instruments of the individual who was perhaps his closest friend.

Trane's spiritual awareness reached its highest point with the recording of A Love Supreme and stayed at that level until his death. In this exalted state he produced one of his most dynamic and far-reaching works. It was totally affirmative music. If one looks at his compositions from this moment until the end of his life, one is struck by the ever-present meaning of what he is trying to say. Pieces such as "Meditations," "The Father and the Son and the Holy Ghost," "Selflessness," "Manifestation," "Evolution," and "Cosmos" all point towards a greater awareness of both the inner and the outer workings of music.

> You know, I want to be a force for real good. In other words, I know that there are bad forces, forces put here that bring suffering to others and misery to the world, but I want to be the force which is truly for good.[2]

In an interview that Alice Coltrane gave after Trane's death, she mentions that he once remarked to her that he was looking for a universal sound, and in thinking about this I was struck by a diagram of Fela Sowande's (see Diagram C). This diagram shows two specific things. First, it illustrates how art is connected up with will, content, form, idea, and imagination, and how this is synthesized through the

Diagram C

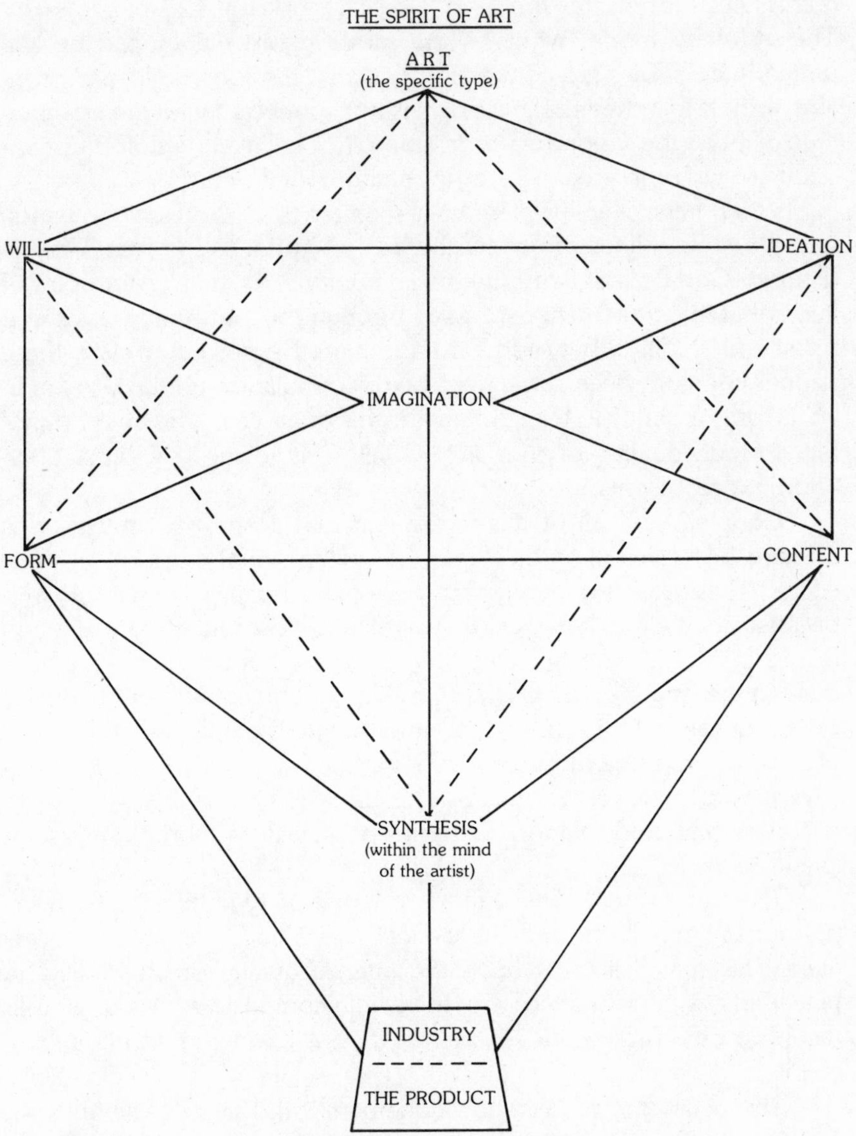

FORM = Architecture, Form, Thought, Signs, Reason, Technique, Objectivity, etc.

CONTENT = Color, Poetry, Intuition, Symbols, Feeling, an Affect, Subjectivity, etc.

FORM = Analysis = Scientific Causality   SYNTHESIS = Mystic Marriage, Virgin Birth

CONTENT = Synthesis = Principle of Synchronicity   ART is hierarchical

INDUSTRY = Work, _not_ as labor, but as _time-occupation_

(The above as association of ideas only)

artist's mind, and with industry out comes the material existence of art (the product). This corresponds to the outside perimeter of the diagram, which represents the psychological mode of artistic expression. The visionary mode, which is the mode expressed by the broken dotted lines, shows the connection between art, idea, will, form, content, and the synthesis of these, but is not connected with the imagination. That is, the visionary expression of art is linked with the unconscious or with the archetype of the thing itself.

When I first saw this diagram, I mentioned to Professor Sowande that the broken lines represent the same symbol as the fourth ray in Godfrey Godson's *Seven Human Temperaments*. The main point of this is that the great artist expressed through the fourth ray serves as a priest and mediator between God and man. Because, however, these temperament rays can sometimes be out of balance, a fourth-ray individual only ascends to the spiritual heights of his creativity by renouncing his individuality for the Divine Will. This to me is what *A Love Supreme* represents.

Coupled with all of this is the fact that Trane as a musician is perhaps best typified by the "griot" or professional musician of West Africa. They both are living archives of the people's traditions; and because they both have great insight and wisdom, they are often feared by the people because they have so many secrets. It also is quite interesting that the griot, by and large, emanates from the lower classes or castes of his tribe group and that he is employed at all levels of society—from the musicians who operate with the chiefs to the ones who play on the village streets. The transference of this concept to American jazz, and to John Coltrane specifically, is more than just an idle thought.

The music on *A Love Supreme* is full of symbolism. The ever-present triplet is there and the theme (Example 53) is always reiterated. This music doesn't have the intense quality of the music he played in live performances, but the whole composition was obviously meant to be a prayer and, in many ways, is a long, tempo-changing chant.

The beginning of "Acknowledgement" and all of "Psalm" is in free tempo. Trane called "Psalm" a narrative, a record, which is the

Example 53

essence of all of *A Love Supreme.* "Acknowledgement" uses the theme (Example 53) of four notes, going up a minor third and back, then up a fourth with the values of an eighth, a quarter, and two eighths, or a complex variation of the pattern of four. Each of these pieces has its own center and this one is around varied combinations of four.

"Resolution" is the freest of the pieces in tonality, but has a very steady tempo. I'm speaking now of Trane's solo, because the piece itself moves through a steady structure, heard in two four-bar phrases. Within this structure Trane plays whatever lines he wants, mostly in phrases or combinations of two and three. "Pursuance" has a loose structure of two groups of three, which are sometimes played separately and sometimes combined. This piece is heard in threes more than the others, although a strong triplet is present in "Resolution." More important is the "central idea" or the "unity of mood" in the works.

The artistry of "Impressions," "Chasin' the Trane," "Alabama," and *A Love Supreme* lies in their central moods. Each has its own flashing scheme of colors. Trane's voice is decidedly different in all of them—wide open on "Chasin' the Trane," skillful on "Impressions," halting on "Alabama," reverent on *A Love Supreme.* With superior symmetry, moving more and more into longer rhythmic lines, his solos continued to increase in length. His sound was changing, more mature, searching, and driving towards infinity. It was a more Eastern voice. In *A Love Supreme* one can hear a slight but constant vibrato.

Trane's lines began to contain more five-note scales. ("Two Bass Hit," from 1958, was in D♭, moving in the black keys. The blues always seem to be more authentically articulated low in the tone.) Trane always had a strong feeling for minor keys. He used more minor thirds moving to fourths, coming from his "Giant Steps" and "Countdown" period. The longer rhythmic lines, especially as they became more metric within the tempo, called for the knowledge of smaller scales. Moving off tonalities gave him greater room to work with rhythms.

On *A Love Supreme,* the piece "Acknowledgement" has a four-note rhythmic line; "Psalms," a speechlike piece starts out around c minor in free time; "Pursuance" outlines a pentatonic scale beginning at c', moving to e♭', to f', to a♭', to B♭, all ascending; "Resolution" moves through changes, all of the pieces through tempos. Dynamically, the music moves very well and with great unity within the band. The communication between Trane and Elvin Jones was in a unique class. When the album was released it was an instant hit and sold so many copies that it won a gold record. Ironically, Trane was never told about this unique achievement in jazz until he happened to walk into Bob Thiele's office and saw the plaque hanging from the wall. Such was the nature of the business. Trane became acclaimed by the critics and the public alike. His band was in demand everywhere, and he had made Impulse Records famous. All the pieces he played on this particular date were on tenor saxophone, which he favored more and more as he moved into his last two years. It has been said quite often that before he made this particular album Trane was spoken to by God, and it is not hard to believe that this is true. The beauty of the words on the cover of the album speak for his ability to give up his energies to a positive spirit. However, when he mentioned his experience to his mother she became extremely sad, because she believed strongly that when a person spoke with God he was nearing the end of his life.

16

John . . . straddles the old and the new like a colossus. Since Bird (and I would even include Ornette Coleman), Coltrane is the most important saxophonist in jazz. One of the many things he accomplished was the breakthrough into the concept that a jazz musician need not—could not—be limited to a solo lasting a few minutes. Coltrane demonstrated that a man could play for a much longer time and that, in fact, the imperatives of his conception often made it necessary for him to improvise at great length. I don't mean he proved that a thirty- or forty-minute solo is necessarily better than a three-minute one. He did prove, however, that it was possible to create thirty or forty minutes of music, and in the process, he also showed the rest of us we had to have the stamina—in terms of imagination and physical preparedness—to sustain these long flights.

When you listen to John . . . he's talking about Negro life from early New Orleans to right now. You see, he has a lot to express. Another thing he did was to underline the diversity of textures that were still possible on the horn. He's done an enormous amount to sensitize listeners to the scope of sound that is possible on the tenor and then on the soprano. There is no question that John Coltrane is a giant in this music.[1]

—Archie Shepp

John Coltrane — 1966, Newport Jazz Festival. A gift for concentration.

Trane was like a scientist in his ability to scrutinize everything that was going on in his life; it was one of his virtues—a constant, ongoing dissecting, looking closely and minutely into all those aspects of one's objective. It is obvious that on the live recording at the Village Gate, March 28, 1965, for the benefit of The Black Arts Repertory Theatre/School, the quartet was going to become freer in tempo. Trane had more than a passing interest in the music coming from the younger musicians, especially Archie Shepp, Pharaoh Sanders, and Albert Ayler.

Kofsky: Have you listened to many of the other younger saxophonists besides Pharaoh?

Coltrane: Yes, Albert Ayler first. I've listened very closely to him. He's something else.

Kofsky: Could you see any relationship between what you were doing and what he was doing? In other words, do you think he has developed out of some of your ideas?

Coltrane: Not necessarily; I think what he's doing, it seems to be moving music into even higher frequencies. Maybe where I left off, maybe where he started, or something.

Kofsky: Well, in a sense, that's what I meant.

Coltrane: Yes. Not to say that he would copy bits and that, but just that he filled an area that it seems I hadn't gotten to.[2]

Trane was personally responsible for getting many young musicians contracts with Impulse. It was through his direct help that Archie Shepp was able to get his first album recorded in 1964. I remember Shepp telling me that they recorded the pieces for the album late at night; and he called Trane who got out of bed and came to the studio because Shepp wanted to take a photograph with Trane for the cover of the album. Trane was always concerned about the younger musician and his struggle to maintain himself in music.

Ayler played at that same benefit, and it was obvious that he was playing some very different sounds. He worked in very small areas and sometimes he spurted out lines like a machine gun. But he could also be extremely lyrical, putting the same hypnotic effect on his audience as Trane. Trane quickly recognized that, and his mind immediately filtered and dealt with all those different sounds.

Throughout the sixties Coltrane had been in touch with Ornette Coleman. It was Trane who first explained to Archie Shepp why he (Shepp) should pay close attention to what Coleman was doing. Trane had been profoundly interested in the band of Sun Ra—not only because Gilmore was in the band, which was reason enough, but also because so many younger musicians were apprenticing in it. In the fifties, Sun Ra was working on more open forms and free structures, thus attracting the younger, more revolutionary musicians. Its alumni include trumpeter Clifford Thornton, trombonist Julien Priester, alto saxophonists Marion Brown and James Spaulding, percussionists Ed Blackwell, Clifford Jarvis, Roger Blank, bassist Richard Evans, and perhaps one of the most promising tenor saxophonists around, Sanders. Besides Gilmore, its mainstays were alto saxophonist Marshall Allen, bassist Ronnie Boykins, baritone saxophonist Pat Patrick, all "dangerous" in their own right. Thornton related that the discipline in that band was to "unlearn" and not play anything familiar. It was another one of the mighty reservoirs out of which Trane dipped.

Sun Ra has a way of looking into the eyes of a person and seemingly looking into his very soul. His band is an institution where people's inner awarenesses are tapped through discipline and dedication to *his* music. The music itself is always changing, always attempting to sound different. Patrick, Gilmore, and Allen have been in the band for almost twenty years and provide the traditional foundation for change. The band practices together very often, especially when a performance is at hand.

I remember a couple years ago seeing Sun Ra. He was not only with his band, but also with his company of dancers at the University of Massachusetts. The music went on for about three and a half hours. It was truly an artistic spectacular to which all of the senses responded. But the highlight of the evening was when John Gilmore played his solo; and Clifford Thornton leaned over to me and asked me if I had ever heard anything like that before. I must admit I hadn't.

It seems unbelievable when I recall that Tyner in our conversations could only remember three times during his entire tenure in the band that they rehearsed. It was a very spontaneous quartet.

Trane only played one piece at the March 28 benefit, "Nature Boy." The piece was written in the forties by Eden Ahbez and made famous by singer Nat King Cole. Its text describes a wise boy who wandered over land and sea in search of the truth and finds out that the greatest thing is to love and be loved in return. Trane begins the piece right at *that* very point in the song. The accompaniment seems very timid at first, and Garrison keeps wanting to fit in some tempo all the way through. But Tyner and Jones relate very much to Trane's new energy level. Trane is very searching in his solo, and his sound has more vibrato and is even more Eastern than on *A Love Supreme.* There is a greater effort on his part to play partial harmonics, which give the tenor a more human sound, coupled with the octave jumping.

166

He draws a line low in the tenor and then answers it high in the harmonic. By the time they get to the end, his solo is so free that he signals the end to the trio by recalling parts of the melodic line of the piece. This was a method that I saw him use on numerous occasions. In fact, he used this method to bring the band back home more often than he used any other. He uses the middle of the horn for circular patterns, ever reaching for the high notes and burrowing for the low ones. Albert Ayler's comment about the evolving nature of the music that night was: "It's not about notes anymore. It's about feelings!"[3]

Trane's playing here was a far cry from A Love Supreme, and it is apparent that his research had taken him into another place—working more in small areas and developing and spinning lines off those small phrases. Miles Davis's observation about Trane's working in small areas and rhythmically expanding the potential of that content by changing accents still held true.

Trane had that stamina of imagination and physical preparedness to make his band an open one, and younger musicians like Shepp took every opportunity sit in with it. Trane was also a fountainhead of ideas, so it was most gratifying when he would unexpectedly turn up to play. Shepp recalls seeing him once at a concert in Copenhagen in 1962 where he played absolutely solo. Shepp had known it could be done on the saxophone, but until that time had never seen it.

In spite of the success of A Love Supreme, it was quite apparent by the early part of 1965 that Trane was going to heed the call for as much freedom as possible in his band. A friend of mine once mentioned that in this sense he may not have seen the consequences. His view was that perhaps Trane was like a river that had overflowed its banks and flooded the area destructively. However, I hope to demonstrate that what he was doing was bringing jazz around to its most natural state—totally improvised playing. This call for "freedom" resulted in "Ascension," his first larger band recording since "Africa" in 1961. "Ascension" was one of the most pioneering projects of Coltrane's life, bringing together some of the better younger players in a session that had the minimum of literate material to work from and which moved, not at any certain bar, but when Trane held up a certain number. This technique of using specific numbers is used by Sun Ra; and Sam Rivers has used it quite often in his big-band arrangements. The band included Freddie Hubbard and Dewey Johnson on trumpet, Trane, Pharaoh Sanders, and Archie Shepp on tenor saxophone, Marion Brown and John Tchicai on alto saxophone, Jimmy Garrison and Art Davis on double bass, McCoy Tyner on piano, and Elvin Jones on percussion. The piece is one long sustained improvisation, alternating group improvisations with individual solos. It was one of the more daring undertakings of an *established* musician thus far in the history of jazz. This was true because, by the time of *A Love Supreme,* Trane had accumulated a loyal following that was truly dedicated to his music; but to now identify himself with the players whom many people resented was putting himself in for a lot of headache. It also marked a direction to which Trane was committing himself, and from which he never backed away—combining musical spirits in an improvised, nonstructured forum. There were two takes of "Ascension," each a little over thirty-five minutes long. They were both issued under the same title and cover, the only distinguishing feature being the edition number etched on the record itself.

Listening to "Ascension" in light of *A Love Supreme* might predispose one to feel that Trane was returning to chaos after order; but it should be remembered that this was an experiment, and that his achievements during the rest of the year would bear out his commitment to a spontaneous music.

All of the musicians were directly or indirectly chosen by Trane. When he called to invite Shepp, Marion Brown was at Shepp's house. When Trane told Shepp he was going to use double instruments and that he had already selected John Tchicai to be one of the alto saxophonists, Shepp mentioned that Marion was there and asked if Trane would like to speak to him. Trane spoke to Marion, told him about the direction of the music, including its improvisatory nature, and Marion agreed to make it. For only the second time in his life, here was the master musician organizing a large band for recording. To Trane, this meant moving from a very safe position as an in-demand artist, to an identification with the younger, more liberated African-American musicians. It was never a question in his mind. He had thought it out, worked it out, and executed it.

The recording I have—marked Edition II—starts out slowly but builds to a peak that is sustained throughout. Trane calls the first line which begins at D♭, then to B♭, back to D♭, up to E♭, which is played twice, then back to D♭. This is repeated, but the second time the E♭ moves up to B♭. The other members of the band enter playing layers of the line and then everyone plays free. There seems to be two tonal changes when Trane plays the above line in a different key. Instead of making a move at a certain bar (there was no set tempo) Trane would signal the changes through a number system. The ensemble's playing was followed by each soloist, and this juxtaposition allowed the soloist to emerge bracing on a lot of energy. All of the players perform by reaching down into the depths of their skills and imagination, with Trane, Shepp, and Sanders sounding as if their lives were at stake. The music has its soft spots. The improvisations are not equal; and it seems that all spirits weren't as in tune or capable as Trane, Shepp, and Sanders. The bassists seem to be undirected sometimes, but for the most part the idea was valid.

In addition to Sun Ra, Trane also listened closely to Cecil Taylor, noting the freedom that was present in his band. This was true whether Shepp, Jimmy Lyons, or Sam Rivers was playing saxophone, and especially true when Sonny Murray was on percussion. Cecil and McCoy Tyner were very close, and Taylor always liked the sounds and placement of Tyner's chords. So Trane had lots of other material to draw from, resulting not only in "Ascension" but also in the following pieces: "Om," using two basses with Sanders and flutist Joe Brazil; "Kulu Sé Mama," using two basses, three percussionists (for the first time), voice, and Sanders; and Meditations, using two percussionists and Sanders. Meditations closed out 1965, and marked the last time Tyner and Jones were to record with Trane.

The last recording sessions of the quartet were May 26, June 10, and August 26, 1965, although the albums themselves weren't released until 1971, fully four years after Trane's death. It was unquestionably the most open, fresh music that the quartet had done, and it showed how Trane's spirit had convinced the other members of the rewards of playing completely spontaneously. This is the direction that Trane was ultimately going in—turning the music full circle and playing by using the language of music itself instead of some predetermined method.

The names of the last compositions of the quartet are "Sun Ship," "Dearly Beloved," "Attaining," and "Ascent." These pieces should be coupled with "Transition," "Suite," and "Dear Lord." All these pieces were recorded around the time of "Ascension." They are the most open and yet the most melodic-rhythmic structures that the quartet had ever recorded in a studio. They are documents of their spiritual unity and of the trio's confidence in the directions of Coltrane. Both Tyner and Garrison have told me that most of the time they addressed Trane as "chief." And a chief is what Coltrane was—a "head man."

Each piece is developed around small rhythmic figures from which each member operates independently, creating sounds which will orally tell the nature of this band and its very intimate communica-

169

tions. Through that communication, their love for music, and for one another, developed a unity in which every effort was combined towards playing the very best music possible. The pieces "Vigil" and "Welcome," which were recorded on the same day as "Ascension," should also be included in this collection because of their place in Trane's overall music.

"Vigil" is another duo piece which Trane plays with Elvin Jones. Like the original style of "Countdown," the piece begins with the percussionist playing a short solo, establishing a tempo. However, instead of trying to play in that tempo or double time that tempo Trane enters in his now very distinguishable style of playing phrases and rhythmic figures within the tempo. Where "Countdown" was two minutes and twenty-one seconds long, "Vigil" is nine minutes and thirty-six seconds long. And even at the end, Trane seems as if he can go on for hours. He's very strong in this piece—operating throughout the horn—but mainly staying and playing, as he does throughout all of these pieces, with the fundamentals of the horn; although occasionally he does flash harmonics here and there. The piece is actually a textbook for any student who wants to learn how to deal with the tenor saxophone, as almost all the pieces from this time are. Above all, "Vigil" is a delightful piece to hear because it still has that beautiful concept of symmetry and form that always flowed from Coltrane's music.

All these pieces are played on tenor saxophone and each has its own certain kind of identity, from "Suite" to "Welcome" and "Dear Lord" which are played in that easy, loping style that Trane liked to use. "Dearly Beloved," a piece built on a line that's going up to C♯ to B, down to A, up to C♯, and down to B, is constructed on a pentatonic scale designed with the syllables of the name of the piece. There is no tempo here and Trane seems often to be straining at the top of the horn, busting out the top of it.

"Transition" is in tempo and is built on one of Trane's more beautiful lines. Here in this piece he does a lot of flashing the harmonics, but it is still a piece played at the fundamentals.

"Sun Ship" is the most active piece. It is built strictly on a rhythmic figure; and it is here that Trane uses those small rhythmic figures, the triplets, which turn out and move up and down from the middle register. "Sun Ship" has the kind of melodic line in which Trane could examine the total potential—where it starts at its intervals, then sequences all throughout the horn, then proceeds to infinite rhythmic variations.

The center of Trane's world was music, and his dedication was always apparent in the quartet. He was possessed by the *idea* of music and had a unique way of working with men. He provided a leadership which is best described in the first ray of Hodson's *Seven Human Temperaments*—that which renounces the individual for the Divine will. Clearly, Trane had accomplished that.

Trane was a man humble to the point of seeming shy (from the exterior), but bursting with musical ideas and visionary mechanisms which were manifested through his technical proficiency. These ideas are structured by the imagination for the purpose of communication through the will. He was a man of great concentration and could take an idea—for example a triplet figure—and play it repeatedly with incredible speed, producing sounds which seemed to spin towards a center—but there was always a wailing, a bursting at the top of the horn, towards infinity. Trane's religion was his music, and his seeking for truths within himself was revealed through his music. The intensity of this search was incredible. Many times when I saw him in the quartet, especially when he played in clubs, he would play one piece, soloing for as long as two hours, then come down from the stand and go to the men's room to practice for a few minutes. In an interview with Leonard Feather, he said, "I never even thought about whether or not they understand what I'm doing . . . the emotional reaction is all that matters—as long as there's some feeling of communication, it isn't necessary that it be understood. After all, I used to love music myself long before I could identify a g minor seventh chord."[4] Tyner once told me that in San Francisco Trane once played so long and so intensely that he burst a blood vessel in his nose and didn't even notice it until Tyner pointed it out to him. So great was his ability to concentrate that he was truly able to examine his inner visions.

17

A higher principle is involved here. Some of his (Coltrane's) latest works aren't musical compositions. I mean they weren't based entirely on music. A lot of it has to do with mathematics, some on rhythmic structure and the power of repetition, some of elementals. He always felt that sound was the first manifestation in creation before music. *I would like to play music according to ideals set forth by John and continue to let a cosmic principle, or the aspect of spirituality, be the underlying reality behind the music as he did.*[1]

—Alice Coltrane

Rashied Ali — 1966, Newport Jazz Festival.

Trane and Alice had moved to Dix Hills, Huntington, Long Island, just before the middle of 1965. They had bought a twelve-room house on three acres and it was here that Trane was to live out the rest of his life. They had a rather large garden which he worked in constantly. But there was always music; and throughout the house there were instruments which included conga drums, a sitar, a piano, the flute and bass clarinet given to him by Mrs. Dolphy, and an assortment of others.

Trane was a rural person; he grew up in the rural South in a quiet, small-town Southern atmosphere. It seemed only natural now that he would want some seclusion. He was making close to $200,000 a year and from 1959 he had his own publishing company, Jowcol, which he used to clear all his own music.

The quartet itself was becoming more of a revolving door band than it had ever been. Everywhere that Trane played people seemed to want to sit in with the band, at least in the larger cities, but I can recall from when I still lived in Pittsburgh that even on Saturday afternoons, when they had matinee open sessions, very few local musicians would get up there and play with John.

He played this year at the Newport Jazz Festival. Curiously enough, he played one short piece, "One Down, One Up," while his good friend and close musical associate Archie Shepp played several numbers with Archie's own quartet. Much to the chagrin of everybody, Shepp and Trane showed up together playing at the newly devised Down Beat Festival in Chicago. But Pharaoh Sanders was the individual who would turn out to be the mainstay horn in the band.

There were a lot of crazy notions about why Trane brought Sanders into the band, but Trane himself made the reasons very plain in his interview with Kofsky:

> *Kofsky:* How do you feel about having another horn in the group, another saxophone? Do you feel that it in any way competes with you or that it enhances what you're doing?
> *Coltrane:* Well, it helps me. It helps me stay alive sometimes, because physically, man, the pace I've been leading has been so hard I've gained so much weight, that sometimes it's been a little hard physically. I feel that I like to have somebody there in case I can't get that strength. I like to have that strength in that band, somewhere. And Pharaoh is very strong in spirit and will, see, and these are the things that I like to have up there.[2]

He further commented about Pharaoh: "What I like about him . . . is the strength of his playing, the conviction with which he plays. He has will and spirit, and those there are the qualities I like most in a man."[3]

The whole question of competition in this situation is out of place. If one wants to look far back into Trane's development and examine the players that he played with, one will discern that it was never a question of competing with anybody. It wasn't a question of competition when he played his historic date with Sonny Rollins; and it certainly wasn't that when he played with the other tenor saxophonists early in his career (even though some like Hank Mobley indirectly made Trane compromise his potential at one time). John Coltrane loved to play music too much for it ever to be a matter of rivalry.

Sanders was fantastic in Trane's band. He had a marvelous technique coupled with a whole host of different sounds. He had developed a flitter technique with his tongue which allowed him to play tones in a rapid trill. He had acquired it while he was in the Sun Ra orchestra, when Sun Ra gave him a mute to play in his instrument. Although Trane first met Sanders in San Francisco in 1961, when he was looking for a mouthpiece replacement, Sanders was originally from Little Rock, Arkansas; he might also have seen the flittering technique down south where it is employed by the blues musicians and in the rural blues touring bands. Sanders first came to New York in the beginning of 1965. I remember Bill Barron telling me that Sanders left his instruments at Barron's while he looked for a permanent place to stay. Barron recollects even then what a pleasant individual Sanders was. Sanders could play extremely high in the tenor, as A. B. Spellman pointed out:

> He went on for minute after minute in a register that I didn't know the tenor had. . . . Those special effects that most tenor men use only in moments of high orgiastic excitement are the basic premises of his presentation. His use of overtones, including a cultivated squeak that parallels his line, is constantly startling. He plays way above the upper register; long slurred lines and squeaky monosyllabic staccatos. . . .[4]

He and Trane locked spirits immediately. He supplied Trane with lines that spurred him on, just as Dolphy had in the first half of the sixties. When Sanders came into the band, voices themselves were used to make sounds. All different shapes came forth—birds, human cries, the voices of the sorrows and the joys of African-American people. The benefits of Sanders's presence were immense, and he and John never collided. They always seemed to be traveling along in the same spiritual direction, using different sounds and soaring on one another's energy.

At the end of September and for the first two weeks of October, the music that Trane came out with points to the master's wisdom. In addition to Sanders, Donald Garrett playing bass clarinet joined Tyner, Garrison, Jones, and Trane. Garrett was an old-time friend of both Archie Shepp and Trane, now living on the West Coast. It seems also more than coincidental that the music of the players coming from the West Coast had been the starting point of the new sixties music. The pieces done in this West Coast collection are all fine music, and the standard done during this performance, "Out Of This World," is played in Trane's unique way of approaching a standard—expanding the distance between harmonic changes so that only the melody is used with any substance. It seems interesting now that Trane thought he had played all he could play of standard pieces in the beginning of 1962. This piece alone contradicts that premise. He begins the piece on the tenor; then after a solo by Sanders and Tyner, he returns and plays the soprano saxophone. His voice is deep in the instrument and perhaps more Eastern than ever before. At times he sounds like a shepherd playing to his flock while they graze, especially when he executes groups of sixteenth notes in fours. The piece was recorded live at the Penthouse in Seattle, Washington. The entire piece takes over twenty-four minutes. This is including all the solos. Trane begins the line on tenor saxophone; and to show the listener almost immediately how he has changed the form of the piece, he plays with the very beginning line of the melody for almost two and a half minutes before he executes the bridge. The piece is in a slow but very even tempo, and Trane is followed by Pharaoh who executes a very beautiful solo on tenor. Now instead of Trane breaking and the other saxophones entering, Sanders enters while Trane is playing his solo; so for a short period both of them are playing together—a decided departure from Trane's pre-1965 era. After Sanders solos, Tyner enters with one of his masterful improvisations. Of course, in any harmonically changing style—especially if the piece is played in this kind of slow but dramatic tempo—Tyner is a wizard. This piece is decidedly in a strong, accented first beat, four beat structure with Tyner stressing that first beat with overwhelming emphasis. Just before Trane reenters, this time on soprano, Tyner gives his very dramatic four-beat chord introduction, and Trane enters playing soprano like a sage—his voice mellow and human-sounding, or like the sound coming from a shenai. Suddenly, Trane moves into a long section in which he weaves in and out of intricate rhythmic patterns and he is joined by Sanders and they play another five or six minutes together, with the trio accompanying. Trane closes out this standard on the tenor saxophone, bellowing the hardest he can on its lowest notes—A♭ and B♭—completely revolutionizing the *form* of the standard but keeping the *content* right there.

But his work on "Cosmos" and "Evolution," in concert with Sanders and including Garrett on "Evolution," was music of such great introspection that I believe it is where Trane became his most visionary. The visionary depths revealed in the music here were matched only by *Om, Meditations* and his March 1966 concert at Philharmonic Hall and his July 1966 tour in Japan. The three horn players conducted a genuine assault on the possibilities of their instruments, especially concerning pitch. In "Cosmos" the line is built on the pentatonic scale, which quickly gets whirled and loses its shape as the concentration on it brings out all the possibilities within the line itself. This rhythmic fixation on the line leads to the development of other lines which sound like animals, cries of the people, and a host of other images. These images were first heard in 1961 but they are now fully developed and functioning. Images and symbols emerge throughout the music as it ranges from very lyrical triplets descending and ascending in a slight curve, to the very aggressive single rhythmic phrase, which repeats itself metrically. The last turns into moving partials. Both Trane and Sanders were revolutionizing not only the instruments and their stated capacities, but also the whole question of what form should bring to life; and to them it was life itself. Their lines link up like the ancient bards calling the spirits. They both grab rhythmic lines and hold onto them with great tenacity, constantly interchanging roles of accompanist and soloist; and near the end their glissando lines sound like sirens. The rhythm really stays on the case. This music is unquestionably at the ritual level in terms of its function.

"Evolution" begins with just the three horns (two tenors and the bass clarinet) and the bass. The sounds coming from the horns are varied. At one moment they sound like the reed section in Ellington's band with Johnny Hodges, and at another they sound like different birds. Then Garrison, who had been accompanying beautifully, always feeling the pulse of the music and moving down the bass, plays a short solo. His playing low on the bass provided a foundation which brought out the high sounds of the horns. The horns reenter and Garrett moves out, playing a solo very high in the bass clarinet, predominated by many moving partials, sounding like chalk moving across a double bass string. Next, Trane enters playing many sliding sounds in the high harmonics, giving the impression of the bow of a bass moving from the wood onto the strings. Then the voices are used. Outrageous music all the way through.

The piece recorded the next day, October 1, 1965, is among the finest—if not *the* finest—playing that Trane did in his career. The piece was called "Om"—Om, the ultimate which makes all things pure, the Deity—and it seems time now to further explain Coltrane's unique fluency with the instrument.

In the accompanying illustration you see a staff with two clefs, the treble and the bass. The first note, that is, the note on the far left-hand side, is C and this note is known as the fundamental. In this note itself

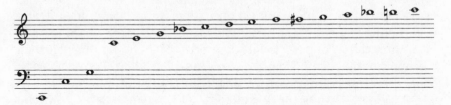

there are constructed all of its overtones or harmonics. For example, the note closest to the far left-hand note C is also C which is the first overtone. Then comes G, the second overtone, or the fifth; then comes C; then the third E; then the third G; then the minor third B♭, followed by a major second C. Then comes the D major second, E major second, F minor second, F♯ minor second, G minor second. A major second, B♭ minor second, B minor second, and C, etc. What this means is that in that fundamental note there are all of these other notes and when one begins to play the overtones or harmonics on a tempered instrument, he begins to play in the *natural scale.* John Coltrane had fluency of the harmonics in all of the stops which allowed him not only an expanded register in the horn but also gave him the ability to create screams by overblowing this system creating a meshing together of the different sounds. The harmonics themselves, however, are created by very sensitive and subtle fingering of the stops. This fingering combination is especially complicated when one sees that on an instrument like the tenor or soprano saxophone the fingerings are not on the holes but are created by a combination of stops. In "Om" Trane pulls all these out, and he no longer is dealing with note patterns as much as he is with the shape of forms or thought patterns. To put this all in a nutshell, he is able to play everything and anything he can hear. With a mind like his and as fast as he could execute his ideas on the instrument, one can begin to see the depths which he could plumb. If one can't see that, one can certainly *hear* it on a piece like "Om."

"Om" is also his most representative world music piece and it is in "Om," a Hindu chanting mechanism, that Trane brings out wooden flutes, bells, a thumb piano, gongs, and cymbals—distinctively a ritual piece done with the utmost reverence. It starts with the thumb piano playing a line of B—A—G—E—D, another pentatonic scale. Then the voices enter, uttering a chant. While this chant is being intoned a wooden flute is played in the background, giving a haunting feeling to the mood. Then the three horns—Sanders and Trane on tenor and Garrett on bass clarinet—begin playing together. Triplets emerge, spinning up and down through the scale. (One should take particular notice of how these lines connect up.) Then, as he always does, Trane comes emerging out of the ensemble playing as though out of the eye of a hurricane; and it is at this point—where all the creative mechanisms that he had learned come into play—that shapes, sounds, images, and visionary points of view come out of his playing.

As complex as this music sounds, it still has tremendous symmetry to it. One line never seems to be standing purely by itself. It seems either to be going from one place to another or it's being used as the launching pad to build another line from. Even on the parts in which he seems to be screaming, he changes the tonalities by executing with his feather touch on the instrument together with emphatic embouchure control, changing the parameters of the tones. This part of his solo ends with his sounding like a whimpering puppy, with that kind of sound coming out of his horn. Then the cymbals enter and Tyner begins his solo. There was certainly no letdown or letup here. The two bassists (and when Garrett is not playing bass clarinet he plays double bass on this record) play an extremely effective duet together, combining arco with pizzicato in a beautiful searing sound. All of this is again in concert with the wooden flute, played most effectively throughout by Joe Brazil. After the double bass duet, Sanders enters and plays an unusually lyrical solo for him, which is especially effective with the staccato playing of Brazil.

There is throughout this entire piece the sense that each player knows where the others are—a sense of wide-open ears. There are also sounds which indicate the use of a Jew's harp, and a sound like the bleating of sheep whose musical source conceals itself. The piece itself lasts twenty-nine minutes and is one long improvisation. Trane's solo in the beginning lasts for eleven minutes; and he and Sanders play together for almost ten minutes at the end.

Right after these dates the band moved to Los Angeles, where Trane met Juno Lewis; and here the last two pieces of this magnificent trip evolved.

The Indian sage, Ghandi, however, is reliably reported to have said: "I do not want the windows and doors of my house to be closed. I want the cultures of all lands to blow freely about my house, but I refuse to be blown off my feet by any of them."[5]

This quote could not be more appropriate in describing "Om" and "Kulu Sé Mama." Outside of the singing voice, this is the first time that Trane uses the voice in this particular manner, that is, a close connection between song and poetry. Lewis is incredible, not only on his singing but also his percussion work. One of the percussion instruments that Lewis plays is a water drum—and it seems more than coincidental that this was the sound that Trane was trying to get in 1961 from the use of double basses. "Kulu Sé Mama" is a chant, and there is a steady pulse held clear through by Jimmy Garrison and the percussion. In fact, the piece is so hypnotic that one time I was listening to it while my little girl, Zena, was riding her hobby horse and she was suddenly put to sleep by the ever-present drone in the music. Although this music certainly has a world view attached to it, it is not as far away from Trane's primary source, Africa, as "Om" was— remembering now also that Trane at this time was not only highly involved in the philosophical works of Africans but also the music and philosophy of East Indians and Chinese. And throughout all the pieces in this late period there is a strong feeling of the pentatonic scale which ranges throughout all of these Eastern musics.

The last piece on this tour was "Selflessness." Drawing from a simple line which is again pentatonic, C—B♭ —G— F— E♭ the piece is just another example of how well Trane and his associates can work on small line material.

By November 1965, Trane was back in New York—this time with Archie Shepp and Carlos Ward in the band plus Rashied Ali. Sanders, like Dolphy before him, had played often with Trane before he became a permanent fixture. Although Shepp and Ward never were permanently in the band, they certainly played off and on with Trane. Each of these men are very strong players with individual styles; Carlos Ward, the young Panamanian, was one of the finest alto players to come on the scene for a long time. Trane closed out November with *Meditations* which included himself, Sanders, Garrison, Tyner, and the two drummers, Ali and Jones. Trane's remarks about *Meditations* are appropriate here:

There is never any end. . . . There are always new sounds to imagine; new feelings to get at. And always, there is the need to keep purifying

181

these feelings and sounds so that we can really see what we've discovered in its pure state. So that we can see more clearly what we are. In that way, we can give to those who listen the essence, the best of what we are. But to do that at each stage, we have to keep on cleaning the mirror.[6]

Meditations was a clear indication of where Coltrane was taking the music rhythmically. For the "Kulu Sé Mama" session in Los Angeles he had used two drummers as well as the poet Juno Lewis on percussion. At this time (*Meditations*) Rashied Ali was firmly in the band, and he had a new, very free approach to playing. He and Jones could play beautifully together and Trane saw this: "I feel . . . the need for more time, more rhythm all around me. And with more than one drummer, the rhythm can be more multi-directional. Someday I may add a conga drummer or even a company of drummers."[7] Nat Hentoff, in the liner notes for *Meditations,* underscores this when he mentions what he witnessed: "In a San Francisco engagement in January 1966, after this record was made, Coltrane had two drummers plus an African percussionist in his complement."[8] However, Jones and Ali were never comfortable playing together, and perhaps nothing points to the differences in these two men more than when Jones breaks into the 6/8 tempo of the "Compassion" part of *Meditations.*

This date, coming less than a year after *A Love Supreme,* really demonstrated what Coltrane had been building up to. Through "Ascension," "Evolution," and "Om" finally evolved *Meditations.* The level of energy that the two percussionists lent to the activities was absolutely rewarding. Trane was obviously going to double all of the instruments. He had worked with the two double basses, and then he brought in Sanders, playing the same instrument he was playing. The drums were just naturally next to be doubled, or expanded as far as could be expanded. By this time Trane was deep into meditation. On "Suite," which he recorded earlier in the year, he even demonstrates how many times a day he is now going through a prayer and meditation session. Learning how to concentrate better helped him bring out shapes in his music.

Meditating is not just a single-level activity. It is not just a clearing out and resting of the mind. Meditation is a penetration to dimensions beyond the third. The whole meditation process, however, has four different levels: First, there is the level of concentration where the mediator is brought to a point where there are no outside interferences. The next is the meditation level itself, that is, meditating on an object which is the receiver of this energy. This is the process by which a person can learn about a thing without using books, by a mental contact. The next level is contemplation, a level where the meditator moves into the inner meaning, cause, and law of the object in order to bring out the mysteries of its truth. The fourth level—a level which very few reach—is the level of adoration, where there is a unity of love in the knowing of the innermost and outermost parts of the object. It was at this level of Trane's meditation that he operated in terms of music; and this is what we hear on *Meditations*.

The piece itself is a suite organized in five parts. First the Trinity, "The Father and the Son and the Holy Ghost," which is introduced by Trane and Sanders with the first harmonic. Each player is playing two notes at the same time and it sounds like birds, or it gives the image of birds gathering. Then there is "Compassion," which is when the piece goes into 6/8. The third part is "Love," which is a bass solo by Jimmy Garrison. (It's interesting that on a later work of Pharaoh Sanders, he called another piece "Love," which was also a bass solo. On this piece, Cecil McBee plays the long bass solo and it appears on Sanders's album *Thempi*.) The fourth part is "Consequences," and what could best be said about this is that to every action there is a reaction. This seems like the "shadow side" of the immense creation to which Trane had already given birth. If one happened to hear only this part of the whole piece one would perceive the work with abysmal misunderstanding. Trane, as wise as he was, certainly knew the consequences of love: hate. The last episode is "Serenity." "Serenity," like "Compassion," is entered into with the use of bells in a 6/8 tempo in which Tyner solos. Tyner also solos on "Compassion." But perhaps the most outstanding qualities of this particular suite are the visions that Trane and Sanders are able to bring out, relying on the strong support of Tyner. More and more, content took precedence over form for Trane, and *Meditations* really epitomized this trend.

Nineteen sixty-five was a transitional year, or perhaps more appropriately one might call it the end of a long transitional period for Trane. He was now fully engulfed and associated with the younger musicians who were consistently reevaluating and changing the parameters of jazz. He had in this year become the most acclaimed musician of his time—winning every poll concerning his identification with the jazz audience. More and more, he was not only looking to the younger musician for resources but becoming amalgamated, transferring his own energies in complete alignment and unity with them. So, paradoxically, in the year that his popularity was most demonstrated he became firmly in alignment with the musicians who were receiving the most admonishment by the public. It only bore out the truth that the late release of his music was constantly misleading the public; when they came out to hear him play, they heard musicianship and music not for their understanding but for their experiencing.

I would certainly say that John Coltrane came to some kind of conclusion in his wisdom at this time. He was so concerned about the insurrections in Watts in 1965 that one of the first things he did was to call Eric Dolphy's mother in Los Angeles to find out if she was OK. This concern for others complemented his personality and was always found in his music. Unfortunately, he was beginning to have a weight problem in this year, and the first physical sign of his impending death began to reveal itself.

18

Traditional, or archaic man, does not recognize any activity as being profane; whether it be hunting, fishing, agriculture, games, sexuality, or what you will; even conflicts, wars, and struggles, have a ritual cause and function, in that they repeat the struggle between two divinities, or commemorate an episode in the divine and cosmic drama. But objects or acts are real, only to the extent in which such objects or acts participate in a reality that transcends them. History, for example, is real, if it repeats a history that had its origin at the beginning of time, or cosmically. A stone, for another example, is real, becomes saturated with being, possesses mana, religious or magical power, either because of its symbolic shape, a shape which existed from time immemorial in the archetypal world before the stone, or because of its origin, as for instance, "pearl" which comes from the watery realms of Neptune, or because the stone is the dwelling place of an ancestor, and so on. Reality is also conferred through what Eliade terms "the symbolism of the center"; thus every traditional society has its own symbolic "center of the world," which—in the case of Western Nigeria—is "Ife." Furthermore, in traditional society, rituals and profane gestures acquire meaning, only because they repeat acts which were originally performed at the beginning of time by the gods, or heroes, or ancestors. [1]

—Fela Sowande

John Coltrane — 1966, Newport Jazz Festival. Fela Sowande: "Imagination really means the ability to give birth to images."

In 1966 McCoy Tyner and Elvin Jones left the band. Trane needed more sound around him, and they had been the nucleus of that sound. Their departure meant another turn in his music, a turn in a path that had almost reached its end. Trane's second wife, Alice, replaced McCoy, and Rashied Ali became the "center" trap drummer, although Trane employed many different percussionists to support Ali whenever he could.

Elvin Jones had been a tower of strength in the band. His bass drum playing was extraordinary, sounding like thunder beneath the horns. Trane had been concerned about his leaving for quite some time. He had been Trane's drummer for five years; often he was cantankerous, and Trane showed the utmost patience in the way he dealt with him. They were equals; there is absolutely no doubt about that. They contributed to the band and to one another with a connection that's seldom seen. On the 1962 recording of "Miles' Mode," Jones plays rolling triplets which sound like a hundred tap-dancing Bill Robinsons in perfect synchronization. He and Ali, as demonstrated by the *Meditations* album, could have been marvelous together, but it just didn't work out. Jones had resisted moving away from the tempo, and after he had made that transformation he was faced with another drummer, so he decided to leave the band. That was essentially the difference between Trane and Jones. Trane completely gave up his ego to music in every way. He gave up his individuality wholly to music and tried to develop in all of his players a sense of submission, making music the object of their meditation.

McCoy's leaving was like John's losing his own son. Tyner had provided direction and was a pillar in the foundation of Trane's ideas. Trane always wanted a steady sound on the piano, even though many times he "strolled" with bass and drums. In the heat of an improvisation, when Trane was really dealing in the hinterland of his visions, it was Tyner's providing the chords in that visionary way he had of placing sounds that totally supported Trane; that kind of support was never recovered in the band after McCoy left. Archie Shepp made a profound point when he said that Trane's genius was in bridging the gap, "[straddling] the old and new like a colossus." All during that time his closest associate was McCoy Tyner. Trane's 1966 music demonstrates that he was truly trying to do as many things as he could possibly do in the band. Tyner had complained for quite some time about the drums and finally it became too much for him.

> There was a thing I wanted to do in music, see, and I figured I could do *two* things: I could have a band that played like the way we used to play,

and a band that was going in the direction that the old one I have now is going in—I could combine these two, with these two concepts going. And it could have been done.[2]

The music played in this new band was certainly as viable as any Coltrane had ever played before. His transitions continued until his death. At the end of 1965 he started playing the bass clarinet, the one that had been given to him by Dolphy's mother. On his next-to-last recording session, February 17, 1967, he played a flute in duo with Sanders playing piccolo. Alice created different textures in the band, and the sound being produced was more non-Western than ever. Alice made great use of the trill to underline her accompanying, and on the piece "To Be" it makes the juxtaposition of the flute and piccolo sound very Eastern. In her own solo, her left hand plays chords while her right keeps spinning lines with a light touch.

In March, 1966, Trane was invited to participate in a production at Philharmonic Hall in New York called "Titans of the Tenor." The other bands included Sonny Rollins, Zoot Sims, Coleman Hawkins, and Yusef Lateef with Bobby Brookmeyer and Clark Terry. Trane brought the last regulars in his band: Garrison, Ali, Alice, Pharaoh, plus Albert Ayler on tenor, Donald Ayler on trumpet, Carlos Ward on alto saxophone and flute, and J. C. Moses, an old friend of mine from Pittsburgh. Trane was said to have paid the Ayler brothers and Ward out of his own pocket because management wouldn't foot the bill for the expanded band. Also, it was well known that the producers did not want the Ayler brothers to play. I remember seeing this event and everybody walking out on stage and recalling bits and pieces of tunes that I knew from Trane's albums. Each of the musicians took solos, and the Ayler brothers did a duet that was going so fast that it sounded like bees in a giant beehive. I knew right then that nobody could possibly capture what had happened in this music after hearing it just once. Trane mentioned in one of his interviews that he wished he could feel what the audience felt when he was playing, but that was just one of the aspects of being a performer that was lost in the whole context of playing music. He himself must have listened to this music several times to try to find out how things fit together or didn't fit together. I recall being afraid myself of what was going on.

Trane had always been concerned with the plight of jazz musicians. He was directly responsible for Archie Shepp's getting his contract with Impulse Records. He repeatedly asked Bob Thiele, his producer at Impulse, about the possibilities of bringing more musicians into the studio. Thiele once commented that they would have signed up at least four hundred new musicians if he had accepted all the names that Trane suggested. Trane's music and its inherent flexibility and growth potential always included others. He was always ready to listen to a new player to see if he sounded different. During most of his career, he had been interested in the cycle-breathing technique of Rahsaan Roland Kirk and, at the end of his life, had outstanding control over his breathing and its use in the horn.

On May 15, 1966, Trane was recorded at the Village Vanguard, a place where he had had his first live recording earlier in the sixties. There are only two pieces that come from this session: "Naima," which Trane first recorded in 1959, and "My Favorite Things," his most acknowledged standard. The first thing that is apparent is the different length of the improvisations. When Trane first recorded "Naima" in the studio it was only a little over four minutes long. The version that I described earlier with Eric Dolphy on bass clarinet was just a little longer than that. This particular version is fourteen and a half minutes long. Trane, his voice now extremely metric, is playing throughout the instrument, especially deep in the tenor and is very lyrical on "Naima" particularly. Every note seems to have a certain specific nuance, a certain place that it has to be, a certain texture, a certain depth, a certain quality. Sanders, on the other hand, approaches the piece in a very staccato style—a style that was best described by A. B. Spellman, perhaps Trane's most accurate ongoing observer. The piece is taken at a very easy tempo. In fact, there is not a tempo but a swirl of sound that has become so evident now in Ali's playing.

Sanders gets many different colors and sounds out of his instrument. When he is working the harmonics he quite often can get the tenor to sound like a violin or a cello, especially when he glissandos throughout the tenor. He has a way of playing a tone in which he never really squarely hits the tone on its mark but takes it to that fine fringe right on the edge of the fundamental and the first overtone. He ends his solo on "Naima" sounding very much like Ben Webster with a heavy vibrato. Sanders was always very imaginative in the band—as Dolphy had been—building constructive lines constantly.

"My Favorite Things" begins with a long bass solo by Jimmy Garrison. Again, one sees the influence of Trane even in Garrison's playing, because he starts off strumming the bass like a harp or a guitar and at certain times he plays very much like a Spanish flamenco guitarist. The length of the piece when Trane first recorded it was thirteen minutes and forty-one seconds; this time it is over twenty-five minutes long—just getting every possible inch out of the piece. After Garrison's solo, Trane comes in playing the soprano as if it were a shenai, probably his best quality of sound, especially deep in the instrument. The solo is very fundamental in its quality; he rarely uses harmonics. It's amazing to realize that Trane must have played these two pieces hundreds of times. I know that every time I saw him playing—and this is especially true in the clubs—there was always a call for "My Favorite Things"; and Trane always seemed to have an affinity for the "Naima," which first developed his double tonality concept, a beautiful example of the restructuring and expansion of form.

Trane made a triumphant trip to Japan in the summer of 1966 and experimented with both the flute and his first instrument, the alto saxophone. This instrument was given to him by the Japanese, and he was having problems with its intonation. Sanders was also given an alto which he clearly had intonation problems with. The music that Trane played in Japan was magnificent. The words of Alice on the album entitled *Concert in Japan* speak highly of the treatment they were afforded there:

> The music in this album was recorded while John and I were touring the beautiful country of Japan. The impressions of this land are as vivid in my mind today as they were seven years ago.
>
> I would like the Japanese people to know that the warm receptions and offerings of flowers and gifts, given to us while we were there, will always be cherished within our hearts forevermore.
>
> We had never seen such ancient, timeless beauty as we saw crafted on your Mt. Fujiyama, valley, and seaside, as well as the profoundly beautiful work of art engraved on the faces of your people.
>
> Your cities and streets were immaculate. You also gave us the best accommodations everywhere we traveled. Thank you for taking us to see the Nagasaki and Hiroshima world memorials where John prayed for your war dead.
>
> Many thanks to Seito and all of the people and musicians who have made this recording possible. The music of this album is reminiscent of so much of the spiritual joy and peace we felt during our most memorable stay in Japan.[3]

Here the mind's effective resonance with nature is at work. The music was recorded July 22, 1966, at the Koseinenkin Hall in Tokyo and the enthusiasm of the audience was unmatched in Trane's playing career. Certainly in his lifetime Trane had met many hostile audiences: when he first went to Europe in the early sixties, the band had tomatoes and other assorted vegetables thrown at them. That, however, had completely changed by 1966. Trane certainly had the ability to energize people with the vitality of his music. However, I would say that his music is not for the uninitiated. By this time the band members—including himself, Garrison, Ali, Alice, and Sanders—were playing as one. Rashied was supplying much power and strength to the band, just as Trane's description of him indicates:

> The way he plays . . . allows the soloist maximum freedom. I can really choose just about any direction at just about any time in the confidence that it will be compatible with what he's doing. You see, he's laying down multi-directional rhythms all the time. To me, he's definitely one of the great drummers.[4]

The piece "Leo," including "Meditations" moving into it, lasts a little over forty-five minutes, with Trane playing for the last eight minutes. He does a little accompanying playing for Sanders during Sanders' solo. Trane's solo was last and Ali provides support and movement, constantly giving Trane a cycle of sound from which to emerge. Trane is now playing more statements that he repeats over and over, each time playing them a little differently. He is stripping the phrase absolutely naked, "purifying" it. This tremendous effort on the part of Trane was done with the confidence that Ali would supply his share of the power, which he more than did.

"Leo," which is introduced by the same motif that introduces "The Father and the Son and the Holy Ghost" segment of *Meditations,* is really Sanders' and Ali's theme song. Pharaoh plays an incredible solo, moving into different levels of the horn—sounding like a string instrument at places, moving tremendously fast in tempo and with tremendous strength of articulation. He also takes the audience through different intensities and mood shapes. All the time this is happening, Garrison and Ali are keeping a sound almost like a drone, low in the musical spectrum. Then Ali solos.

Rashied Ali is such a great percussionist that he is one of those players that you even like to watch practice. He has a beautiful way of using the bass drum, which he usually has two of. He uses the drums to create a ground swell of sound, so instead of moving in just a linear direction it's moving almost like a spiral. During his solo he plays the drums in a most musical fashion. All kinds of patterns come from his solo. Then at the end he uses the cymbal and then goes to the high hat. This is all combined with Sanders and his connecting up with a beautiful duet in which Sanders plays the bass clarinet. The whole thing has an Eastern sound to it. Again, Coltrane's world view is being transferred to the other members of the band.

If for no other reason, bringing Alice into the band would have been appropriate at this time, if only because of the need to promote more women players. Unquestionably, there has been tremendous male chauvinism in jazz and too often women have been treated as mere sex objects or exploited as Billy Holiday was by members of the orchestra. But there is certainly more to Alice Coltrane than just her symbolic value in the band. She plays a tremendous solo here, and she has a beautiful way of interspersing the white and the black keys in a sequenting, pentatonic scale pattern that makes her music sound very exotic.

Trane enters playing a line beginning on E, going up to E, then back to D, to B to A and then to B. He takes this fragment and builds until he has a structure as solid as the pyramids. His triplets now are played in fast tempo, holding the middle note and moving either the bottom or top note up or down minor steps, and of course always unfolding in a beautiful metric montage. Music should never be like a competitive poll where one says this or that was his best playing, but of all the documents I have uncovered up to this date, I find Trane's playing on "Leo" and "Peace On Earth" during this tour to be at the height of his exalted mood.

19

In short, his tone is beautiful because it is functional. In other words, it is always involved in saying something. You can't separate the means that a man uses to say something from what he ultimately says. Technique is not separated from its content in a great artist.[1]

—Cecil Taylor

John and Alice Coltrane — 1966, Newport Jazz Festival. The teacher and his student.

The photographs in Simpkins' book of Trane's trip to Japan show how much weight he has gained, and one actually shows Trane holding his side where obviously he had developed pain. Interestingly enough, *Ascension* had been the number one album of 1966 in the polls—just another indication to Trane that he had been going in the right direction. After all, jazz had started from blowing instruments in a free style. Certainly that was what Dixieland was about. And now Coltrane had brought it back to that; but the crucial change was the revolutionary aspects of playing the instrument.

He knew that the music that he was playing needed greater and greater study. He and Michael Olatunji had worked out a process by which Trane would use the Olatunji Center of Africal Culture as a practicing and playing situation for himself and his colleagues. He also envisioned a teaching institution where young players could come and not only work on their instruments but deal with the theoretical and philosophical aspects of jazz.

During the time that he and Alice were married, he had counseled her not only on music but on how to deal with the record companies if something should happen to him. After his death, it was her instigation that created a situation by which his music could continue to be channeled through Impulse Records.

His recording output during 1967—his last year—was sparse; but the quality and strength, especially on the piece "Ogunde," show no detrimental effects from his illness. On February 22 he rounded out a cycle which he started with Arthur Taylor in 1959, then with Elvin Jones, and last with Rashied Ali—with a duo on drums. This last one is named for four planets: Mars, Venus, Jupiter, and Saturn, and lasts approximately thirty minutes.

Trane's improvisations expressed all the things that he experienced. When asked if there was any stopping point for himself, Trane replied, "No. . . . You just keep going all the way, as deep as you can. You keep trying to get right down to the crux."[2] He had a great friendship with the Nigerian drummer Olatunji, and they planned a trip to Africa where Trane wanted to collect musical sources. I just can't help thinking here about the analogy of Moses not going into the Promised Land and Trane never having the opportunity to visit Africa. The connecting factors, which are factors that ruled his life, only confuse the real meaning of his outpouring if left without purpose. In the spring of 1967 he played a concert for the benefit of the Olatunji Cultural Center.

The Friday before he died, Trane was asked about what he would like to have put on the liner notes about the music for the album *Expression:*

> "I would like to put out an album . . . with absolutely no notes. Just the titles of the songs and the personnel. By this point I don't know what else can be said in words about what I'm doing. Let the music speak for itself."[3]

He died on Monday, July 17, 1967, of a liver ailment. Trane was survived by his mother; his wife Alice; three sons, John Jr., Ravi, and Oranyan; and his two stepdaughters, Michelle and Saida. I remember his death. I had been married two days and my wife and I were spending our honeymoon in San Francisco. On July 17 we decided to take a trip to Sausalito, a small seaside town right outside of San Francisco. As we were eating in a little restaurant, the news of Trane's death came over the radio. No words can describe how stunned I was. The owner of the restaurant, who was a great Coltrane fan, closed the bar and we sat around while he played albums and talked about Trane. That evening, my wife and I went to the club called Both/And where Roland Kirk was playing. I recall first hearing Kirk and Trane play together years before that time. Kirk announced that the music that he played that night would be in tribute to Coltrane. It was by far the best playing I had ever heard Rahsaan Roland Kirk play.

EPILOGUE

In other words we can explain the over involvement with FORM at the expense of CONTENTS as widening and/or deepening and/or acceleration of the traffic stream that moves continually in a downward direction between conscious and unconscious, while narrowing or otherwise restricting the upward traffic stream to the extent that it has virtually been put out of action. But it is this upward traffic stream that produces both science and art. Therefore the student who has perhaps no more than the potentials of the creative individual, but who is forced to approach his work and research within the framework of a THEORY AND METHOD pattern in which the purely structural element of FORM takes precedence OVER CONTENT, either loses his creative potentials or is forced to develop it outside the boundaries of Education. This would seem to explain why—as Mumford states . . . "too often the major contributions to knowledge, from Newton to Einstein, from Gilbert to Faraday, have been made outside the university's walls."[1]

—Arthur Koestler

John Coltrane — Near the end.

In October 1975 I went down to Boston and saw McCoy Tyner's quintet playing in the Jazz Workshop. There were so many things at the time that reminded me of the influences of Trane that I immediately felt nostalgic about the music. Tyner's tenor saxophonist, Azar Lawrence, played so many lines that were favorite phrases of Trane's that I remember thinking back about all the tenor saxophonists that Trane influenced. It's hard to think of any single player outside of Sanders, Archie Shepp, or Sam Rivers, who has not been either directly or indirectly affected by John Coltrane. When Trane left jazz, he left it at a place where just in terms of musicianship a tenor saxophonist had to be able to, as a basic criteria, play all the fundamentals and the harmonics of the instrument in tempo so quickly that it would turn cream into butter. The instrument itself went through a metamorphosis and became an extension of his mind.

That was only one aspect of the influence I saw that evening. There were only two shows, one starting at 10:30 and the other at 12:30. Each show lasted for an hour and a half with a half-hour break between shows. When I was first listening to jazz in clubs this was unheard of. It was Trane's insistence on being able to play longer, even if it was only one piece, that changed the format in the Jazz Workshop from an ongoing, ever-busy, folks-walking-in-and-out situation to only two performances an evening.

The overwhelming influence, however, was Tyner's bringing different instruments into his band—the double clarinet from Yugoslavia, the koto from Japan, and other flutes and non-Western instruments that he has incorporated in his bands over the years. Now he has a percussionist whose specific responsibility is to create different sounds and different moods within the context of the musical situation.

John Coltrane was an artist and a presence who had to be seen and heard in person to be experienced as the real thing. (It seems incredible that over his last twelve years he was only on TV once, in a thirty-minute show that Ralph Gleason had during the early sixties called "Just Jazz.") John Coltrane was in fact such an artist and presence that he can rightly be called an "orisha." That is what the Yoruba people call an individual when his name, and the magic that he brought to the world, are remembered and deified long after his death.

NOTES

INTRODUCTION—pp. 1—19

1. Fela Sowande, *The Role of Music in African Society,* Washington, D.C., Howard University, 1969, p. 17.
2. J.C. Thomas, *Chasin' The Trane: The Music and Mystique of John Coltrane,* New York, Doubleday and Co., 1975, p. 116.
3. Fela Sowande, *Aspects of Nigerian Music* [n.p.], 1967, p. 24.
4. Fela Sowande, "Black Folklore," in *Black Lines,* Black Studies Department, University of Pittsburgh, Fall 1971, pp. 13, 14, mimeograph.
5. Thomas, *Chasin' the Trane,* p. 188.

CHAPTER 1—pp. 21—27

1. Fela Sowande, "Black Folklore," in *Black Lines,* Black Studies Department, University of Pittsburgh, Fall 1971, pp. 21—22, mimeograph.
2. Janheinz Jahn, *Muntu,* New York, Grove Press, Inc., 1961, p. 217.
3. Sowande, "Black Folklore," p. 4.

CHAPTER 2—pp. 29—38

1. Fela Sowande, *The Role of Music in African Society,* Washington, D.C., Howard University, 1969, p. 20.
2. For other examples of Chambers's accompaniment, see the following Miles Davis recordings: "S'posin'" (Nov. 16, 1955, Prestige 7014); "Airegin" (Oct. 26, 1956, Prestige 7094); "Sid's Ahead" (Apr. 3, 1958, Columbia 1193); and "Porgy and Bess" (July 22, 1958, Columbia 1274).
3. Oswald Spengler, *The Decline of the West,* trans. Charles F. Atkinson, 2 vols., New York, Alfred A. Knopf, Inc., 1928, 1:62.
4. Sowande, *The Role of Music in African Society,* p. 21.

CHAPTER 3—pp. 39—47

1. Fela Sowande, "Nigerian Traditional Music," in *Aspects of Nigerian Music* [n.p.], 1967, pp. 8—9.
2. C.O. Simpkins, *Coltrane: A Musical Biography*, New York, Herndon House, 1975. (See the tenth photograph insert in the center of the book, following p. 150.)
3. Ralph Ellison, *Shadow and Act*, New York, Random House, Inc., 1964, p. 225.
4. Louis Armstrong, quoted in "Bop Will Kill Business Unless It Kills Itself First," *Down Beat*, April 7, 1948, p. 2.
5. Marshall W. Stearns, *The Story of Jazz*, New York, Oxford University Press, 1958, p. 227.
6. In the drumming practices of India, most of the drummers must first learn how to sing all the different rhythms before they can apply it to their playing.
7. John Coltrane (with D. DeMichael), "Coltrane on Coltrane," *Down Beat*, September 29, 1960, pp. 26—27.
8. Fela Sowande, "The Development of a National Tradition of Music," in *Aspects of Nigerian Music* [n.p.], 1967, pp. 57—58.
9. The personnel included Donald Byrd, trumpet; Coltrane, tenor sax; Horace Silver, piano; Paul Chambers, bass; Kenny Burrell, guitar; and Philly Joe Jones, drums.
10. Fela Sowande, *The Role of Music in African Society*, Washington, D.C., Howard University, 1969, p. 27.

CHAPTER 4—pp. 49—54

1. Fela Sowande, "The Development of a National Tradition of Music," in *Aspects of Nigerian Music* [n.p.], 1967, pp. 54—55.
2. *Ibid.*, p. 54.
3. *Ibid.*, pp. 57—58.
4. A view of Miles Davis may be found in my book *Miles Davis: A Musical Biography*, New York, William Morrow and Co., Inc., 1974.
5. Fela Sowande to William Cole, 21 March 1974.
6. Interview with McCoy Tyner, Amherst, Mass., 21 March 1974.
7. To date, no tapes have come forward that support this. However, in my own conversations with Max Roach, Brown's close musical associate, he indicated that Trane and Brown had played together and he felt that a tape would be brought out sometime.

CHAPTER 5—pp. 55—64

1. John Coltrane, liner notes for *A Love Supreme* (Impulse Records, Stereo A-77), December 1964.
2. John Coltrane (with D. DeMichael), "Coltrane on Coltrane," *Down Beat*, September 29, 1960, p. 27.
3. *Ibid.*

4. Miles Davis, quoted in Nat Hentoff, liner notes for *Giant Steps* (Atlantic Records SD 1311), 1959.
5. John Coltrane, quoted in Nat Hentoff, *Ibid.*
6. *Ibid.*
7. Fela Sowande, "The Catholic Church and the Tone-Languages of Nigeria," in *Aspects of Nigerian Music* [n.p.], 1967, p. 45.

CHAPTER 6—pp. 65—74

1. Fela Sowande, "The Development of a National Tradition of Music," in *Aspects of Nigerian Music* [n.p.], 1967, pp. 51—52.
2. D.H. Lawrence, *Fantasia of the Unconscious,* New York, Albert and Charles Boni, 1930, pp. 98—99.
3. Fela Sowande, *The Role of Music in African Society,* Washington, D.C., Howard University, 1969, p. 27.
4. Jolande Jacobi, *The Psychology of C.G. Jung,* London, Routledge & Kegan Paul, 1969, p. 34.
5. John Coltrane (with D. DeMichael), "Coltrane on Coltrane," *Down Beat,* September 29, 1960, p. 27.

CHAPTER 7—pp. 75—84

1. Fela Sowande, *Theory and Method,* Washington, D.C., Howard University, 1971, p. iv.
2. John Coltrane (with D. DeMichael), "Coltrane on Coltrane," *Down Beat,* September 29, 1960, p. 26.
3. Mark Gardner, liner notes for *Tenor Madness* (Prestige 7657), April 1969.
4. Nat Hentoff, liner notes for *Giant Steps* (Atlantic Records SD 1311), 1959.
5. Coltrane (with DeMichael), "Coltrane on Coltrane," p. 27.
6. Valerie Wilmer, "Conversation with Coltrane," *Jazz Journal,* December 1962, p. 2.
7. Coltrane (with DeMichael), "Coltrane on Coltrane," p. 26.
8. *Ibid.*
9. *Ibid.*

CHAPTER 8—pp. 85—98

1. Fela Sowande, *Black Experience of Religion,* Washington, D.C., Howard University, 1970, p. 4.
2. Fela Sowande, "Black Folklore," in *Black Lines,* Black Studies Department, University of Pittsburgh, Fall 1971, pp. 21—22, mimeographed.
3. Zita Carno, "The Style of John Coltrane," *Jazz Review,* October 1959, pp. 17—21; November 1959, pp. 13—17.
4. Fela Sowande, *Theory and Method,* Washington, D.C., Howard University, 1971, p. ii.

5. Zita Carno, "The Style of John Coltrane."
6. Frank Kofsky, *Black Nationalism and the Revolution in Music,* New York, Pathfinder Press, Inc., 1970, p. 226.

CHAPTER 9—pp. 99—111

1. Fela Sowande, *The Role of Music in African Society,* Washington, D.C., Howard University, 1969, p. 21.
2. "John Coltrane, Finally Made," *Newsweek,* July 24, 1961, p. 64.
3. John Coltrane, quoted in Nat Hentoff, liner notes for *Giant Steps* (Atlantic Records SD 1311) 1959.
4. John Coltrane (with D. DeMichael), "Coltrane on Coltrane," *Down Beat,* September 29, 1960, p. 27.
5. John Coltrane, quoted in Valerie Wilmer, "Conversation with Coltrane," *Jazz Journal,* January 1962, p. 2.
6. Coltrane (with DeMichael), "Coltrane on Coltrane," p. 27.
7. *Ibid.*
8. *Ibid.*
9. John Coltrane, quoted in Nat Hentoff, *Giant Steps.*
10. Fela Sowande, "The Development of a National Tradition of Music," in *Aspects of Nigerian Music* [n.p.], 1967, pp. 62—63.

CHAPTER 10—pp. 113—122

1. Lama Anagarika Govinda, "Meditation and Art," in *Maitreya,* Vol. 1, Berkeley, Shambhala Publications Inc., 1970, p. 9.
2. Several pieces they recorded together are: "Just For The Love," "Nita" (September 21, 1956); "All Morning Long" (November 15, 1957); "Come Rain Or Come Shine," "Lush Life" (January 10, 1958).
3. John Coltrane (with D. DeMichael), "Coltrane on Coltrane", *Down Beat,* September 29, 1960, p. 27.
4. Ralph J. Gleason, liner notes for *Coltrane's Sound* (Atlantic Records SD 1419), 1960.
5. Coltrane (with D. DeMichael), "Coltrane on Coltrane," p. 27.
6. Fela Sowande, *Theory and Method,* Washington, D.C., Howard University, 1971, p. 19.
7. Stanley Dance, "Tyner Talking," *Down Beat,* October 24, 1963, pp. 18—19.
8. Frank Kofsky, *Black Nationalism and the Revolution in Music,* New York, Pathfinder Press, Inc., 1970, p. 233.

CHAPTER 11—pp. 123—130

1. Fela Sowande, *The Role of Music in African Society,* Washington, D.C., Howard University, 1969, p. 15.

2. John Coltrane, quoted in Dom Cerulli, liner notes for *Africa/Brass* (Impulse Records, Stereo A-6), 1961.
3. John Coltrane, quoted in Ralph J. Gleason, liner notes for *Olé Coltrane* (Atlantic Records SD 1373), 1961.
4. Cerulli, *Africa/Brass.*
5. *Ibid.*
6. John Coltrane, quoted in Ralph J. Gleason, *Olé Coltrane.*
7. John Coltrane (with D. DeMichael), "Coltrane on Coltrane," *Down Beat,* September 29, 1960, p. 27.

CHAPTER 12—pp. 131—135

1. Fela Sowande, "The Catholic Church and the Tone-Languages of Nigeria," in *Aspects of Nigerian Music* [n.p.], 1967, pp. 45—46.
2. Fela Sowande, "Black Folklore," in *Black Lines,* Black Studies Department, University of Pittsburgh, Fall 1971, p. 22, mimeograph.

CHAPTER 13—pp. 137—146

1. Lama Anagarika Govinda, "Meditation and Art," in *Maitreya,* Vol. 1, Berkeley, Shambhala Publications Inc., 1970, pp. 9—10.
2. John Coltrane, quoted in Nat Hentoff, liner notes for *Coltrane "Live" at the Village Vanguard* (Impulse Records, AS-10), 1961.
3. Richard Wilhelm, *I Ching* (Princeton: Princeton University Press, 1967), pp. xxiii—xxiv, quoted in Fela Sowande, *Nigerian Music and Musicians: Then and Now,* n.p., p. 79.
4. Coltrane, quoted in Hentoff, *Coltrane "Live" at the Village Vanguard.*
5. *Ibid.*
6. *Ibid.*
7. *Ibid.*
8. Frank Kofsky, *Black Nationalism and the Revolution in Music,* New York, Pathfinder Press, Inc., 1970, pp. 234—235.
9. *Ibid.,* p. 242.
10. *Ibid.*
11. Fela Sowande, "The Development of a National Tradition of Music," in *Aspects of Nigerian Music* [n.p.], 1967, p. 63.

CHAPTER 14—pp. 147—153

1. Fela Sowande, "The Catholic Church and the Tone-Languages of Nigeria," in *Aspects of Nigerian Music* [n.p.], 1967, pp. 42—44.
2. Frank Kofsky, *Black Nationalism and the Revolution in Music,* New York, Pathfinder Press, Inc., 1970, p. 235.
3. Sowande, "The Catholic Church and the Tone-Languages of Nigeria," pp. 42—44.

CHAPTER 15—pp. 155—162

1. Fela Sowande, "The Philosophy of Music," in *Aspects of Nigerian Music* [n.p.], 1967, pp. 19—20.
2. John Coltrane, quoted in Frank Kofsky, *Black Nationalism and the Revolution in Music,* New York, Pathfinder Press, Inc., p. 241.

CHAPTER 16—pp. 163—171

1. Archie Shepp, quoted in Nat Hentoff, liner notes for *New Thing at Newport* (Impulse Records, AS-94), 1965.
2. Frank Kofsky, *Black Nationalism and the Revolution in Music,* New York, Pathfinder Press, Inc., 1970, p. 234.
3. Albert Ayler, liner notes for *The New Wave in Jazz* (Impulse Records, AS-90), 1965.
4. Leonard Feather, "For Coltrane the Time Is Now," in *Melody Maker,* December 19, 1964, p. 6.

CHAPTER 17—pp. 173—184

1. "Alice Coltrane Interviewed by Pauline Rivelli," in *Black Giants,* ed. by Pauline Rivelli and Robert Levin, New York and Cleveland, World Publishing Co., 1970, p. 122.
2. Frank Kofsky, *Black Nationalism and the Revolution in Music,* New York, Pathfinder Press, Inc., 1970, p. 233.
3. John Coltrane, quoted in Nat Hentoff, liner notes for *Meditations* (Impulse Records, AS-9110), 1965.
4. A.B. Spellman, quoted in Nat Hentoff, *Ibid.*
5. Fela Sowande, "The Teaching of Music in Nigerian Schools," in *Aspects of Nigerian Music* [n.p.], 1967, p. 29.
6. Coltrane, quoted in Hentoff, *Meditations.*
7. *Ibid.*
8. Nat Hentoff, *Ibid.*

CHAPTER 18—pp. 185—192

1. Fela Sowande, "Nigerian Traditional Music," in *Aspects of Nigerian Music* [n.p.], 1967, p. 6.
2. John Coltrane, quoted in Frank Kofsky, *Black Nationalism and the Revolution in Music,* New York, Pathfinder Press, Inc., 1970, p. 232.
3. Alice Coltrane, liner notes for *Concert in Japan* (Impulse Records, AS-9246-2), 1973.
4. John Coltrane, quoted in Nat Hentoff, liner notes for *Coltrane "Live" at the Village Vanguard Again* (Impulse Records, AS-9124), 1966.

CHAPTER 19—pp. 193—196

1. Cecil Taylor, "John Coltrane," in *Jazz Review,* January 1959, p. 34.
2. John Coltrane, quoted in Nat Hentoff, liner notes for *Coltrane "Live" at the Village Vanguard Again* (Impulse Records, AS-9124), 1966.
3. John Coltrane, quoted in Nat Hentoff, liner notes for *Expression* (Impulse Records, AS-9120), 1967.

EPILOGUE—pp. 197—199

1. Arthur Koestler, *The Act of Creation,* New York, Dell Publishing Co., Inc., 1966, pp. 180—181, quoted in Fela Sowande, *Theory and Method,* Washington, D.C., Howard University, 1971, p. 37.

RECORDING DATES AND PERSONNEL

The following is a listing of the recordings on which John Coltrane played. I have omitted the record labels since I am primarily concerned with the dates and personnel involved. On the personnel listings, the names with one star are the leaders of those specific sessions. In the cases where various personnel replacements were used on individual takes, I have included all players in one group. The pieces with two stars are John Coltrane's compositions.

For a discography including labels and broadcast dates, I recommend the one compiled by Jorgen Grunnet Jepsen. It would be best for anyone interested in the extant recordings of Coltrane to consult the latest Schwann Catalog, since records are still being released (with new combinations of cuts) even now, and records are always going out of print. As of June 1976 there were sixty Coltrane records listed in Schwann.

Date and Place	Pieces	Personnel	Instruments
November 21, 1949 New York	Tally Ho	*Dizzy Gillespie	trumpet, vocal
	Say When	Don Slaughter	trumpet
	You Stole My Wife	Elmon Wright	
	I Can't Remember	Willie Cook	
		Matthew Gee	
		Sam Hurt	trombone
		Charlie Greenlea	
		Jimmy Heath	alto sax
		John Coltrane	
		Jessie Powell	tenor sax
		Paul Gonsalves	

January 9, 1950 New York

Coast to Coast
Oo-La-La
Honeysuckle Rose
Carambola

Al Gibson — bars
John Acea — piano
John Collins — guitar
Al McKibbon — bass
Specs Wright — drums
Tiny Irvin — vocal

* Dizzy Gillespie — trumpet, vocal
Don Slaughter ⎫
Elmon Wright ⎬ trumpet
Willie Cook ⎭
Matthew Gee ⎫ trombone
Sam Hurt ⎬
Charles Greenlea ⎭
Jimmy Heath ⎫ alto sax
John Coltrane ⎬
Jessie Powell ⎫ tenor sax
Paul Gonsalves ⎬
Al Gibson — bars
John Acea — piano
Floyd Smith — guitar
Al McKibbon — bass
Specs Wright — drums
Carlos Duchesne — conga
Francisco Pozo — bongo
Tiny Irvin ⎫ vocal
Joe Carroll ⎬

Date and Place	Pieces	Personnel	Instruments
March 1, 1951 Detroit	Love Me	*Dizzy Gillespie	trumpet
	Tin Tin Deo	John Coltrane	alto, tenor sax
	We Love to Boogie	Milt Jackson	vibes, piano
	Birks Works	Kenny Burrell	guitar
		Percy Heath	bass
		Kansas Fields	drums
April 7, 1952 Cincinnati	Velvet Sunset	Gene Redd	trumpet, vibes
	Moonglow	Joe Mitchell	trumpet
	Ain't Misbehavin'	*Earl Bostic ⎫	alto sax
	Linger Awhile	Pinky Williams ⎭	
		John Coltrane	tenor sax
		Joe Knight	piano
		Jimmy Shirley	guitar
		Ike Isaacs	bass
		Specs Wright	drums
August 15, 1952 Los Angeles	You Go to My Head	Gene Redd	trumpet, vibes
	The Hour of Parting	Joe Mitchell	trumpet
	Smoke Gets in Your Eyes	*Earl Bostic ⎫	alto sax
	For You	Pinky Williams ⎭	
		John Coltrane	tenor sax
		Joe Knight	piano
		Harold Grant	guitar
		Ike Isaacs	bass
		Specs Wright	drums

1952 Nashville

Bittersweet
Fat Sam from Birmingham

Tommy Turrentine — trumpet
John Coltrane — alto, tenor sax
*Gay Crosse — tenor sax, vocals
Stash O'Laughlin — piano
Alvin Jackson — bass
Oliver Jackson — drums

August 5, 1954 Los Angeles

Burgundy Walk
Sunny Side of the Street
Sweet as Bear Meat
All of Me
Used To Be Duke
Skokiaan
Poor Butterfly
Madame Butterfly
Warm Valley
Autumn in New York
Sweet Lorraine
Time on My Hands

Harold Baker — trumpet
Lawrence Brown — trombone
Jimmy Hamilton — clarinet
*Jimmy Hodges — alto sax
John Coltrane — tenor sax
Cal Cobbs — piano
John Williams — bass
Louis Bellson — drums

October 27, 1955 New York

Ah-Leu-Cha
Budo
Stablemates
How Am I To Know?
Just Squeeze Me
S'posin'
Miles' Theme

*Miles Davis — trumpet
John Coltrane — tenor sax
Red Garland — piano
Paul Chambers — bass
Philly Joe Jones — drums

Date and Place	Pieces	Personnel	Instruments
November, 1955 Detroit	Trane's Strane Nixon, Dixon and Yates Blues High Step	Curtis Fuller John Coltrane Pepper Adams Roland Alexander *Paul Chambers Philly Joe Jones	trombone tenor sax bars piano bass drums
March, 1956 Los Angeles	Dexterity East Bound Easy To Love Visitations J. P. Jones Stablemates	John Coltrane Kenny Drew *Paul Chambers Philly Joe Jones	tenor sax piano bass drums
May 7, 1956 New York	Weejah On It Polka Dots and Moonbeams Avalon	Donald Byrd Hank Mobley } John Coltrane } *Elmo Hope Paul Chambers Philly Joe Jones	trumpet tenor sax piano bass drums
May 11, 1956 New York	In Your Own Sweet Way Diane Trane's Blues Woody'n You It Could Happen to You Surrey With the Fringe on Top	*Miles Davis John Coltrane Red Garland Paul Chambers Philly Joe Jones	trumpet tenor sax piano bass drums

	Salt Peanuts		
	Four		
	The Theme, I		
	The Theme, II		
May 24, 1956 New York	Tenor Madness	*Sonny Rollins	tenor sax
		John Coltrane	tenor sax
		Red Garland	piano
		Paul Chambers	bass
		Philly Joe Jones	drums
June 5, 1956 New York	Dear Old Stockholm	*Miles Davis	trumpet
	Bye Bye Blackbird	John Coltrane	tenor sax
	Tadd's Delight	Red Garland	piano
		Paul Chambers	bass
		Philly Joe Jones	drums
September 7, 1956 New York	Just You, Just Me	Hank Mobley	tenor sax
	Tenor Conclave	Al Cohn	tenor sax
	Bob's Boys	Zoot Sims	tenor sax
	How Deep Is the Ocean	John Coltrane	tenor sax
		Red Garland	piano
		Paul Chambers	bass
		Art Taylor	drums
September 10, 1956 New York	All of You	*Miles Davis	trumpet
	'Round Midnight	John Coltrane	tenor sax
	Sweet Sue	Red Garland	piano
		Paul Chambers	bass
		Philly Joe Jones	drums

Date and Place	Pieces	Personnel	Instruments
September 21, 1956 New York	**Just for the Love **Nita We Six Omicron	Donald Byrd John Coltrane Horace Silver *Paul Chambers Kenny Burrell Philly Joe Jones	trumpet tenor sax piano bass guitar drums
October 26, 1956 New York	If I Were a Bell Well You Needn't 'Round about Midnight You're My Everything Half Nelson Oleo I Could Write a Book Airegin Tune Up Blues by Five When Lights Are Low My Funny Valentine Trane's Blues Ahmad's Blues When I Fall in Love	*Miles Davis John Coltrane Red Garland Paul Chambers Philly Joe Jones	trumpet tenor sax piano bass drums

November 30, 1956 New York	Mating Call	John Coltrane	tenor sax
	Soultrane	*Tadd Dameron	piano, arranger
	Gnid	John Simmons	bass
	On a Misty Night	Philly Joe Jones	drums
	Super-Jet		
	Romas		
March 22, 1957 New York	Anatomy	Webster Young	trumpet
	Interplay	Idrees Sulieman	
	Soul Eyes	Bobby Jaspar	tenor sax
	Light Blue	John Coltrane	
	C.T.A.	Mal Waldron	piano
		Kenny Burrell	guitar
		Paul Chambers	bass
		*Art Taylor	drums
April 6, 1957 New York	The Way You Look Tonight	Lee Morgan	trumpet
	Ball Bearing	*John Griffin	
	Smoke Stack	Hank Mobley	tenor sax
	All the Things You Are	John Coltrane	
		Wynton Kelly	piano
		Paul Chambers	bass
		Art Blakey	drums
April 16, 1957 New York	Monk's Mood	John Coltrane	tenor sax
	Ruby, My Dear	*Thelonious Monk	piano
	Nutty	Wilbur Ware	bass
	Trinkle Tinkle	Shadow Wilson	drums

Date and Place	Pieces	Personnel	Instruments
April 18, 1957 New York	Eclypso Solacium Minor Mishap Tommy's Time	Idrees Sulieman John Coltrane Tommy Flanagan Kenny Burrell Doug Watkins Louis Hayes	trumpet tenor sax piano guitar bass drums
April 19, 1957 New York	Potpourri J.M.'s Dream Doll Don't Explain Falling in Love Blue Calypso	Bill Hardman Jackie McLean John Coltrane * Mal Waldron Julian Euell Art Taylor	trumpet alto sax tenor sax piano bass drums
April 20, 1957 New York	Dakar **Mary's Blues Route 4 Watches' Pit Velvet Scene Cat Walk	* John Coltrane Cecil Payne ⎱ Pepper Adams ⎰ Mal Waldron Doug Watkins Art Taylor	tenor sax bars piano bass drums
May 17, 1957 New York	The Way You Look Tonight One by One From This Moment On	Idrees Sulieman Sahib Shihab John Coltrane * Mal Waldron Julian Euell Ed Thigpen	trumpet alto sax, bars tenor sax piano bass drums

May 17, 1957 New York

Cattin'	*Paul Quinichette	tenor sax
Anatomy	*John Coltrane	tenor sax
Vodka	Mal Waldron	piano
Sunday	Julian Euell	bass
Exactly Like You	Ed Thigpen	drums
Tea for Two		

May 31, 1957 New York

**Straight Street	Johnny Splawn	trumpet
**Chronic Blues	*John Coltrane	tenor sax
While My Lady Sleeps	Sahib Shihab	bars
Bakai	Red Garland	piano
Violets for Your Furs	Mal Waldron	piano
I Hear a Rhapsody	Paul Chambers	bass
Time Was	Al Heath	drums

June 26, 1957 New York

Epistrophy (2 takes)	Ray Copeland	trumpet
Crepuscule with Nellie	Gigi Gryce	alto sax
Well You Needn't	Coleman Hawkins	tenor sax
Blues for Tomorrow	John Coltrane	tenor sax
Abide with Me	*Thelonious Monk	piano
Off Minor	Wilbur Ware	bass
	Art Blakey	drums

August 16, 1957 New York

**Trane's Slo Blues	*John Coltrane	tenor sax
Toni's Dance	Earl May	bass
Like Someone in Love	Art Taylor	drums
I Love You		
**Slowtrane		

Date and Place	Pieces	Personnel	Instruments
August 23, 1957 New York	You Leave Me Breathless **Bass Blues **Traneing In Soft Lights and Sweet Music Slow Dance	John Coltrane *Red Garland Paul Chambers Art Taylor	tenor sax piano bass drums
September 15, 1957 New York	**Blue Train **Locomotion **Moment's Notice **Lazy Bird I'm Old Fashioned	Lee Morgan Curtis Fuller *John Coltrane Kenny Drew Paul Chambers Philly Joe Jones	trumpet trombone tenor sax piano bass drums
September 20, 1957 New York	Dealin' Wheelin' Robbin's Nest Things Ain't What They Used To Be	Prestige All Stars: John Coltrane Paul Quinichette } Frank Wess Mal Waldron Doug Watkins Art Taylor	tenor sax tenor sax, flute piano bass drums
October, 1957 New York	Not So Sleepy Love and the Weather Turtle Walk If I'm Lucky Strictly Instrumental	Winners' Circle: Donald Byrd Frank Rehak Gene Quill John Coltrane	trumpet trombone alto sax tenor sax

Al Cohn — bars
Eddie Costa — piano
Freddie Green — guitar
Oscar Pettiford — bass
Philly Joe Jones }
Ed Thigpen } — drums

October 9, 1957 New York

With a Song in My Heart

Donald Byrd — trumpet
Curtis Fuller — trombone
John Coltrane — tenor sax
*Sonny Clark — piano
Paul Chambers — bass
Art Taylor — drums

Speak Low
Come Rain or Come Shine
News for Lulu
Sonny's Crib
Softly

November 15, 1957 New York

Donald Byrd — trumpet
John Coltrane — tenor sax
*Red Garland — piano
George Joyner — bass
Art Taylor — drums

Our Delight
They Can't Take That Away from Me
Woody'n You
Undecided
I Got It Bad
Soul Junction
What Is There To Say
Birks Works
Hallelujah
All Morning Long

Date and Place	Pieces	Personnel	Instruments
December 13, 1957 New York	Billie's Bounce Solitude Two Bass Hit Soft Winds Lazy Mae	Same personnel as November 15, 1957	
December, 1957 New York	Ain't Life Grand El Toro Valiente Midriff Late Date The Kiss of No Return The Outer World	Donald Byrd Idrees Sulieman Bill Hardman Ray Copeland Melba Liston Frank Rehak Jimmy Cleveland Sahib Shihab Bill Graham John Coltrane Al Cohn Bill Slapin Walter Bishop Wendell Marshall * Art Blakey	trumpet trombone alto sax tenor sax bars piano bass drums
December, 1957 New York	Tippin' Pristine	Donald Byrd John Coltrane Walter Bishop Wendell Marshall * Art Blakey	trumpet tenor sax piano bass drums

December 20, 1957 New York

Under Paris Skies
Filide
Two Sons
Paul's Pal
Clifford's Kappa
I Hadn't Anyone

*Ray Draper — tuba
John Coltrane — tenor sax
Gil Goggins — piano
Spanky DeBrest — bass
Larry Richie — drums

1957–1958 New York

Besame Mucho

**Michel Legrand and his Orchestra
John Coltrane — tenor sax

January 3, 1958 New York

Ammons' Joy
Groove Blues
The Real McCoy
It Might as Well Be Spring
That's All
Cheek To Cheek
Jug Handle
Blue Hymn

John Coltrane — alto, tenor sax
*Gene Ammons — tenor sax
Paul Quinichette }
Jerome Richardson — flute
Pepper Adams — bars
Mal Waldron — piano
George Joyner — bass
Art Taylor — drums

January 10, 1958 New York

Lush Life
Nakatini Serenade
The Believer
Come Rain or Come Shine
Lover

Donald Byrd — trumpet
*John Coltrane — tenor sax
Red Garland — piano
Paul Chambers — bass
Louis Hayes — drums

February 7, 1958 New York

Russian Lullaby
Theme for Ernie
Good Bait
You Say You Care
I Want to Talk about You

John Coltrane — tenor sax
*Red Garland — piano
Paul Chambers — bass
Art Taylor — drums

221

Date and Place	Pieces	Personnel	Instruments
March 7, 1958 New York	Lyresto Why Was I Born Freight Train Big Paul I Never Knew	*John Coltrane Tommy Flanagan Kenny Burrell Paul Chambers Jimmy Cobb	tenor sax piano guitar bass bass
March 13, 1958 New York	Well's Fargo West 42nd Street W.F.P.H. Snuffy Rhodomagnetics	*Wilbur Harden John Coltrane Tommy Flanagan Doug Watkins Louis Hayes	flute tenor sax piano bass drums
March 26, 1958 New York	Rise 'n Shine I See Your Face before Me If There Is Someone Lovelier than You Little Melonae **By the Numbers	John Coltrane *Red Garland Paul Chambers Jimmy Cobb	tenor sax piano bass bass
April 2, 1958 New York	Two Bass Hit Straight No Chaser Milestones	*Miles Davis Julian "Cannonball" Adderley John Coltrane Red Garland Paul Chambers Philly Joe Jones	trumpet alto sax tenor sax piano bass drums
April 3, 1958 New York	Dr. Jekyll Sid's Ahead	Same personnel as April 2, 1958	

April, 1958 New York Plaza

Jazz at the Plaza
My Funny Valentine
If I Were a Bell
Oleo

* Miles Davis	trumpet
John Coltrane	tenor sax
Julian "Cannonball" Adderley	alto sax
Bill Evans	piano
Paul Chambers	bass
Philly Joe Jones	drums

May 23, 1958 New York

Black Pearls
Lover Come Back to Me
Sweet Sapphire Blues

Donald Byrd	trumpet
* John Coltrane	tenor sax
Red Garland	piano
Paul Chambers	bass
Jimmy Cobb	drums

May 26, 1958 New York

Green Dolphin Street
Stella by Starlight
Put Your Little Foot Out

* Miles Davis	trumpet
Julian "Cannonball" Adderley	alto sax
John Coltrane	tenor sax
Bill Evans	piano
Paul Chambers	bass
Jimmy Cobb	drums

June 25, 1958 New York

Wild Man
'Round Midnight
The Jitterbug Waltz

Miles Davis	trumpet
Jerome Richardson	clarinet, bars
Phil Woods	alto sax
John Coltrane	tenor sax
Herbie Mann	flute
Betty Glaman	harp
Eddie Costa	vibes
Bill Evans	piano

Date and Place	Pieces	Personnel	Instruments
		Paul Chambers	bass
		Kenny Dennis	drums
		*Michel Legrand	arranger, director
July 3, 1958 Newport Jazz Festival	A-Leu-Cha	*Miles Davis	trumpet
	Straight No Chaser	Julian "Cannonball" Adderley	alto sax
	Two Bass Hit	John Coltrane	tenor sax
	Fran-Dance	Bill Evans	piano
		Paul Chambers	bass
		Jimmy Cobb	drums
July 11, 1958 New York	Spring Is Here	Wilbur Harden	trumpet
	Invitation	*John Coltrane	tenor sax
	I'm a Dreamer	Red Garland	piano
	Love Thy Neighbour	Paul Chambers	bass
	Don't Take Your Love Away	Jimmy Cobb ⎱	drums
	Stardust	Art Taylor ⎰	
	I'll Get By		
	My Ideal		
August 18, 1958 New York	Dial Africa	*Wilbur Harden	trumpet, fluegelhorn
	Domba	Curtis Fuller	trombone
	Gold Coast	John Coltrane	tenor sax
	Tanganika Strut	Tommy Flanagan	piano
		Alvin Jackson	bass
		Arthur Taylor	drums

August 25, 1958 New York

B. J.
Anedao
Once in a While

*Wilbur Harden	trumpet, fluegelhorn
Curtis Fuller	trombone
John Coltrane	tenor sax
Howard Williams	piano
Alvin Jackson	bass
Arthur Taylor	drums

September 12, 1958 New York

Manhattan

Art Farmer	trumpet
Doc Severinsen	
Ernie Royal	
Bob Brookmeyer	trombone
Frank Rehak	
Tom Mitchell	
Hal McKusick	alto sax
John Coltrane	tenor sax
Sol Schlinger	bars
Bill Evans	piano
Barry Galbraith	guitar
Milt Hinton	bass
Charlie Persip	drums
Jon Hendricks	narrator
*George Russell	conductor, arranger

October 13, 1958 New York

Shifting Down
Like Someone in Love
Double Clutching
Just Friends

Kenny Dorham	trumpet
*John Coltrane	tenor sax
*Cecil Taylor	piano
Chuck Israels	bass
Louis Hayes	drums

Date and Place	Pieces	Personnel	Instruments
November, 1958 New York	Essil's Dance Doxy I Talk to the Trees Yesterdays Angel Eyes Oleo	*Ray Draper John Coltrane John Maher Spanky DeBrest Larry Ritchie	tuba tenor sax piano bass drums
December 26, 1958 New York	Do I Love You Because You're Beautiful Then I'll Be Tired of You Something I Dreamed Last Night Bahia Time after Time **Goldsboro Express	Freddie Hubbard *John Coltrane Red Garland Paul Chambers Art Taylor } Jimmy Cobb }	trumpet tenor sax piano bass drums
January 15, 1959 New York	Bags and Trane Three Little Words Be-Bop The Night We Called It a Day The Late, Late Blues Centerpiece Stairway to the Stars Blues Legacy	*John Coltrane *Milt Jackson Hank Jones Paul Chambers Connie Kay	tenor sax vibes piano bass drums
February 3, 1959 Chicago	Grand Central The Sleeper Weaver of Dreams	*Julian "Cannonball" Adderley John Coltrane Wynton Kelly	alto sax tenor sax piano

March 2, 1959 New York

Wabash
Limehouse Blues

Paul Chambers — bass
Jimmy Cobb — drums

Freddie Freeloader
So What
Blue in Green

*Miles Davis — trumpet
Julian "Cannonball" Adderley — alto sax
John Coltrane — tenor sax
Wynton Kelly — piano
Bill Evans
Paul Chambers — bass
Jimmy Cobb — drums

April 22, 1959 New York

Flamenco Sketches
All Blues

Same personnel as
March 2, 1959

May 4–5, 1959 New York

**Cousin Mary
**Giant Steps
**Count Down
**Spiral
**Syeeda's Flute Song
**Mr. P.C.

*John Coltrane — tenor sax
Tommy Flanagan — piano
Paul Chambers — bass
Art Taylor — drums

November 24, 1959 New York

Little Old Lady
I'll Wait and Pray

*John Coltrane — tenor sax
Wynton Kelly — piano
Paul Chambers — bass
Jimmy Cobb — drums

Date and Place	Pieces	Personnel	Instruments
December 2, 1959 New York	**Naima **Harmonique My Shining Hour **Like Sonny **Fifth House **Some Other Blues	Same personnel as November 24, 1959	
June 28, 1960 New York	Cherryco The Blessing	*Don Cherry *John Coltrane Charlie Haden Ed Blackwell	trumpet tenor and soprano sax bass drums
July 8, 1960 New York	Focus on Sanity Bemsha Swing The Invisible	*Don Cherry *John Coltrane Percy Heath Ed Blackwell	trumpet tenor and soprano sax bass drums
Summer, 1960 New York Birdland	**Exotica **One and Four **Simple Like	*John Coltrane McCoy Tyner Steve Davis Billy Higgins	tenor sax piano bass drums
October 21, 1960 New York	**Village Blues My Favorite Things	*John Coltrane	tenor and soprano sax

October 24, 1960 New York

Summertime
Blues to Elvin
**Blues to Bechet
**Blues to You
**Mr. Day
***Mr. Syms
***Mr. Knight
**Central Park West
Body and Soul
**Satellite
***26-2
**Untitled Original

McCoy Tyner — piano
Steve Davis — bass
Elvin Jones — drums

Same personnel as October 21, 1960

October 26, 1960 New York

But Not for Me
Everytime We Say Goodbye
**Liberia
The Night Has a Thousand Eyes
**Equinox

Same personnel as October 21, 1960

March 20, 1961 New York

Someday My Prince Will Come

*Miles Davis — trumpet
Hank Mobley } — tenor sax
John Coltrane }
Wynton Kelly — piano
Paul Chambers — bass
Jimmy Cobb — drums

Date and Place	Pieces	Personnel	Instruments
March 21, 1961 New York	Teo	*Miles Davis John Coltrane Wynton Kelly Paul Chambers Jimmy Cobb	trumpet tenor sax piano bass drums
May 23, 1961 New York	Greensleeves (2 takes) Song of the Underground Railroad	Booker Little Britt Woodman Carl Bowman Julius Watkins Donald Corrado Bob Northern Robert Swisshel Bill Barber Eric Dolphy *John Coltrane Laurdine Patrick McCoy Tyner Art Davis Elvin Jones	trumpet trombone euphonium french horn tuba alto sax, bass clarinet, flute tenor sax reeds piano bass drums
May 25, 1961 New York	**Olé **Dahomey Dance Aisha Original Untitled Ballad	Freddie Hubbard Eric Dolphy *John Coltrane	trumpet alto sax, flute tenor and soprano sax

June 7, 1961 New York

**Africa (2 takes)
**Blues Minor

McCoy Tyner — piano
Reggie Workman ⎫
Art Davis ⎬ bass
Elvin Jones — drums

November 2–3, 1961 New York
Village Vanguard

**Spiritual
Softly as in a Morning Sunrise
**Chasin' the Trane

Same personnel as May 23, 1961

Eric Dolphy — bass clarinet
*John Coltrane — tenor and soprano sax
McCoy Tyner — piano
Reggie Workman ⎫
Jimmy Garrison ⎬ bass
Elvin Jones — drums

November 5, 1961 New York
Village Vanguard

**India
**Impressions

Same personnel as November 2–3, 1961

End of November, 1961
Copenhagen
(Bootleg—John Norris,
Coda, 893 Youge Street,
Toronto, 5, Ontario)

My Favorite Things
**Blue Train
**Naima
**Mr. P.C.
I Want to Talk about You
**Impressions
**Spiritual

Eric Dolphy — bass clarinet, flute, alto sax
*John Coltrane — tenor sax
McCoy Tyner — piano
Reggie Workman — bass
Elvin Jones — drums

Date and Place	Pieces	Personnel	Instruments
December 21, 1961 New York	Greensleeves It's Easy To Remember	*John Coltrane McCoy Tyner Jimmy Garrison Elvin Jones	tenor and soprano sax piano bass drums
April 11, 1962 New York	The Inch Worm **Big Nick Soul Eyes	Same personnel as December 21, 1961	
June 21, 1962 New York	**Miles' Mode	Same personnel as December 21, 1961	
June 29, 1962 New York	**Tunji (Toon-gee) Out of This World	Same personnel as December 21, 1961	
September 18, 1962 New York	Nancy What's New **Up 'Gainst the Wall	Same personnel as December 21, 1961	
September 26, 1962 New York	Stevie In a Sentimental Mood Angelica My Little Brown Book The Feeling of Jazz **Big Nick Take the Coltrane	*John Coltrane *Duke Ellington Aaron Bell Jimmy Garrison } Sam Woodyard } Elvin Jones	tenor and soprano sax piano bass drums

November 13, 1962 New York

Too Young To Go Steady
All or Nothing at All
They Say It's Wonderful
I Wish I Knew
You Don't Know What Love Is
Say It Over and Over Again

* John Coltrane — tenor and soprano sax

McCoy Tyner — piano
Jimmy Garrison — bass
Elvin Jones — drums

March 6–7, 1963 New York

They Say It's Wonderful
Lush Life
Autumn Serenade
My One and Only Love
Vilia
Dedicated to You
You Are Too Beautiful

* John Coltrane — tenor and soprano sax

McCoy Tyner — piano
Jimmy Garrison — bass
Elvin Jones — drums
Johnny Hartman — vocal

April 29, 1963 New York

** After the Rain
Dear Old Stockholm

* John Coltrane — tenor and soprano sax

McCoy Tyner — piano
Jimmy Garrison — bass
Roy Haynes — drums

July 7, 1963 Newport

My Favorite Things
I Want To Talk about You

Same personnel as
April 29, 1963

October 8, 1963 New York
Birdland

** The Promise
** Afro-Blue
I Want To Talk about You

* John Coltrane — tenor and soprano sax

McCoy Tyner — piano
Jimmy Garrison — bass
Elvin Jones — drums

Date and Place	Pieces	Personnel	Instruments
November 18, 1963 New York Birdland	**Your Lady **Alabama	Same personnel as October 8, 1963	
April 27, 1964 and June 1, 1964 New York	**Crescent **Lonnie's Lament **Wise One **The Drum Thing **Bessie's Blues	Same personnel as October 8, 1963	
December 9, 1964 New York	**A Love Supreme, Part I Acknowledgement **A Love Supreme, Part II Resolution **A Love Supreme, Part III Pursuance **A Love Supreme, Part IV Psalm	Same personnel as October 8, 1963	
February 17–18, 1965 New York	Nature Boy **Brazilia Chim Chim Cheree **Song of Praise	*John Coltrane McCoy Tyner Jimmy Garrison ⎱ Art Davis ⎰ Elvin Jones	tenor and soprano sax piano bass drums

234

March 28, 1965 New York Village Gate	*John Coltrane McCoy Tyner Jimmy Garrison Elvin Jones	Nature Boy	tenor sax piano bass drums
May 26, 1965 New York	Same personnel as March 28, 1965	**Dear Lord	
June 10, 1965 New York	Same personnel as March 28, 1965	**Transition **Suite— Prayer and Meditation: Day Peace and After Prayer and Meditation: Evening Affirmation Prayer and Meditation: 4 A.M.	
June 16, 1965 New York	Same personnel as March 28, 1965	**Living Space	
June 28, 1965 New York	Same personnel as March 28, 1965	**Welcome **Vigil	
June 28, 1965 New York	Freddie Hubbard } Dewey Johnson	**Ascension, part 1 **Ascension, part 2	trumpet

Date and Place	Pieces	Personnel	Instruments
		Marion Brown	alto sax
		John Tchicai	
		*John Coltrane	tenor sax
		Archie Shepp	
		Pharoah Sanders	
		McCoy Tyner	piano
		Art Davis	bass
		Jimmy Garrison	
		Elvin Jones	drums
July 2, 1965 Newport Jazz Festival	**One Down, One Up	*John Coltrane	tenor and soprano sax
		McCoy Tyner	piano
		Jimmy Garrison	bass
		Elvin Jones	drums
		The Rev. Norman O'Connor	narrator
August 26, 1965 New York	**Sun Ship	*John Coltrane	tenor sax
	**Attaining	McCoy Tyner	piano
	**Dearly Beloved	Jimmy Garrison	bass
	**Ascent	Elvin Jones	drums
	**Amen		
September 22, 1965 New York	**Joy	Same personnel as August 26, 1965	

September 30, 1965 Seattle,
Washington The Penthouse

**Cosmos
Out Of This World, part 1
Out Of This World, part 2
**Evolution, part 1
**Evolution, part 2
Tapestry in Sound

*John Coltrane ⎫ tenor sax
Pharaoh Sanders ⎬
McCoy Tyner — piano
Donald Garrett — bass clarinet
Jimmy Garrison — bass
Elvin Jones — drums

October 1, 1965 Seattle,
Washington

**Om, part 1
**Om, part 2

*John Coltrane ⎫ tenor sax
Pharaoh Sanders ⎬
Joe Brazil — flute
McCoy Tyner — piano
Donald Garrett — bass and bass
    clarinet
Jimmy Garrison — bass
Elvin Jones — drums

October, 1965 Los Angeles

**Selflessness

*John Coltrane ⎫ tenor sax
Pharaoh Sanders ⎬
Donald Garrett — bass clarinet,
    bass
McCoy Tyner — piano
Jimmy Garrison — bass
Elvin Jones ⎫ drums,
Frank Butler ⎬ percussion
Juno Lewis — percussion

237

Date and Place	Pieces	Personnel	Instruments
October, 1965 Los Angeles	Kulu Sé Mama	*John Coltrane	tenor sax
		Pharaoh Sanders	bass clarinet,
		Donald Garrett	bass
		McCoy Tyner	piano
		Jimmy Garrison	bass
		Elvin Jones	drums
		Frank Butler	drums
		Juno Lewis	vocal, percussion
November 23, 1965 New York	**The Father and the Son and the Holy Ghost	*John Coltrane	tenor sax
	**Compassion	Pharaoh Sanders	
	**Consequences	McCoy Tyner	piano
	**Serenity	Jimmy Garrison	bass
	**Love	Elvin Jones	drums
		Rashied Ali	
February 2, 1966 San Francisco	**Manifestation	*John Coltrane	tenor sax,
	**Reverend King		bass clarinet
	**Peace on Earth	Pharaoh Sanders	tenor sax, flute
	**Leo	Alice Coltrane	piano
		Jimmy Garrison	bass
		Rashied Ali	drums
		Ray Appleton	percussion
		Joan Chapman	tamboura

May 28, 1966 New York
Village Vanguard

**Naima
My Favorite Things

*John Coltrane — tenor and soprano sax, bass clarinet

Pharaoh Sanders — tenor sax, flute
Alice Coltrane — piano
Jimmy Garrison — bass
Rashied Ali — drums
Emanuel Rahim — percussion

July 22, 1966 Tokyo, Japan

**Meditations
**Leo, parts 1, 2, 3
**Peace on Earth, parts 1 and 2

*John Coltrane
Pharaoh Sanders } — tenor and Yamaha sax, bass clarinet

Alice Coltrane — piano
Jimmy Garrison — bass
Rashied Ali — drums

February 15, 1967 New York

**To Be
**Offering

Same personnel as July 22, 1966

February 22, 1967 New York

**Mars
**Venus
**Jupiter
**Saturn

*John Coltrane — tenor sax
Rashied Ali — drums

March 17, 1967 New York

**Expression
**Ogunde

*John Coltrane — tenor sax, flute
Alice Coltrane — piano
Jimmy Garrison — bass
Rashied Ali — drums

WORKS CITED

Ayler, Albert. Liner notes for *The New Wave in Jazz*. Impulse Records AS-90, 1965.

Carno, Zita. "The Style of John Coltrane." *Jazz Review,* October 1959, pp. 17—21; November 1959, pp. 13—17.

Cerulli, Dom. Liner notes for *Africa/Brass*. Impulse Records Stereo A-6, 1961.

Cole, Bill. *Miles Davis: A Musical Biography*. New York: William Morrow & Co., 1974.

Coltrane, Alice. Liner notes for *Concert in Japan*. Impulse Records AS-9246-2, 1973.

Coltrane, John, with DeMichael, D. "Coltrane on Coltrane." *Down Beat,* September 29, 1960, pp. 26—27.

Dance, Stanley. "Tyner Talking." *Down Beat,* October 24, 1963, pp. 18—19.

Ellison, Ralph. *Shadow and Act*. New York: Random House, 1964.

Feather, Leonard, "For Coltrane the Time Is Now." *Melody Maker,* December 19, 1964, p. 6.

Gardner, Mark. Liner notes for *Tenor Madness*. Prestige Records 7657, 1969.

Gleason, Ralph J. Liner notes for *Coltrane's Sound*. Atlantic Records SD-1419, 1960.

_____ . Liner notes for *Olé Coltrane*. Atlantic Records SD-1373, 1961.

Govinda, Lama Anagarika. *Maitreya*. Vol. 1. Berkeley: Shambhala Publications Inc., 1970.

Hentoff, Nat. Liner notes for *Coltrane "Live" at the Village Vanguard*. Impulse Records AS-10, 1961.

_____ . Liner notes for *Coltrane "Live" at the Village Vanguard Again*. Impulse Records AS-9124, 1966.

_____ . Liner notes for *Expression*. Impulse Records AS-9120, 1967.

_____ . Liner notes for *Giant Steps*. Atlantic Records SD-1311, 1959.

_____ . Liner notes for *Meditations*. Impulse Records AS-9110, 1965.

_____ . Liner notes for *New Thing at Newport*. Impulse Records AS-94, 1965.

Jacobi, Rolande. *The Psychology of C. G. Jung.* London: Routledge & Kegan Paul, 1969.

Jahn, Janheinz. *Muntu.* New York: Grove Press, 1961.

Koestler, Arthur. *The Act of Creation.* New York: Dell Publishing Co., 1966.

Kofsky, Frank. *Black Nationalism and the Revolution in Music.* New York: Pathfinder Press, 1970.

Lawrence, D. H. *Fantasia of the Unconcious.* New York: Albert and Charles Boni, 1930.

Rivelli, Pauline, and Levin, Robert, eds. *Black Giants.* New York and Cleveland: World Publishing Co., 1970.

Simpkins, C. O. *Coltrane: A Musical Biography.* New York: Herndon House, 1975.

Sowande, Fela. *Aspects of Nigerian Music* [n.p.], 1967.

————. *Black Experience of Religion.* Washington, D.C.: Howard University, 1970.

————. "Black Folklore," in *Black Lines.* Mimeographed. Pittsburgh: Black Studies Department, University of Pittsburgh, Fall 1971.

————. *Theory and Method.* Washington, D.C.: Howard University, 1971.

————. *The Role of Music in African Society.* Washington, D.C.: Howard University, 1969.

Spengler, Oswald. *The Decline of the West.* Translated by Charles F. Atkinson. 2 vols. New York: Alfred A. Knopf, 1928.

Stearns, Marshall W. *The Story of Jazz.* New York: Oxford University Press, 1958.

Taylor, Cecil. "John Coltrane." *Jazz Review,* January 1959, p. 34.

Thomas, J. C. *Chasin' the Trane: The Music and Mystique of John Coltrane.* New York: Doubleday & Co., 1975.

Wilhelm, Richard, ed. *I Ching.* Princeton: Princeton University Press, 1967.

Wilmer, Valerie. "Conversation with Coltrane." *Jazz Journal,* December 1962, p. 2.

FOR FURTHER
REFERENCE

"About John Coltrane (as viewed by Bob Thiele)." *Jazz,* May 1968, p. 22.

Alder, Vera Stanley. *The Finding of the Third Eye.* New York: Samuel Weiser, 1970.

Arrigoni, A. "Qualcosa sta cambiando." *Music Jazz,* June 1960, pp. 17—21.

Atkins, R. "John Coltrane and Dizzy Gillespie in Britain." *Jazz Monthly,* February 1967, pp. 11—12.

"Ayler, Coleman Quartets Play for Trane Funeral." *Melody Maker,* August 1967, p. 3.

Balliett, Whitney. "Jazz Concerts: Memorial at Carnegie Hall." *New Yorker,* April 27, 1968, p. 158.

BeBey, Francis. *African Music: A People's Art.* New York and Westport: Lawrence Hill & Co., 1975.

Berendt, Joachim E. *The New Jazz Book: A Historical Guide.* New York: Hill & Wang, 1959.

————. "Free Jazz: der neue Jazz der sechziger Jahre." *Melos,* October 1967, pp. 349—351.

————. "Jazz Meets the World." *World Music,* 1968, p. 9.

Berger, D. "John Coltrane." *Jazz Hot,* August 1967, p. 5.

Black Creation. New York: Institute of Afro-American Affairs at N.Y.U., Fall 1972.

Blavatsky, Helene. *The Secret Doctrine.* New York: Theosophical Publishing Co., 1888. Reprinted Madras, 1962.

Blume, A. "An Interview with John Coltrane." *Jazz Review,* January 1959, p. 25.

"Bob Thiele Talks to Frank Kofsky about John Coltrane." CODA Publications, May 28, 1968.

Bolognani, M. "John Coltrane: sensibilitia o transtormiso?" *Music Jazz,* November 1967, pp. 37—38.

Brown, D. Record review: *Coltrane Legacy. Coda,* 1971, p. 16.

Buin, Y. "Coltrane ou la mise `a mort." *Jazz Hot,* May 1967, pp. 14—17.

Burns, J. and Cooke, J. "Record Reviews." *Jazz Monthly,* November 1969, p. 5.

Cash, W. J. *The Mind of the South,* New York: Alfred A. Knopf, 1941. Reprinted London: Thames & Hudson, 1971.

"Caught in the Act." *Down Beat,* August 6, 1959, p. 14.

Cerulli, Dom. Record review. *Down Beat,* December 26, 1957, p. 39.

"Chronique des disques: John Coltrane." *Jazz Hot,* July-August 1972, p. 29.

"Cinq personnages en quete de 'Trane.'" *Jazz Hot,* January 1962, pp. 16—21.

Clar, M. "John Coltrane: Soultrane." *Jazz Review,* April 1959, p. 24.

Cole, William S. "John Coltrane and Sonny Rollins: What Else Is There To Say?" University of Pittsburgh, n.p., 1970.

Coleman, R., "Coltrane." *Melody Maker,* July 11, 1964, p. 6.

"John Coltrane." *Jazz & Pop,* September 1967, p. 26.

"Coltrane: Anti-Jazz or the Wave of the Future?" *Melody Maker,* September 28, 1963, p. 11.

"Coltrane Dead of a Liver Ailment." *Bill Board,* July 29, 1967, p. 12.

"Coltrane Dies in New York." *Melody Maker,* July 22, 1967, p. 1.

"John Coltrane Dies." *Down Beat,* August 24, 1967, pp. 12—13.

"John Coltrane, 1926—1967." *Jazz Magazine,* August 1967, pp. 16—23.

"Coltrane, John William, 1926—, Saxophonist Finally Made," *Newsweek,* July 24, 1961, p. 64.

"Coltrane, John William, 1926—1967, Saxophonist." *British Book Year,* 1968, p. 588.

"John William Coltrane, 1926—1967: Tribute." *Down Beat,* September 7, 1967, pp. 15—17.

"Combo review." *Variety,* July 26, 1961, p. 55.

"Congo Republic Issues Set of Stamps Honoring Black Musicians and Depicting Miles Davis, Ella Fitzgerald, Count Basie, and John Coltrane." *New York Times,* June 3, 1973, sec. 2, p. 8.

"Controverse autour de Coltrane." *Jazz Hot,* May 1960, pp. 28—29.

Cooke, J. "Better Times Ahead." *Jazz Monthly,* January 1963, pp. 4—5.

————. "In Memoriam." *Jazz Monthly,* September 1967, p. 2.

————. "Late Trane." *Jazz Monthly,* January 1970, pp. 2—6.

Cordle, O. "The Soprano Saxophone: From Bechet to Coltrane to Shorter." *Down Beat,* July 20, 1972, pp. 14—15.

Curnon, Wystan. "The Jazz Avant-Garde." *Comment,* April 1968, pp. 41—43.

Dance, Stanley. "Jazz." *Music Journal,* September 1967, p. 92.

Dargenpierre, J. C., Poulain, M., and Terot, F. "John Coltrane." *Jazz Monthly,* February 1967, pp. 11—12.

Davis, John P., ed. *American Negro Reference Book.* Englewood Cliffs, New Jersey: Prentice-Hall, 1965, p. 764.

Dawbarn, B. "What Happened?" *Melody Maker,* November 18, 1961, p. 15.

————. "Saxists: Always the Innovators." *Melody Maker,* June 14, 1969, p. 16.

_____. "Coltrane." *Melody Maker,* October 15, 1966, p. 8.

_____. "I'd Like To Play Your Clubs: Interview with John Coltrane." *Melody Maker,* November 25, 1961, p. 8.

Delmore, M. "John Coltrane est mort." *Jazz Hot,* August 1967, pp. 15—16.

_____. "Coltrane 1963: vers la composition." *Jazz Hot,* December 1963, pp. 10—11.

Delmore, M., and Lenissois, C. "Coltrane vedette d'Antibes." *Jazz Hot,* September 1965, pp. 5—6.

DeMichael, D. "John Coltrane and Eric Dolphy Answer the Jazz Critics." *Down Beat,* April 12, 1967, pp. 20—23.

_____. "Old Wines, New Bottles." *Down Beat,* September 13, 1963.

Dexter, Dave, Jr. *The Jazz Story from the 90's to the 60's.* Englewood Cliffs, New Jersey: Prentice-Hall, 1964.

"Disques du Mois: Ascension." *Jazz Magazine,* May 1970, p. 48.

"Disques du Mois: Cannonball and Coltrane." *Jazz Magazine,* April 1972, p. 30.

"Disques du Mois: The Coltrane Legacy." *Jazz Magazine,* December 1970, pp. 52—53.

"Disques du Mois: Selflessness." *Jazz Magazine,* April 1970, p. 36.

"E tornato John Coltrane." *Musical Jazz,* December 1963, pp. 16—17.

Ebony, special issue. August 1969, pp. 81—96.

Editors of Ebony. *The Negro Handbook.* Chicago: Johnson Publishing Co., Inc., 1966.

Essence, December 1971, p. 42.

Feather, Leonard. "Coltrane, Does It Now Mean a Thing, If It Ain't Got That Swing?" *Melody Maker,* April 16, 1966, p. 6.

_____. "Honest John: The Blindfold Test." *Down Beat,* February 19, 1959, p. 39.

_____. "Jazz: Going Nowhere ('anti-jazz')." *Show,* January 1967, pp. 12—14.

"Finally Made." *Newsweek,* July 24, 1961, p. 64.

Fremer, B. "John Coltrane." *Orkester Journalen,* March 1958, p. 12.

Fresia, E. "Discografia." *Music Jazz,* February 1964, p. 42.

Gardner, Barbara. "Jazzman of the Year: John Coltrane." *Down Beat,* special issue, 1962, p. 66—69.

Garland, Phyllis, "Requiem for Trane." *Ebony,* November 1967, pp. 66—68.

_____. "The Sound of Soul." Chicago: H. Regnery Co., 1969, p. 188.

Gaspard, J. J. "Miles Davis." *Musica,* October 1959, p. 29.

Gerber, A. "Disques du Mois: Live in Seattle." *Jazz Magazine,* January 1972, p. 27.

_____. "Disques du Mois: Sun-Ship." *Jazz Magazine,* December 1971, pp. 37—38.

_____. "Huit faces de Coltrane." *Jazz Magazine,* June 1972, pp. 25—31.

_____. "Huit faces de Coltrane." *Jazz Magazine,* July 1972, pp. 14—17.

Gibson, J., and Lenissois, C. "Les fabuleux de mons coltraniens sont revenus le 1er Novembre." *Jazz Hot,* December 1963, pp. 9—10.

_____. "Les concerts Coltrane." *Jazz Hot,* December 1962, pp. 17—19.

Gibson, M. "John Coltrane: The Formative Years." *Jazz Journal*, June 1960, pp. 9—10.

Gillis, F., and Merriam, A. P. *Ethnomusicology and Folkmusic: An International Bibliography of Dissertations and Theses*. Middlet~vn, Conn.: Society for Ethnomusicology and Wesleyan U. Press, 1966 (special series in ethnomusicology vol. 1).

Gitler, I. "Trane on the Track." *Down Beat*, October 16, 1958, pp. 16—17.

Gleason, Ralph. Record review. *Down Beat*, January 14, 1956, p. 26.

Goddet, L. "La chronique de disques: Transition." *Jazz Hot*, January 1971, p. 34.

Gold, Don. Record review. *Down Beat*, January 23, 1958, pp. 20, 24.

Goldberg, Joe. *Jazz Masters of the 50's*. New York, London: Collier-Macmillan Co., 1965.

Goldman, A. H. *Freakshow*. New York: Atheneum, 1971.

Goodman, J. "Looking for the Black Message." *New Leader*, January 1, 1968, pp. 26—28.

"Grand Prix pour Coltrane." *Jazz Magazine*, April 1962, p. 16.

Green, B. "A Matter of Form." *Jazz Journal*, June 1967, pp. 11—12.

Grigson, L. "Directions in Modern Jazz." *Jazz Monthly*, September 1961, p. 17.

Guastone, G. "Quattro chiacchiere con Gianni Basso su cinque sassofonisti." *Music Jazz*, November 1960, p. 19.

Haitch, Elisabeth. *Initiation*. Palo Alto, California: The Seed Center, 1965.

Heckman, D. "After Coltrane." *Down Beat*, March 1, 1967, pp. 18—19.

———. "The Month's Jazz." *American Record Guide*, December 1967, p. 339.

Heline, Corinne. *Color and Music in the New Age*. La Canada, California: New Age Press, 1964.

Hennessey, M. "Coltrane: Dropping the Ball and Chain from Jazz." *Melody Maker*, August 14, 1965, p. 6.

———. "Forty-Seven Minutes of Magnificent Coltrane." *Melody Maker*, July 31, 1965, p. 8.

Hentoff, Nat. "John Coltrane: Challenge Without End." *International Musician*, March 1962, pp. 12—13.

———. Record review. *Down Beat*, October 6, 1956, p. 12; November 14, 1956, p. 28; December 12, 1956, p. 39; April 18, 1956, p. 28.

Hobson, W. "The Amen Corner." *Saturday Review*, April 29, 1961, p. 51.

"Hommage a John Coltrane." *Jazz Magazine*, September 1967, pp. 12—15.

Houston, B. "Always Expect the Unexpected." *Melody Maker*, July 29, 1967, p. 6.

Hunt, D. C. "Coleman, Coltrane and Shepp: The Need for an Educated Audience." Jazz & Pop, October 1968, pp. 18—21.

Hunt, Roland. *The Eighth Key to Color*. London: Fowler & Co., 1965.

Idestam-Almquist, D. "In Memoriam." *Orkester Journalen*, September 1967, pp. 6—7.

"Impulse, Mrs. Coltrane in Legacy Agreement." *Down Beat*, September 5, 1968, p. 13.

"In Memoriam." *Broadway Musical Incorporated,* October 1967, pp. 26—27.

"Interview with Albert Ayler." *Down Beat,* November 17, 1966, p. 17.

"Interview with George Russell." *Down Beat,* May 29, 1958, p. 15.

Ioakimidis, D. "Sonny Rollins et John Coltrane." *Jazz Hot,* December 1962, pp. 30—34.

———. "Sonny Rollins et John Coltrane en parallele." *Jazz Hot,* September 1967, pp. 24—27, October 1967, pp. 22—25, November 1967, pp. 22—24.

James, M. "The John Coltrane Quartet in Amsterdam." *Jazz Monthly,* January 1964, p. 10.

"Jazz Gallery, New York." *Variety,* May 25, 1960, p. 66.

Jazz & Pop, Editorial, September 1967, p. 7.

Jazz & Pop, Editorial, September 1968, pp. 123—129.

Jepson, J. G. *A Discography of John Coltrane.* Denmark: Karl Emil Knudsen, 1969.

Jones, L. "A Coltrane Trilogy." *Metro,* December 1961, pp. 34—36.

Jones, LeRoi. *Black Music.* New York: William Morrow & Co., 1967.

Jones, M. "It's True: We'll Never Hear Their Likes Again." *Melody Maker,* December 30, 1967, p. 6.

———. "Putting the Greats on Record." *Melody Maker,* January 25, 1969, p. 8.

Kart, L. "The Coltrane Legacy." *Down Beat,* May 13, 1971, p. 22.

Koechlin, P. "L'ombre de Coltrane sous le Soleil de Parker," *Jazz Hot,* January 1964, p. 10.

———. "Coltrane à Paris." *Jazz Hot,* September 1965, p. 10.

Kofsky, Frank. "Brief Interview with John Coltrane." *Jazz & Pop,* March 1968, pp. 22—23.

———. "John Coltrane." *Jazz & Pop,* September 1967, pp. 23—31.

———. "John Coltrane and the Jazz Revolution; the Case of Albert Ayler." *Jazz,* 1960, pp. 20—22 n. 9; pp. 24—25 n. 10.

———. "A Note on Jazz Rhythm." *Jazz,* January 1967, pp. 16—17.

———. "Revolution, Coltrane, and the Avant-Garde." *Jazz,* July 1965, pp. 13—16 n. 7; pp. 18—22 n. 8.

Kopulos, G. "John Coltrane: Retrospective Prospective." *Down Beat,* July 22, 1971, pp. 14—15.

Korall, B. "I've Talked Enough: Interview with Sonny Rollins, John Coltrane and Ornette Coleman." *Melody Maker,* September 15, 1962, pp. 8—9.

"L'enterrement de Coltrane." *Jazz Hot,* November 1967, p. 7.

"Le Dossier Coltrane." *Jazz Magazine,* May 1960, pp. 22—27.

"Le 17 juillet 1967 . . . Disparaissait John Coltrane." *Jazz Hot,* February 1972, pp. 16—17.

Lees, Gene. "L'homme Coltrane." *Jazz Magazine,* November 1961, pp. 34—35.

———. "Consider Coltrane." *Jazz,* February 1963, p. 7.

Lemery, D. "Comme un Seul Homme." *Jazz Magazine,* February 1965, pp. 30—34.

"Lettere al directtore: Pro e Contro Coltrane." *Musical Jazz,* July 1960, pp. 10—12.

Lindgren, G. "Coltrane's Konturer: en stor stilbildares maagfacetterade musikatiska insats belyses." *Orkester Journalen,* January 1968, pp. 8—9.

———. "Coltrane's Konturer." *Orkester Journalen,* March 1968, pp. 10—11; April 1968, p. 10.

———. "Coltrane's Konturer Naagra ytterligare synpunkter pace John Coltrane's musik." *Orkester Journalen,* May 1968, pp. 8—9.

Litweiler, J. "Caught in the Act." *Down Beat,* October 19, 1967, p. 44.

———. Record review: *Transition. Down Beat,* December 24, 1970, p. 22.

Locke, D. "Cosmic Music." *Jazz Monthly,* July 1969, p. 23.

Masson, J. R. "La Nuit des Magiciens." *Jazz Magazine,* January 1963, pp. 22—29.

Mathieu, Bill. Record review. *Down Beat,* April 9, 1964.

McRae, B. "A B Basics: A Column for the Newcomer to Jazz." *Jazz Journal,* September 1967, p. 8.

———. "John Coltrane: The Impulse Years." *Jazz,* July 1971, p. 26.

Melody Maker, September 28, 1963, p. 11; June 3, 1965, p. 10; April 16, 1966, p. 6.

Morgenstern, D. "Modern Reeds—and How They Grew." *Down Beat,* May 14, 1959, p. 17.

Mortara, A. "Coltrane (e altri); la Crisidel Parkerismo." *Music Jazz,* March 1961, pp. 18—22.

———. "John Coltrane; la Maturazione di Uno Stile." *Music Jazz,* May 1961, pp. 10—14.

Mutwa, Vusamazulu Credo. *Indaba, My Children.* Johannesburg, South Africa: Blue Crane Books, 1965.

"New Jazz." *Newsweek,* December 12, 1966, p. 108.

"New Wave in Jazz." *Melody Maker,* April 3, 1971, p. 24.

New York Times, 18, 19, 22 July; 13 August 1967.

Nketia, Kwabena. *The Music Of Africa.* New York: W. W. Norton & Co., 1974.

Noames, J. L. "Jazz à New York." *Jazz Magazine,* October 1965, p. 21.

Pagan, Isabelle M. *Racial Cleavage.* London: The Theosophical Pub. House, 1937.

Palmer, B. "Jazz on Record." *Rolling Stone,* April 15, 1971, p. 48.

"Plugged Nickel, Chi." *Variety,* March 16, 1966, p. 65.

Polillo, A., and Testoni, G. C. "Impressioni su Coltrane." *Music Jazz,* January 1963, pp. 10—14.

Postgale, J. "The Black and White Show 1970—80: A Speculation on the Future of Jazz." *Jazz Monthly,* December 1970.

Postif, F. "John Coltrane: une Interview." *Jazz Hot,* January 1962, pp. 12—14.

———. "New York in Jazz Time." *Jazz Hot,* December 1960, p. 25.

Priestley, B. Record reviews; *Selflessness. Jazz Monthly,* June 1970, p. 12.

Quersin, B. "La Passe Dangereuse." *Jazz Magazine,* January 1963, pp. 39—40.

Record review: *Africa/Brass. Jazz,* November 1970, p. 31.

Record review: *Africa/Brass. Jazz Monthly,* December 1970, pp. 19—20.

Record review: *Giant Steps. Oakland Tribune,* 1960.

Record review. *Jazz,* October 1969, pp. 29—30.

Record review: *Live in Seattle. Coda,* 1972, p. 24.

Record review. *Metronome,* January 1958, p. 20; February 1958, p. 34.

Reisner, R. G. *The Jazz Titans.* Garden City, New York: Doubleday & Co., 1960.

Rivelli, Pauline. "Alice Coltrane." *Jazz & Pop,* September 1968, pp. 26—30.

Santucci, U. "Jazz and Microstruttura and John Coltrane." *Music Jazz,* July—August 1963, pp. 12—17.

Schallplattenbes prechungen: *Transition. Jazz Podium,* March 1972, p. 82.

Seidel, R. "John Coltrane: Caught in the Act (John Coltrane Memorial Concert)." *Down Beat,* November 11, 1971, pp. 24—26.

"Sentiano ora le Opinioni di Alcuni Noti Musicisti." *Musical Jazz,* January 1963, pp. 15—16.

"Seven Steps to Jazz." *Melody Maker,* May 14, 1966, p. 8.

"Shepp Big Band Stars in Coltrane Tribute." *Down Beat,* August 20, 1970, p. 12.

Sinclair, John. Record review. *Jazz,* August 1964, pp. 16—17.

Smith, Lillian. *Killers of the Dream.* New York: Norton Press, 1949. Rev. ed. Garden City: Doubleday Anchor, 1963.

Smith, W. Record review: *Selflessness. Jazz & Pop,* March 1970, p. 52.

Spellman, A. B. *Black Music.* New York: Schocken Books, 1970.

———. "Heard and Seen." *Metro,* November 1961, p. 8.

———. "John Coltrane 1926—1967." *Nation,* August 14, 1967, pp. 119—120.

———. "Small Band Jazz." *New Republic,* August 17, 1968, pp. 40—41.

———. "Trane + 7 = A Wild Night at the Gate." *Down Beat,* December 30, 1965, p. 15.

Steiner, Rudolf. *Education as an Art.* Blauvelt, New York: Rudolf Steiner Pub., 1970.

Stenbeck, L. "Coltrane och guds Rarlek." *Orkester Journalen,* July-August 1965, p. 7.

Sundin, B. "Coltrane musik angelagen och Kravende." *Orkester Journalen,* December 1962, pp. 10—11.

Taggert, J., ed. "Poems for John Coltrane: An Anthology." *Jazz Monthly,* October 1970, p. 31.

Taylor, Cecil. "John Coltrane." *Jazz Review,* January 1959, p. 34.

Tepperman, B. Record review: *Trane's Reign. Coda,* 1971, p. 19.

Tercinet, A., and others. "Special Coltrane." *Jazz Hot,* October 1970, pp. 6—25.

Thornton, C. "Caught in the Act: Black Solidarity Festival." *Down Beat,* July 23, 1970, p. 30.

Toomajian, S. "Caught in the Act." *Down Beat,* September 21, 1967, p. 26.

"Trane et Woody à Paris." *Jazz Magazine,* September 1965, pp. 7—8.

"Trane Stops the Gallery." *Sunday News,* May 15, 1960.

Tynan, John. Record review. *Down Beat,* May 15, 1958, p. 24.

———. "Take 5." *Down Beat,* November 23, 1961, p. 40.

Variety Magazine, July 26, 1961, p. 55; March 16, 1966, p. 65.

Voce, S. "Basic Trane-ing." *Jazz Journal,* August 1967, p. 10.

Walker, M. "John Coltrane" (discography). *Jazz Monthly,* August 1966, pp. 11—13; September 1966, pp. 30—31; October 1966, pp. 23—24; November 1966, pp. 29—31.

West, H. I. "How Jazz Was Orphaned." *American Music Digest,* 1970, pp. 34—35.

"Who's on First." *Down Beat,* March 10, 1966, p. 8.

Williams, Martin. "The Bystander." *Down Beat,* May 10, 1962, p. 39.

————. "Coltrane, Coleman Up to Date." *Jazz,* November 1966, pp. 4—5.

————. "John Coltrane: Man in the Middle." *Down Beat,* December 14, 1967, pp. 15—17.

————. "Coltrane Triumphant." *Saturday Review,* January 16, 1965, pp. 73—74.

————. "Coltrane Up to Date." *Saturday Review,* April 30, 1966, p. 67.

————. *Jazz Masters in Transition, 1957—1969.* London: Collier-Macmillan, 1970.

————. *The Jazz Tradition.* New York: Oxford University Press, 1970.

————. "Legacy of John Coltrane." *Saturday Review,* September 16, 1967, p. 69.

————. Record review. *Down Beat,* January 18, 1962, p. 30.

Williams, R. "Jazz record: Live in Seattle." *Melody Maker,* April 17, 1971, p. 28.

Wilmer, Valerie. *Jazz People.* London: Alison & Busby, 1970.

————. "When You Lose an 'Elder Brother'" (interview with McCoy Tyner). *Melody Maker,* August 19, 1967, p. 8.

Wilson, John S. *Jazz: The Transition Years 1940—1960,* New York: Appleton-Century-Crofts Division of Meredith Publishing Co., 1966.

Wilson, Russ. *Oakland Tribune,* June 4, 1959.

Wiskirchen, G. "Jazz on Campus." *Down Beat,* May 1, 1969, pp. 45—46.

Zimmerman, P. D. "Death of a Jazz Man." *Newsweek,* July 31, 1967, pp. 78—79.

INDEX OF NAMES AND SUBJECTS

Note: Page numbers of photographs are shown in italic type. Page numbers of certain songs, pieces, and albums are given in the Index of Music Discussed.

Dixieland, 18, 195
Dixon, Bill (trumpet), 145
Dolphy, Eric (alto sax, bass clarinet, flute), 6, *100*, 102, 125, 126—29, 139, 141, 143, 144, 149, 152, 157, 158, 176, 189. *See also* Orchestras
Dolphy, Mrs. (mother of Eric), 158, 175, 184, 188
Dorham, Kenny (trumpet), 3, 81
Down Beat, 121, 125, 145
Down Beat Festival, 175
Drew, Kenny (piano), 69, 74
Drugs, 3, 53—54, 98, 115, 149. *See also* Alcohol, "D and D Band," *and under Coltrane listing:* Alcohol, Drugs
Drum, 24, 43, 43 (n. 6), 45, 73, 79, 110—111, 119, 125, 158, 180—182, 187—88, 195. *See also* Abakwa, Africa, Jones, Elvin; Taylor, Art

East Coast, music scene, 80
Eastern considerations, 17, 64, 110, 181. *See also* African music, Indian music, Indonesian music, Javan music, *and under Coltrane listing:* Eastern considerations, African music, Non-Western elements
Eckstine, Billy (singer), 144
Edison, Harry Sweets (trumpet), 118
Einstein, Albert, 16, 197
Ellington, Duke (piano, composer, leader), 27, 79, 83, 149, 151, 178
Energy, 70—73. *See also* Jung, C. G.
European music, 19, 37, 102, 107. *See also under Coltrane listing*
European tours, 115, 190, 191
Evans, Bill (piano), 2, 110
Evans, Richard (bass), 166

Farmer, Art (trumpet), 117
Feather, Leonard (critic), 171
Feminine elements, 42, 75, 107. *See also* Art, Creation, Masculine elements, Philosophy, *and under Coltrane listing:* Philosophy, Vision
Five Spot (club), 79
Flanagan, Tommy (piano), 104
Folk music, 9
France, acclaim in, 126
Franklin, Aretha (singer), 24

"Free jazz," 19, 152
"Free structure," 165—70, 195
Fuller, Curtis (trombone), 69, 74

Gardner, Mark (critic), 78
Garland, William Red (piano), 1, 2, 34—35, 37, 47, 88, 97, 110, 117
Garner, Erroll (piano), 35
Garrett, Donald (bass clarinet, bass), 177, 178, 180
Garrison, Jimmy (bass), 6, 7, 23, 34, 52—54, *86*, 95, *124*, 125, 133, 139, 140, 142, 152, 157, 166, 167, 169, 177, 178, 181, 183, 188, 189, 190, 191
Garvey, Marcus (Black nationalist), 14
Getz, Stan (tenor sax), 130
Gillespie, Dizzy (trumpet), 3, 27, 42, 43, 91, 152
Bands, leader of, 26, 27, 43, 64
Gilmore, John (tenor sax), 141, 165—66
Gleason, Ralph (critic), 116 (n. 4), 199
Glenn, John (tenor sax), 26, 129
God, 85, 160. *See also* Religion, Triplets, Unity, *and under Coltrane listing:* God, Religion, Triplets
God—Man—Nature. *See* Unity.
Golson, Benny (composer, tenor sax), 26, 117
Gordon, Dexter (tenor sax), 31
Govinda, Lama Anagarika (philosopher), 113, 137
Granoff Studios, 26
Gray, Wardell (alto sax), 31
Greenlee, Charles (husband of Mary Blair), 84
Greenwich Village, music scene in, 2, 116, 139, 188. *See also* Village Gate, Village Vanguard.
Griffin, Johnny (tenor sax), 78
Grill. *See* Crawford Grill #2

Haden, Charlie (bass), 122
Haley, Alex (author), 13
Hamlet, North Carolina, 23
Hard bop, 8, 18, 32, 33, 36, 80—81, 91. *See also* Bebop, Bop, *and under Coltrane listing:* Bebop, Hard bop
Hard blues. *See* Blues
Harden, Wilbur (trumpet), 98, 115, 126
Harlem, music scene in, 42
Harlem Renaissance, 14

Vanguard Records, 140
Vega Records, 126
Vertical Playing, 33, 47, 80
  Vertical Patterns, 36
  See also Harmonics/harmony, Space, *and under Coltrane listing:* Harmony/harmonics, Space
Village Gate (club), 116, 165
Village Vanguard (club), 139, 189
Vinson, Eddie Cleanhead (alto sax), 26, 31
  Band, leader of, 67
Visible/invisible, 32, 33, 134. *See also* Art, Creation, Philosophy, *and under Coltrane listing:* Philosophy, Vision
Voice, 2, 24, 26, 36, 43, 46, 47, 51, 61, 143, 147. *See also* Africa, Music, Sanders, Pharaoh, Tradition/roots, Yoruba language, music, *and under Coltrane listing:* African music, traditional, Voice

Wall's, Dan (club), 41
Ward, Carlos (alto sax, flute), 181, 188
Ware, Wilbur (bass), 59, 60, 64, 78
Watkins, Doug (bass), 3, 81, 115
Webb, Chick (drums), 35
Webb, Joe, 26, 67
Webster, Ben (tenor sax), 31, 189
West coast, musicians, influences of, 102, 176. *See also* San Francisco

Western approach/considerations, 12, 17, 32. *See also* European music, Western music, *and under Coltrane listing:* European music
White, Andrew, v
William Penn High School, 24, 25. *See also under Coltrane listing:* Schooling
Wilson, Shadow (drums), 60
Workman, Reggie (bass), 53, 66, 125, 133, 144, 152
Work songs, 84. *See also* African-American Music
World view, 85, 91, 137. *See also* Art, Creation, Eastern considerations, Feminine element, God, Islam, Masculine element, Philosophy, Religion, Sowande, Fela, Triplets, Unity, Visible/invisible, *and under Coltrane listing:* World view, Communication, God, Nature, Philosophy, Religion, Triplets, Vision

Yoruba language, music, 17, 24, 26, 61, 70, 87, 131, 147, 199. *See also* African music, African tradition/roots, Drum, Triplets, Voice, *and under Coltrane listing:* African concerns, African music, traditional, Triplets, Voice
Young, Lester (tenor sax), 27, 31

INDEX OF MUSIC DISCUSSED

Note: Individual songs and pieces are shown with quotation marks. Albums appear in italic type.